PROACTIVE SECURITY
ADMINISTRATION

Second Edition

PROACTIVE SECURITY ADMINISTRATION

George E. Curtis
Utica College

R. Bruce McBride
Utica College

Prentice Hall

Boston   Columbus   Indianapolis   New York   San Francisco   Upper Saddle River
Amsterdam   Cape Town   Dubai   London   Madrid   Milan   Munich   Paris   Montreal   Toronto
Delhi   Mexico City   Sao Paulo   Sydney   Hong Kong   Seoul   Singapore   Taipei   Tokyo

Editorial Director: Vernon R. Anthony
Acquisitions Editor: Eric Krassow
Editorial Assistant: Lynda Cramer
Director of Marketing: David Gesell
Marketing Manager: Adam Kloza
Senior Marketing Coordinator: Alicia Wozniak
Marketing Assistant: Les Roberts
Production Editor: Steve Robb
Project Manager: Susan Hannahs

Senior Art Director: Jayne Conte
Cover Designer: Suzanne Behnke
Cover Art: Fotolia
Full-Service Project Management: Seshan Ram,
Integra Software Services, Pvt. Ltd.
Composition: Integra Software Services, Pvt. Ltd.
Text Font: 10/12, Minion Regular

Credits and acknowledgments for content borrowed from other sources and reproduced, with permission, in this textbook appear on the appropriate page within text.

Library of Congress Cataloging-in-Publication Data
Curtis, George E., 1942-
  Proactive security administration / George E. Curtis, R. Bruce McBride. — 2nd ed.
    p. cm.
  Includes bibliographical references and index.
  ISBN-13: 978-0-13-507150-2 (alk. paper)
  ISBN-10: 0-13-507150-X (alk. paper)
  1. Internal security—United States.   2. Law enforcement—United States.   3. Private
security services—United States.   4. Police, Private—United States.   5. Police
administration—United States.   I. McBride, R. Bruce.   II. Title.
  HV8141.C87 2010
  363.20973—dc22

                                                    2010015440

Prentice Hall
is an imprint of

www.pearsonhighered.com

ISBN 10:   0-13-507150-X
ISBN 13: 978-0-13-507150-2

4 2022

BRIEF CONTENTS

CONTENTS

PREFACE

NEW TO THIS EDITION

- A new chapter on risk management for security services
- A new chapter on security services in certain industries
- A new chapter on the role of security services in compliance efforts
- An expanded chapter on the legal implications for the performance of security services
- An expanded chapter on national security under the organizational structure of the U.S. Department of Homeland Security and its state and local counterparts
- An expanded chapter that explores future trends implicating security services and directions that the performance of security might take

ABOUT THIS BOOK

Our principal objective in writing this text was to discuss the current critical issues concerning the proactive delivery of security services (i.e., the prevention of security incidents and the detection of those that occur). We have endeavored to accomplish three important goals: to achieve relative balance in discussing the administration of security by the public and private sectors and the need for greater cooperation; to incorporate current policies for the administration of security set forth in the USA PATRIOT Act, Gramm-Leach-Bliley Act, Health Insurance Portability and Accountability Act, Sarbanes-Oxley Act, and the myriad other legislative efforts to ensure domestic security; and to discuss at length the need to utilize technology in the protection of critical assets, especially those utilized in the Information Age.

To add value and currency to the original text, we have enhanced it with the content listed above in the "New to This Edition" section.

In Chapter 1, we provide an extensive historical and conceptual background of the delivery of security services. Volunteer watchmen were replaced by paid police as the United States changed from an agrarian to an industrial society. We note that major national investigations were handled by private security companies such as Pinkerton. By the end of World War II, several models of security services had emerged, including contract, public/proprietary, executive protection, and the growing service sectors and sales industries. The chapter then follows the development of modern security technology from traditional locks to biometric readers. We conclude this chapter with the current state of security services, including the merger of national companies into international security service conglomerates.

Chapter 2 focuses on the legal bases for public and private sector security operations and legal issues that affect the administration of security services. The discussion includes an overview of the sources of law; the structure of court systems; principles of criminal and civil liability that apply to security personnel and their employers; requirements for the protection of employee, customer, or client information; laws governing the execution of common security measures; and the legal issues affecting public–private relationships.

Chapter 3 presents a security service organizational scheme and an overview of strategic planning and budgeting. Because of the inclusion of security services into many public sector agencies, we created a four-level organizational model based on the range of resources and law enforcement powers. The proactive model includes a great deal of planning, particularly strategic planning.

Chapter 4 is a new chapter that deals with the assessment and mitigation of enterprise security risk. We emphasize the need to identify risks, vulnerabilities, and threats to assets and then develop countermeasures to minimize or prevent attacks. Organizations are challenged to undertake risk assessment and consider the criteria essential to the preparation and execution of a strategic plan for the administration of security at the enterprise level.

Chapter 5 deals with securing assets and explores the conventional and technological threats to physical assets: employees, facilities, equipment, and infrastructure. Perimeter security and access control remain the focus in the security plan of many businesses. Yet it is internal operations and procedures that are often not addressed in the security plan. The issue over contract or proprietary officers is also presented from a mission-driven perspective. Special attention is then focused on special populations and situations that include conventional criminal behavior (e.g., workplace violence) and fire safety.

Chapter 6 explores the conventional and technological threats to the information, data, and intellectual property assets of an organization. The discussion includes an overview of conventional economic crimes and cyber crimes, the threats those crimes pose to the information assets of government and private sector organizations, the need to secure those assets by implementing proactive prevention and detection strategies and measures, and the technologies available to manage the implementation of those measures.

Chapter 7 is a new chapter that focuses on securing assets in specific industries. It reviews the general security concerns for colleges and universities, schools, hospitals, the maritime industry, laboratories, shopping malls and retail, and the gaming industry. Each area will require additional outside readings in terms of developing issues and trends.

Chapter 8 examines the methods of conducting investigations and the proactive benefits of the investigation of a security incident or crime. The discussion focuses on the administration of investigations, the legal constraints on the public sector with respect to investigations, and a brief overview of cyber crime and fraud investigations. Methods for analyzing attacks are discussed as part of the organization's administration of a proactive security strategy. The theme is that the actual process of investigation is only part of the overall response to a security incident and that preparation, real-time monitoring, and post-event attack analysis are essential to the development of security countermeasures and constant revision of security policy.

Chapter 9 is an expanded chapter from the first edition that begins with the development of national security under the aegis of the Department of Homeland Security. The various agencies that constitute this Department are reviewed in terms of their contributions to security. The chapter explores the risks presented by emergencies and the planning strategy required to deal with the administration of an emergency response using the National Incident Management Systems. The discussion describes the various infrastructures that require protection, the methods of responding to that task, the financial and management issues related to emergency response, and current issues related to weapons of mass destruction and terrorism.

Chapter 10 examines the personnel or human resource issues pertaining to the administration of security operations. The chapter discusses educational requirements for security personnel; the necessity, criteria, and procedures for the performance of background checks; legal issues affecting employment and collective bargaining; and the administration of rewards and other methods of motivating security personnel and providing for career development.

Chapter 11 is a new chapter dealing with increasing governmental mandates for compliance with regulatory and private-sector standards for the performance of security services in numerous contexts. This chapter focuses on the necessity for compliance, particularly in the private sector, and the legal implications for the failure to comply with those standards.

Chapter 12 explores the need for training and the components of an effective ongoing training program for the different levels of security operation and positions within a security unit. The chapter reviews various topic areas in security training and methods of delivery.

Chapter 13 discusses the unique challenges posed to security administration of organizations that compete internationally and governments that must capture criminals who have committed an attack beyond the country's borders.

Chapter 14 is an expanded version of the previous chapter which examines future directions and trends in security administration. The theme of the chapter is that proactive security administration requires constant reexamination and revision of the strategic security plan in the light of constant economic, cultural, political, and legal challenges.

We begin each chapter by highlighting those terms the student should become familiar with during the first reading of the chapter. We conclude each chapter with two features designed to familiarize students with the process of conducting research related to security on the Internet and to enable them to understand and apply critical issues discussed in each chapter. Web links for future study are also presented in each chapter.

ACKNOWLEDGMENTS

We would like to thank the many students, officers, investigators, and administrators we have taught in college classrooms and training academies for their insight, ideas, and concerns on the administration of security service organizations. Today many are senior administrators and policy makers in police and security service organizations.

A number of current administrators provided critical insights. They include Thomas Ryan, former State University of New York at Oswego police administrator and senior partner, CRJ Associates; the security directors and police chiefs of the State University of New York; and Mark Fettinger and the training and management staff at the New York State Office of Public Safety, Division of Criminal Justice Services.

Several members of industry organizations and law enforcement agencies have shared their knowledge and expertise with us over the years, much of which is reflected in this effort. They include Don Rebovich, executive director for the Center for Information Management and Identity Protection and our colleague at Utica College; Joseph Giordano, the director of the Economic Crime Management program at Utica College; Suzanne Lynch, assistant executive director of the Economic Crime Institute at Utica College; Thomas Lenahan, professor emeritus at Herkimer County Community College; Martin Biegelman, director of the Financial Integrity Unity at Microsoft; Ken Jones, former Deputy Chief Inspector, U.S. Postal Inspection Service, and currently a director of Forensic Advisory Services for KPMG LLP; and Ray Philo, the Chief of Police for the Town of New Hartford, New York.

Special acknowledgments go those executives who teach at the Executive Development Institute of the International Association of Campus Law Enforcement Administrators, who are always sharing new concepts and trends. They include Sue Riseling, University of Wisconsin, and John King, Tufts University.

George Curtis thanks his family—Lorraine, Michael, and Melissa—for allowing him to usurp family time and for their support and encouragement in completing this task. He also appreciates the collaborative and supportive environment nurtured by colleagues at Utica College, as well as the constant encouragement and support of graduate and undergraduate students.

Bruce McBride gives thanks to his family—Barbara, Robbie, Megan, and Brian—for their patience and support. He also says thank you to his colleagues and friends at Utica college.

Finally, we thank the reviewers of this edition: D.C. Jim Dozier, Sam Houston State University; Daniel K. Maxwell, University of New Haven and University of Phoenix; and Larry Snyder, Herkimer County Community College. We also thank the reviewers of the first edition: Neal Strehlow, Fox Valley Technical College; Norman Bates, Northeastern University; and David Mullins, Webster University.

ABOUT THE AUTHORS

George E. Curtis, J.D., is Dean of the School of Business and Justice Studies and Executive Director of Economic Crime Institutes at Utica College and is a member the New York State Bar Association, the Association of Certified Fraud Examiners, the Association of Certified Fraud Specialists, and ASIS International.

R. Bruce McBride, Ed.D., is Professor of Criminal Justice at Utica College and is a member of ASIS International, the International Association of Campus Law Enforcement Administrators, and the Criminal Justice Educators Association of New York State. He is the former Assistant Vice Chancellor for University Police of the State University of New York.

1

■ ■ ■

Development of Security in the United States

KEY TERMS

alarm services, ASIS International, assets, biometric security, Brinks, CCTV, cell phone, client, corporate/proprietary services, critical infrastructure, cyberspace, Department of Homeland Security, executive protection, frontier, fusion center, homefront security, IACP, Internet, magnetic strip, National Advisory Committee on Criminal Justice Standards and Goals, Securitas, security, security services, Texas Rangers, U.S. Marshals Service, watch and guard

INTRODUCTION

Security is generally defined as achieving safety, protection, and freedom from threats and danger. Historically, all communities have enacted rules and procedures, built fortifications, installed locks and alarms, and obtained arms to protect themselves from various threats. As discussed by the National Advisory Committee on Criminal Justice Standards and Goals (1976: 3–11), the concept of security begins with providing for one's personal protection and expands to the family and then to the larger societies of community, political entity, and nation. In modern society, people cannot work, play, or socialize unless they feel safe and secure in their own environments. For this discussion, *security* is viewed as providing safety and protection to people and protecting assets and property. Our definition of *assets* is rather broad because it includes such items as money, equipment, employees, information, and professional reputation. In the area of property, we include the concept of critical infrastructure, which means the service and delivery system for food, water, electricity, transportation, and electronic commerce.

The issue of security has taken on a new meaning since the events of September 11, 2001. Within hours after the attacks on the World Trade Center in New York City and the Pentagon in Arlington, Virginia, many state and municipal police departments began patrol-security operations at various sites such as water reservoirs, nuclear power plants, railroad yards, and major public buildings. Private corporations and public security forces began reviewing emergency response plans in order to respond to a potential second wave of terrorist attacks and its aftermath. These efforts were immediately apparent at airports with the suspension of flight service for several days followed by the immediate initiation of new passenger- and baggage-screening procedures and the eventual federal government takeover of airport security. From a public administration standpoint, the most notable effect was the reorganization of the federal government under the auspices of the new Department of Homeland Security. Within a month and a half, additional powers were given to federal law enforcement agencies under the USA PATRIOT Act with regard to antiterrorism operations, such as money transfer monitoring, search warrants, and electronic eavesdropping.

The importance of domestic security for the 2009–2010 fiscal year is indicated by the federal budget, which allocated $50 billion for homeland security funding including equipment and training for state and local emergency responders. Today one notes the more subtle changes that continue to take place in terms of the importance of national threat levels by color codes, the deployment of extra police and security officers and metal detection devices at municipal buildings and corporate headquarters, concrete bomb barriers around building perimeters, removal or trimming of shrubbery around office complexes, and increased demand of personal identification to purchase plane, train, and bus tickets. Taken together, these changes illustrate the nationwide effort that has occurred to focus public law enforcement and private sector security services on protecting the nation.

There are, however, operational, legal, and philosophical differences between public law enforcement and private sector security. The differences are noticed immediately in criminal justice education courses and curricula. Textbooks and monographs regarding security issues remain schematically and contextually split between public sector policing and private security. Simply stated, the private sector is viewed as being primarily responsible for an organization's perimeter, internal security of personnel and corporate assets, and safety of employees and visitors. Public-sector state, county, and local police enforce state and federal laws in providing public safety. Somewhere in between remains a wide range of private, state, and federal agencies that enforce statutes, conduct agency-related investigations, and provide both national and agency security.

There has always been mistrust between security officers, often deemed "watchmen," and the "real police." The real police have law enforcement powers and use weapons, while security officers often lack enforcement powers and ability to use weapons. However, as a police officer, one of the authors frequently "shook doors" and undertook security assignments including executive protection, building security surveys, and crime prevention/risk-assessment projects. As an administrator over a state university system, co-workers and clients often referred to the police department as "security" based on the agency's historical beginnings.

The reality is that many private sector security operations have modern equipment for protecting transportation facilities, health and higher education organizations, and nuclear plants. Municipal and state governments spend millions of dollar each day for "security," to protect important infrastructure sites such as public buildings, monuments, water and electric power facilities, and cyber business operations.

Thus, the discussion of "security" has to be considered in a larger context under the term *security services,* which includes a wide range of agencies in both the public and private sectors that provide the assistance encompassed by our definition. But first, to obtain a broad overview of security services in the United States, one has to review the agency types and numbers of public police officers, private security officers, security officers working for public agencies, investigative agents, privately hired contract and proprietary security officers and investigators, computer security specialists, and auxiliary, volunteer, and reserve officers. This does not include communications specialists, analysts, technical support personnel, consultants, vendors, or equipment manufacturers.

Numerically, there are more private security officers than police officers. At this time, it is difficult to calculate the number of personnel who could be classified as security officers because of the wide range of activities classified as security—a conservative estimate is approximately 2 million. According to the Bureau of Justice Statistics (2007), in calendar year 2004, there were approximately 1.1 million police personnel, of which 740,000 were sworn police officers. This figure does not include federal officers and investigators with police powers. These figures were collected from about 1900 police departments that participated in the Census of State and Local Law Enforcement Agencies administered that year. There continues to be more nonsworn personnel involved in private security or public safety operations each year.

The issues of national security, exemplified by the formation of the new cabinet-level Department of Homeland Security in April 2003, indicate the need for the inclusion of a wide range of services, specialty areas, and agencies. The new federal department, for example, has more than 170,000 members with twenty-two separate agencies, including, those with long historical traditions such as the Coast Guard, Secret Service, Border Patrol, and Customs. On the state and county levels, police departments have formed units and subunits to deal with the security of public buildings, utilities, transportation networks, and cyber information systems. In summary, there is an expanding and interacting role for all public and private sector agencies and corporations to contribute to the domestic security of the United States under the broad term of security services. There is also a need for public sector and private sector agencies to begin working better and smarter in addressing community security needs. For now, we consider the main differences between policing and security services in the United States. In many instances, the image is hazy because, as stated, many police departments find themselves involved in security operations. Even before 9/11, the operational situation was sometimes confusing in that police officers might work their regular assignment and then take on part-time security work in their off-hours. From our perspective, the primary role of U.S. police departments is to provide a wide range of law enforcement services to a geographic entity. Unlike other countries, the United States has a decentralized system with a federal system of government composed of state, county, and local (i.e., city, town, and village) entities with various police powers. In theory, the enforcement of laws and suppression of crime are provided to all citizens in a distinct geographic district. In some areas, crime and accident victims have a choice in calling either the state, county, or local police department to respond to a complaint or emergency situation.

Security service companies and agencies, which may include a unit in a large government agency, have primary missions in protecting assets—such as people, property, and information—of a defined client. The client might be an individual, a company, or a governmental entity. In many cases there is a formal contractual or operational agreement stating the client's responsibility for paying for the service. Hence, this becomes the contextual outline for private security and private policing. If the client does not want the service or is unable to pay for it, the relationship ends. While some security service units have law enforcement powers, these powers are granted only by the state as a means to protecting assets. This grant of law enforcement power is very common with public hospital, university, and mental health facility police who have state powers, but their primary client is the organization to which they are assigned.

Even in communities with state, county, or municipal policing services, some clients pay an additional cost. For example, a household may be protected by a city police department that it supports by taxes, but if it wants additional protection such as a residential alarm service, a gated community neighborhood, or a twenty-four–hour bodyguard detail, the household has to pay for it. It is true that people who have higher incomes can buy extra protection and security!

AN HISTORICAL OVERVIEW

The development of security in the United States mirrors the creation and expansion of the United States from an English colony to a world power. Ironically, many interstate security services and investigations were operated by private companies before being replaced by the federal government or state police agencies. Since World War II, a number of security service provider models have been established that continue to remain in business. Many of these companies are now engaged in providing global services or have become a subsidiary of global security service conglomerates. In tracing this development, this chapter also focuses on the development of technology from the Industrial Revolution of the mid-1800s to the present Information Age and its impact on security operations and equipment.

THE COLONIAL PERIOD

Based on the English experience in the late 1700s, the first security services for colonial cities and towns were provided by paid and volunteer watchmen. Their main purpose was to sound warning alarms for house fires and attacks by Indians. The sheriff, who was the main officer for the colonial court system, provided the enforcement of laws. The British army, assisted by citizen militias, provided the mainstay of security. The cost of military expenses related to the French and Indian War and frontier security led to the imposition of taxes on legal documents and imports by the Crown. These costs for providing armed forces became just one of the underlying causes of the American Revolution.

The creation of the United States of America in 1781 resulted in the creation of a limited standing army assisted by state militias. National border security was first provided by the Coast Guard to deal with smugglers and shipwrecked sailors and to warn of possible attacks by pirates and foreign powers. The U.S. Customs Service was also created to deal with border and port entry issues, collect duties on imported goods, and process cargo and mail. Eventually in growing urban areas, the watchman system was eventually replaced by paid police. The growth of public police departments mirrored the population expansion brought on by immigration and the growth of the factory system for producing goods. The factory system resulted in wholesale movements of people from farms to urban centers, which caused extraordinary problems of poverty, crime, and lawlessness. Citing various sources, Lersch (2002) posits that the formation of early police departments was undertaken to protect the property of political and business elites and was viewed as a way to control immigrants, the poor, and freed slaves. Nevertheless, by 1840, uniformed police overseen by civilian governments replaced the armed forces in providing public safety services.

SECURITY IN THE NINETEENTH CENTURY

The concept of the frontier is important in studying security services in the United States. By strict definition, the frontier is territory that is unsettled and not under the jurisdiction of a formal governmental authority. The American frontier began along the Eastern seaboard in the late 1700s and slowly expanded to the West Coast to encompass the entire country by 1890. Security for frontier settlements initially was provided by the military and U.S. Marshals Service, which today remains as the law enforcement arm of the U.S. court system. The main enemies of new settlers were attacking Indian tribes, bandits, and cattle and horse thieves. As westward expansion spread across the Mississippi River and into the Southwest, state governments often provided security to frontier settlements through state-sponsored militias or citizen police such as the Texas Rangers. Founded after the revolution against Mexico in 1836, the Rangers provided protection for settlers against hostile Indian war parties and Mexican bandits throughout the nineteenth century. As Utley (2002) discussed, the Rangers often ignored international boundary lines and pursued raiding parties and wanted criminals into Mexico but frequently did not take prisoners back to Texas. As settlements became towns and towns became cities, formal law enforcement bureaucracies were established.

The rise and expansion of railroads contributed to the development of national public safety services on the American frontier. Railroad companies were often granted powers by state legislatures to create police or detective forces to protect their property interests anywhere near the railroad right of way. As Simonsen (1998: 16) describes, Chicago businessman Allen Pinkerton formed a private guard service in 1850 that eventually provided security and investigative services to transportation companies and industrial clients. Poulin and Nemeth (2005) credit Pinkerton with having the most influential impact on the development of the security industry for tracking down interstate criminals and protecting private property. Other firms that were created during this era included the Wells Fargo Company, Brinks, Burns, and others. During the Civil War the federal government relied on these private companies for war intelligence. It is often reported that the Pinkerton National Detective Agency was the actual "secret service" for the Union army during the Civil War. After the war, these agencies were used by individuals and local governments to pursue interstate investigations and wanted persons. These private detective agencies actively pursued the Jesse James gang and other bank and railroad bandit groups such as the Daltons, Renos, and the Youngers in the Midwest and Southwest United States.

As the United States continued to grow as a rising industrial power after the Civil War, one of the roles for private protection agencies was to prevent labor unrest and undertake intelligence efforts against labor organizers and strikers. The major intent of most union protests was for resolution of differences between labor and management, but some groups felt that violence was the only way to create rapid change for working people. One major group, the International Workers of the World, felt that capitalism would not change unless company owners were removed with violence. Industrial giants, such as Andrew Carnegie, John D. Rockefeller, and a wide range of local and regional business owners, who were afraid of loss of production and destruction of property, hired private watch companies and often requested the support of state and federal troops and police to arrest organizers and quell strikes. Pitched gun battles often occurred between union men and employer guards during strikes at coal mines, steel mills, and railroad facilities between 1870 and 1910 over reduced wages, general working conditions, and prohibitions against workers forming or joining labor unions. Discussing the role of Pinkerton and other private security companies in labor disputes, Clifford (2004) discusses that "Pinkerton men" and other operatives were used for undercover work, strikebreaking, and an armed force for various battles. For the Pullman railroad car strike of 1894, more than 3,600 Pinkerton men were sworn in as special deputies to confront striking car repairmen. In many of these case studies, the owners replaced the strikers with lower paid workers who were often newly arrived immigrants to the country. Although there was a lull in labor battles during World War I, renewed violence occurred during the Great Depression from 1930 to 1939 in all major industries. This trend ended with federal legislation, such as the National Labor Relations Act, that allowed workers to form unions.

Not until the early twentieth century was the interstate pursuit of crimes and investigations gradually changed from private detective agencies to federal and state organizations. Historically, each major federal and state law enforcement agency started with a specific role and then expanded to other areas. For example, the Federal Bureau of Investigation (FBI), created in 1908 as an agency to investigate federal crimes, did not emerge as an important law enforcement agency until the 1930s when there was national concern for interstate kidnapping and bank robbery. The FBI's mission to deal with internal security and counterterrorism began in World War II when agents were assigned to domestic intelligence-gathering assignments to prevent espionage and sabotage by foreign agents. This mission expanded after 1945 to address the growth of the Russian empire and the threat of domestic Communist Party activity. The most profound innovations occurred, however, during the late 1930s under Director J. Edgar Hoover. Hoover, who served as director for 48 years, established high standards for personnel and their training in the FBI, then titled "Bureau of Investigation." One great change involved having criminal records switched from the International Association of Chiefs of Police to the FBI, thus creating a national criminal information data bank. Another was the creation of the FBI crime laboratory that later became the model for state and regional laboratories.

SECURITY MODELS DURING AND AFTER WORLD WAR II

Internal security during World War II was an important national undertaking. The term *homefront security* was used as citizens volunteered for plane spotting, shore patrol, civil defense, and emergency medical services. Citizen and local police were organized and trained to keep watch and report any suspicious activity near railroad yards, factories, and defense plants. Thousands of men who were hired to provide plant security were trained by local police and federal trainers, thus forming the nucleus of the "private security" industry. By the end of World War II, the following security service models were firmly in place.

CONTRACT WATCH AND GUARD SERVICES   These services provide monitoring and physical patrol of company perimeters, buildings, and parking lots. Within the past ten years, many public agencies, including the military, have outsourced their perimeter security needs to private vendors as a means of reducing personnel and deployment costs. These services are provided by national contract agencies such as Wackenhut, Guardsmark, Allied Barton, Securitas, and various regional and local private companies. Note that Burns, Pinkerton, and Wells Fargo were merged into Securitas in 2003.

CONTRACT INVESTIGATIVE SERVICES   These investigation services obtain information on a wide range of areas such as criminal incidents, civil lawsuits, domestic breakups, unusual employee behavior, corporate merger intelligence, and background clearances for high-risk positions. Private law firms also use these services to locate witnesses and review evidence obtained from the state prosecutor. In the public sector, many agencies and corporations contract with private services to deal with agency affairs involving fraud and mismanagement. The leading contract companies include Garda, Securitas, and Kroll Inc. There are also a wide variety of regional and local agencies that provide these services. As noted later in this chapter, a number of national companies provide international services.

SECURITY TRANSPORT AND CASH MANAGEMENT   Historically linked to the pre–Civil War era, these services continue to transport money, jewelry, and valuable documents and other items between locations by rail, sea, air, and ground transport. The most noted are the Brinks Corporation and Loomis, which can trace their beginnings to transportation in the American West. The greatest change in these services is the international transport of cash and valuables as needed by a global economy.

CORPORATE/PROPRIETARY AND PUBLIC AGENCY SECURITY SERVICES   Based on the mission of the organization, such services are created by a corporation or a public entity to include perimeter security, investigative services, audits, employee background checks, financial fraud, fire safety, emergency management, business continuity, risk management, and parking services. Often these security services are granted powers to enforce penal and traffic laws related to service populations. Examples include campus and public authority police departments that were created to deal with protecting a defined clientele. Also established were investigative units for most federal agencies such as the Securities and Exchange Commission, which conducts reviews of potential abuse and fraud in the securities industry. In the 1980s, many internal security units added computer security to deal with increasing incidents of cyber crime and electronic intrusions into computer systems and networks.

EXECUTIVE PROTECTION   Terrorism and kidnap for ransom have long historical traditions, and industrial leaders, media celebrities, and government officials have often relied on personal guard services. Executive protection includes providing security for persons during events or around the clock in their residences and workplaces as well as entering behind-the-scene negotiations to ransom kidnapped victims. The most noted public executive protection agency perhaps is the U.S. Secret Service, which is now part of the new Department of Homeland Security. Originally created to deal with currency counterfeiting gangs, the mission of this agency expanded to protection of the president and vice president of the United States after the assassination of President William McKinley in 1901.

ALARM SERVICES   The first alarm system consisted of telegraph lines connected to private homes and businesses that were linked to electrical contacts on doors and windows (Hess and Wrobleski, 1996: 19–20). Over time, these telegraph systems were replaced by alarm services provided over telephone lines. Today many national and local alarm services provide businesses and homes with a wide variety of alarm and fire protection services based on motion and heat detection technology. Alarms are connected to a central alarm station, which in turn notifies the police department where the home or business is located. Corporations that perform this service include Honeywell, ADT, Siemens, and Simplex. A negative consequence of the growth of alarm services in the 1970s was the profusion of false alarm calls activated by pets, electric storms, and homeowner misuse. This was an important topic addressed by the National Advisory Task Force on Private Security in 1979, which made more than twenty recommendations for service improvement, including licensing alarm dealers, properly training alarm users, setting standards for equipment, and imposing sanctions for repeated false reports. Today in some areas, false alarms have become such a problem that police departments are not responding unless they receive a backup phone call from the owner or a victim.

TECHNICAL CONSULTING AND SUPPLY SERVICES   One of the overlooked areas in the security industry is a vast network of consultant and supply services. Today it is impossible for any administrator to keep track of the many changes that occur in the security industry each year. Equipment supply companies generally range from local lock and alarm equipment services to national companies that produce and sell advanced computerized systems. Similarly, thousands of consultants offer their expertise on issues that include organization and management, training, and personnel selection including executive searches, perimeter and internal control cost applications, and advanced technological systems protection. Consultants often prepare bid specifications for equipment selection. A recent listing of exhibitors (Security Management, 2009) attending a national conference gives a sample of the type of vendor services available under this heading (see Exhibit 1-1).

It is important to note that many national companies offer a wide range of service types just discussed. For example, Wackenhut Security offers watch and guard, executive protection, and even airport emergency planning. The company also contracts for private jail services. As discussed later in this chapter, the global economic environment has created the need for the creation of international conglomerations that offer these services on an international basis.

Access Control	Integrated Security Systems
Alarms	Intrusion Detection Equipment
Asset Recovery, Tracking	Key Controls
Biometrics	Lighting
Blast Mitigation	Locks
Bullet Resistant Systems	Modular Vaults
Central Station Monitoring	Night Vision Devices
Chemical Trace Detection	Parking
CCTV Systems	Perimeter Protection
Command and Control Stations	Product Testing
Communications	Protective Barriers
Computer Services	Risks
Covert Video	Safes and Security Containers
Digital Video Recorders	Security Doors
Document Destruction	Signal Transmission Systems
Door and Door Hardware	Security Software
Electronic Article Surveillance	Surveillance and Still Cameras
Explosive Detection and Engineering	Tactical Lighting
Fire Safety	Trade Secrets
First Aid/Emergency Equipment	Truth Verification
Global Position Systems	Uniforms and Protective Apparel
Guard Dogs	Video Encryption
Guard Services	Weapons and Weapons Disposal
Guard Tour Systems	X-ray, Metal, Weapons and Bomb Detection
Hazardous Materials	Equipment

EXHIBIT 1-1   Sample of Security Service Vendors ASIS Convention—2009

THE 1960s

By the mid-1960s, traditional security enterprises had increased dramatically as a result of rising crime rates, racial riots, antiwar and civil rights protests, campus demonstrations, and building takeovers. This increasing violent crime was exemplified by the assassinations of President John F. Kennedy, his brother and presidential candidate Robert Kennedy, and civil rights activists such as Martin Luther King and Medgar Evers. On the streets, there was alarming concern about the robbery, theft, drug use and sale, criminal mischief, and general disorder brought about by increased drug sales. As discussed by Pittman (1974), there was increased use of drugs in African American, Hispanic, and white neighborhoods by persons under twenty-one years of age. Concurrently, there was national acceptance by persons of varied backgrounds of drug use including marijuana, cocaine, amphetamines, and hallucinogens that contributed to increased personal and property crime rates. Most alarming was the increased rate of juvenile crime committed by children between the ages of twelve and eighteen. Using Uniform Crime Report data for the early 1970s, Griffin and Griffin (1978: 67–68) reported that just over 2 million persons under the age of eighteen were arrested for criminal offenses, the most common being assault, property crimes, and violations of drug laws. Since that time, this figure has not widely fluctuated, and juveniles continue to constitute approximately 18 to 20 percent of all arrests in this area.

Against this background, private corporations and public enterprises increased their efforts to improve perimeter security and to deal with internal personal safety issues related to the organization. For example, the use of campus and hospital security forces occurred during the late 1960s based on the increase of crime and campus disorders over civil rights, the Vietnam War, and student governance. As presented by Powell (1981: 9), college and university campuses became prime targets for outside criminals "who realized that a campus population was made up of mostly young people who had little concern for security or crime and administrators whose main interest was education, not protection or enforcing the law."

With the rampant growth of private security services, the need for national standards in the industry became apparent because of the lack of administrative regulations for security providers. The National Advisory Committee on Criminal Justice Standards and Goals, which was in the early 1970s conducting a series of investigations into the inner workings of the criminal justice system, included the private security industry. Its task force report on *Private Security,* which was issued in 1976, created some fifty standards dealing with hiring, training, and the operation of private security businesses. Many of these standards called for increased cooperation between private security providers and public law enforcement. Although these were simply recommendations, they became the benchmarks for state and federal legislation related to the security industry into the twenty-first century.

Professional Associations

During the 1960s, professional associations in both the public and private sectors addressed personal and operational standards and national policy issues. For police chiefs, the International Association of Chiefs of Police (IACP), originally founded in 1893 as the National Chiefs of Police Union, was created to further professional development and networking among police chiefs for the apprehension of wanted persons. By the 1960s, the IACP had become a leading group for setting nationwide policy standards for officer recruitment, training, operational policies, and executive development. Articles on programs, innovations, and technology appear in *The Police Chief,* the association's monthly magazine.

The American Society for Industrial Security (now termed ASIS International) was established in 1955 to promote professional standards and networking for the private security industry. In 1977 ASIS established the certified protection professional program, which is a nationally recognized course and examination for certifying security managers. Many of the main topics covered in the review curriculum and testing have been presented in this text, including security management practices, human resource administration, risk and vulnerability assessment, investigative methods and resources, legal issues including tort liability, physical security, emergency management, and protection of sensitive information. The association also offers certifications for Physical Security Professional and Professional Certified Investigator. The Physical Security Professional certification is designed for security services personnel whose main tasks involve threat analysis, integrated security systems design, and security assessment. The Professional Certified Investigator certification is designed for those who deal mainly in investigation, and the knowledge and skill areas include case management, evidence collection, and case presentation. Another innovative course is a two-week Executive Development program offered in conjunction with the Wharton School of Finance, University of Pennsylvania. Topics in this program include strategic thinking, leadership, finance and management, and other related areas. These and other training opportunities can be found at www.asisonline.org. Local, state, and regional ASIS chapters offer a number of training programs at their meetings. The chapters publishes *Security Management,* which is offered each month to members in hard copy and online.

Not surprisingly, many law enforcement and security personnel belong to both organizations. Both groups offer a number of excellent training programs and model program policy standards. IACP, ASIS, and other security groups provide political policy review and often address Congress and state legislatures on a wide range of safety and security issues. Their national conventions are "go-to" affairs for major politicians including the president and the attorney general of the United States. These annual conferences also attract national and international speakers and must be held in large cities with major hotels and a convention center that can accommodate the thousands of attendees.

Other professional associations for security personnel were also established during this time for a wide range of industry groups such as colleges and universities, hospitals, investigative groups, and alarm companies. The International Association of Campus Law Enforcement Administrators (IACLEA) was founded in 1958 to address personnel and law enforcement operational standards and campus safety issues. Like other associations, IACLEA provides executive training, legal information, and executive peer reviews of campus operations. Regional and state associations of campus law enforcement administrators include the Northeast Association of Campus Security Administrators. Health care and safety directors in the nation's hospitals founded the International Association for Healthcare Security & Safety to create communication and training among executives. It offers a number of basic and supervisory training courses to health care personnel.

Several professional associations focus on specific aspects of security services including investigations. Some of the more prominent of those organizations are the International Association of Financial Crimes Investigators (IAFCI), Association of Certified Fraud Examiners (ACFE), Institute of Internal Auditors (IIA), High Technology Crime Investigators Association (HTCIA), and the International Association of Computer Investigative Specialists (IACIS). Each of these organizations conducts conferences and educational and training sessions each year and maintains a Web site with valuable links and publications for its members. Several of the organizations provide certification programs (e.g., the certified financial crimes investigators [CFCI], certified fraud examiner [CFE], and the certified forensic computer examiner [CFCE]) to validate the knowledge and expertise of their membership. For an exhaustive list of professional associations that covers both state and national listings, please go to www.mainesecurity.com/Security_Organizations.htm.

Technological Innovations in Security

Technological innovations for security applications continue to expand at a fast pace. Each year, the authors attend several major security conferences that display new systems programs and hardware. The showroom floors at these events are divided into closed-circuit television systems (CCTV), computer monitoring, computer record systems, radio communications, and miscellaneous devices, including locks, alarms, electronic detection systems, motor vehicles, and weapons. In our visits to security sites throughout the United States, we see this technology being applied in all kinds of criminal justice situations.

Perhaps the most high-tech facility recently reviewed was a new county correctional facility in Rochester, New York. The facility consists of four 3-tiered pods housing approximately fifty-five inmates per pod. By computer, one officer in a control booth controls each pod area, which includes opening and closing individual cells and controlling access into the pod. Meals, limited recreation, medical calls, and visitor time can all be regulated. Monitoring is provided by CCTV and computer systems linked to a central station for the entire facility. The CCTV cameras are so powerful that the operator can direct the camera to pick out a person's facial features. To enter each secure area, correctional personnel have electronic proximity access cards, which are programmed to allow access to specific areas based on the officer's rank and duties. Planners anticipate that one officer who wears a wireless alarm unit could control each pod. If the alarm is activated, the computer would locate the source and location of the alarm call so that help could be summoned. Ironically, the same company that developed the personal alarm system is presently considering selling the unit to college campuses and health care facilities in order to provide personal protection for employees and students.

Outside the correctional center, patrol personnel have wireless laptop computers in their patrol units for report writing, data checks, and communications transmissions. Many police departments now equip their personnel on foot patrol with handheld units that can be used for data checks on persons and cars. Patrol units can also be tracked through vehicle locating systems, which is part of a computerization effort in enhanced 911 communications centers. Computer-aided dispatching allows communicators not only to take complaints but also to complete a number of checks that match the complainant, location, and suspect with state and national crime data. Many patrol vehicles today have in-car cameras that can video-record activity inside the unit as well as interactions in the front and backseat of the vehicle. These are often used to record high-speed chases or complaints where citizens allege that they were mistreated by officers.

Many organizations have integrated security systems, which rely on a combination of access control alarms, video monitoring, patrol detection, and personal identification banks that are operated by computers and activated by intrusions or breaks in the system. Then there are still agencies that rely on locks and keys.

While this has helped security service operations to be effective, the introduction of computer technology has opened new avenues to criminals for theft and destruction of proprietary data. Today, the world communicates for business, educational, and social reasons through cyberspace. *Cyberspace* is a metaphor for the nonphysical terrain created by computer systems that communicate with each other. As a result, we now have terms such as *cyber crime, cyber predator, spoofer,* and *hacker,* which are discussed in later chapters.

THE NOT-SO-DISTANT PAST

Until the 1930s, individuals performed law enforcement and security measures on foot, bicycles, and horses. Automobiles did not become the major medium for patrol until after World War II. Before the 1930s, officers were assigned to specific beats and routinely reported to station houses for instructions and information updates. In large cities in the mid-1800s, different precincts used the telegraph to communicate with each other and headquarters. Other methods were used for patrol communications. In one rural village, a railroad-type semaphore signal was used to alert foot officers that they had to return to the station to hear a complaint or receive instructions. In the twentieth century, veteran officers recall walking their beats with a time box to log that they had checked certain locations. The officers inserted a certain key into the box that would record that the specific location had been checked. A punch was then recorded on a circular paper disk, and the disk was turned in at the end of the shift for verification. Today computerized handheld units can record or scan watch areas.

The authors are always amazed at how "old-school" patrol tactics reappear in the modern world. For example, bike patrols provide an excellent method for security patrol in crowded or limited vehicle access areas such as shopping malls, college campuses, city centers, tourist sites, and recreation areas. Officers on bikes with portable radios are able to cover a wide area and have increased interactions with citizens. At some locations, officers on horses are being used for the same reasons. Horseback patrols have been used for airport perimeter security because horse patrols can cover fields and wooded areas to guard against trespassers or terrorists setting up for a portable ground-to-air missile attack.

Locks and Alarms and Perimeter Security

The core of security hardware for many years was the traditional lock and key. Developed in the colonial period, the key is inserted into a tumbler device and causes the tumbler to move and thus open the door. Ironically, traditional keys remain the basic form for security in many locations. One of the authors recalls carrying a ring of twenty keys that could open various doors and gates. Each activity had to be recorded on a paper form and there was always the fear of losing the key set because rekeying the entire facility to ensure security would be a financial and operational nightmare. The problem of lost and copied keys remains an ever-present problem. There is also the issue of who could have master keys that open any lock in the facility.

With the development of the telegraph and telephone, businesses were able to be connected to a central alarm company for fire and burglary protection. These early systems relied on humans to pull the alarm or simple electrical connections at a door or window to activate a telegraph code to a central station. Today's burglar and fire detection systems use electronic and digital connections to either identify a threat (sudden heat surge), review a motion (a break in a radio wave signifying that there is a motion in an area or a need for help), or allow authorized persons into a building or sections of a building. Through a computer network, these systems also allow supervisors to monitor employee and authorized guest movement in the facility. The most common systems today include:

- Magnetic strip readers—a card with a magnetic strip is swiped through the reader; entry is either granted or denied.
- Proximity readers—the person who wears a badge simply waves it near a scanner to be granted access. The identifying binary digits on the card are matched to the main access computer for access or denial of access.
- Key punch—a code is punched into a pad and access is allowed or denied.
- Smart card—a plastic card is embedded with a computer chip and holds a wide range of information concerning its owner such as personal characteristics and medical history.

The latest development is in biometric security. Such a technology allows entry after a person's fingerprint, hand, or retina has been scanned and matched in a data file for access to a particular area. Proponents of biometrics posit that it is the best way to establish a person's identity because magnetic strip readers and proximity readers can be lost or stolen. Biometric systems are becoming very inexpensive, but they are being developed for major security needs (e.g., passenger identification) as a result of September 11 attacks. Biometric systems can interface with proximity cards to identify both a fingerprint and the owner of the card. The next generation of biometrics will be a multimodal system that matches a person's facial and voice characteristics. Futurists also point to the use of DNA, ear characteristics, computer keystroke, personal signature, and perhaps body odor as identity elements. As discussed, later, any access control system has strengths and weaknesses.

Communications Technology

The first innovation in communications technology was base-to-car radio communications whereby officers could radio from remote areas to base stations on beat conditions and could be dispatched to calls after complainants phoned or walked into the station. The early police radios relied on vacuum tubes, which were bulky and could be placed only on vehicles or in large backpacks. With the development of the transistor that began in the 1940s, Bell Telephone, General Electric, Motorola, and other vendors developed a battery-powered portable radio so that foot patrol officers could talk to their base and to each other. By today's standards, the first portable radios were comparatively large. They also had varying broadcasting distance and required constant recharging from electrical sources. Today's radios are handheld and can be combined with cell phone technology, which includes picture transmissions. The development of the cell phone mirrored that of police portable radios; both are wireless transmitting devices. Bellis (2003) reports that cell phone technology began in 1947 and was actually available for public use by the mid-1970s. Unfortunately, there was not enough airwave space available for commercial applications until the Federal Communications Commission, the regulatory agency for all radio transmissions, granted phone companies the right to employ alternative cell technologies with the 800-mhg bands in 1987. This allowed companies to create a number of base stations to divide the service between a large number of local cell towers. Cell phones increase the capability for field units to speak to each other in continuous conversation. Small security companies can use them instead of a police/fire frequency for business purposes. Base stations for communications have evolved from the one-channel base to the car system prevalent in the 1960s. Caller identification, digital recording of complaints and dispatch instructions, trunk systems to handle a large volume of calls, and multifrequency scanning are all common functions found in communications centers.

Closed-Circuit Television

The development of television, video, and cable technology for general use contributed to the development of closed-circuit television systems, which relies on high-density TV receiving digitized transmissions through fiber-optic cable from a remote camera. The authors recall that early CCTV monitoring systems were black and white and were not able to show activity in "real time." The development of cheap fiber-optic cable and digital technology has addressed this problem and large amounts of picture information can be transferred from the camera to the video monitor. Video cameras range in size from traditional weatherproof outdoor cameras of approximately 5 feet in length to a camera the size of a small book of matches for covert video surveillance purposes. Today's cameras also have 360-degree ease of movement and are often hidden inside domes attached to ceiling connections.

Related to the use of cameras was the development of video recording technology, which allows sound and visual recordings to be saved on magnetic tape. The first audio recorders were made after 1947 and were used to record radio programs. At the same time, recorders were being developed to tape television programs, which before the early 1950s had to be broadcast live. Research and development by a number of U.S. and Japanese companies for a home video recording unit led to the invention of Betamax and VHS recording devices by 1973. The commercial applications were immediately used by security services to record and store images for intelligence and security purposes. Today digital audio and video recordings can be sent from a remote site camera to a main station by using the Internet and then stored on computer disk instead of magnetic tape. The development of wireless broadband technology with camera features can now record from stationary positions to a command center.

At our favorite wine store, the owner had a contest in which customers were asked to identify all of the store's camera sites; the winner would win a 10 percent discount. In all, he had 11 cameras including one hidden in a clock. While this is a humorous example, the incident indicated the extent to which general retail, mall, sporting, educational, and public areas are now being watched for crime and event monitoring. An emerging issue in many cities is the increased use of CCTV in dense crowd or crime-prone areas. As will be discussed throughout this book, CCTV cameras are being increasingly used by a wide range of public and private sector agencies to monitor street activity and search for wanted persons, and for investigative review purposes. Through analytics software, systems can be programmed to look for persons acting suspicious or entering restricted locations. Studies continue to show that the use of CCTV in a specific area generally results in a reduction of public offenses. There are a number of caveats to this conclusion including the rate of active response by security services and law enforcement to an incident.

Computer Technology

From the late 1970s, computer technology slowly developed for a variety of security management applications such as data retrieval, recordkeeping, crime mapping, intelligence analysis, and computer-aided dispatch. As discussed by Negroponte (1995), in 1972 there were only 150,000 computers in use. Today it is estimated that one company will sell more than 100 million computers. The computer revolution occurred with the introduction of the personal computer, which slowly replaced the bulky mainframe units that powered office machines. In 1992, small laptop units were introduced and became "must-have" equipment for many computer users while traveling or in remote locations. The laptop has been improved so much that some people use it exclusively instead of a desk PC. Battery storage has improved, and now users can use a wireless network connection rather than hooking into a phone line. Closely tied to the development of the laptop computer was the CD-Rom drive, which enabled storage of about 5 billon or more bits on compact disks. These drives have been very important for storage of records and information. As Negroponte states, each CD-Rom can store more than 100 classic books (1995: 68). The development of inexpensive computer units that could communicate with each other by phone lines opened the way for the practice of hacking, by which computer criminals could essentially burglarize networks by inserting and erasing data and altering procedural commands. Most damaging is the insertion of viruses or instructional commands that basically copy themselves over and over again thus destroying the host system. In their review of corporate crime in the twentieth century, Rosoff, Pontell, and Tillman (2002) state that viruses have cost governments and private corporations billions of dollars to repair network systems. One of the more notorious events for this century was the Love Bug of 2000. This virus infected not only corporations and private e-mail accounts but also high security systems including the National Security Agency. Since 2000 a number of viruses have been created by bored computer hackers and professional data thieves around the world and these have invaded a number of systems.

The worst possible scenario envisioned by security planners is the use of the computer by terrorists to hack into infrastructure systems. Several case studies have shown that hackers follow world events. For example, Chinese hackers attempted to gain access to various Defense Department data banks after a surveillance plane collided with a jet interceptor that was attempting to monitor Americans. From a terrorism standpoint, there is fear that hackers will be able to shut down or modify computers controlling air traffic systems, water control, railroad switches, or the banking industry, thereby causing immediate panic. As a result, the National Infrastructure Protection Center has become an important element of the homeland security effort to deal with these threats and respond to actual emergency events.

Magnetic Cards

The key to most commerce today is an electronic card reader which reads information on the magnetic stripe of a payment card that is installed at point of sale (POS) terminals such as ATM machines and gas pumps for credit and debit card transactions. Before electronic cards, most credit cards were plastic and the embossed account number and expiration date on the front of the card were used to make an imprint on paper. These paper transactions were then sent in batches to a card company for payments and billing. Today, most cards have a magnetic strip that has three precise tracks so that the card can be read at point of sale terminals anywhere in the world. As outlined by Furchgott (2003), each track contains important information regarding a security code for card verification and a name and account number, expiration data, account limits, and a personal identification number (PIN) verification key. This information is captured by the card reader and then transmitted to the credit company's processing center. For security applications, the same process is used to unlock doors after the card is read. Information regarding time and date of entrance is also recorded. In many locations, one of the tracks on the card contains information that would limit the user's access to certain buildings or rooms based on day and time.

Closely associated with magnetic cards are smart cards; as mentioned earlier, they contain a computer chip and can hold a wide range of personal and financial information. At certain college campuses, these cards are used for identification, food services, library access, residence hall access, and debit use. Like any card of convenience, these cards are often stolen, and PIN codes left in wallets or on dressers are used by the thief to obtain access to the account.

As with any application, the human factor determines how much security is obtained by a particular card program. Persons with magnetic access cards are known to give the cards to friends. It is not uncommon at schools for one student to use his or her card to gain access to a location and then allow strangers to follow him or her into it. For financial applications, criminals use portable skimmers to capture the information from the magnetic stripe on a card and then download it to a personal computer for creating counterfeit cards to access accounts. It is estimated that millions of dollars are stolen through skimming scams annually.

According to Suzanne Lynch (personnel communication, December 9, 2009), because of increasing global fraud, the majority of the industrialized nations in Europe, Asia, South America, and Canada have moved toward implementing smart card technology in credit and debit cards. Smart-chip cards are imbedded with an encrypted chip that stores the same information as on a magnetic stripe along with other data that identify the validity of a transaction. Chip cards still have a magnetic stripe on their back as a "fallback" in the event the terminal is inoperative. Many countries, such as the United Kingdom, utilize both chip and a PIN in terminals to make a purchase or obtain cash at an ATM. Losses from many types of card frauds have been significantly reduced due to this technology.

The United States is the only industrialized nation that has not switched to or planned to switch to the use of smart-chip card technology. Banks that issue credit and debit cards, as well as the merchants that accept the cards, feel that the fraud losses are at an "acceptable level" and that upgrading the payment infrastructure would be too expensive. The upgrades would require banks replacing all magnetic stripe cards with cards embedded with chips and either replacing or upgrading ATMs and merchant point of sale terminals to "read" the information stored on the chip. This lack of global acceptance has angered many banks since there is an increase in cross-border fraud whereby foreign banks have experienced increased card losses in the United States. Organized fraudsters come to the United States with the specific intent of using cards with the backup magnetic stripe to commit fraud. A recent case example involved a large organized criminal group traveling to the United States from Europe to withdraw thousands of dollars from ATMs using information skimmed from the magnetic stripe and re-encoded on a piece of plastic along with the stolen PIN from UK customers. These cards could not be used in the United Kingdom because of the chip and PIN necessary to withdraw fund from UK ATMs.

Data Banks

Nationally, the development of national computer data banks for law enforcement and security purposes began with the National Crime Information Center (NCIC) developed by the FBI in 1967. NCIC remains the main data bank for information on wanted persons, stolen vehicles, missing persons, and stolen and recovered personal property. Today a wide range of state and regional computers maintain data on all types of crime information including suspect information, address/location history, motor vehicle and driver history, and modus operandi. The main disadvantage of these data banks is that only agency members can access one data bank for investigative purposes in what is called the "data silo." One of the reasons for the creation of Department of Homeland Security was to merge the computer data banks of various federal agencies into interacting systems for counterterrorism purposes. This is exemplified by the creation of intelligence or fusion centers in major cities and states by the Departments of Justice and Homeland Security. To address terrorist threats and major criminal enterprises, the goal of these centers is to gather and analyze intelligence and share information to specific agencies in a region and to databases in the United States. Thus, fusion centers "provide a mechanism where law enforcement, public safety, and private partners can come together with a common purpose and improve the ability to safeguard our homeland and prevent criminal activity" (Department of Homeland Security, 2009). Personnel assigned to a fusion center hail from state and local police forces, correctional agencies, federal attorney's office, federal agencies such as Customs and Border Protection, Office of Homeland Security, transportation authorities, and selected private organizations.

The effort here is to make connections when suspicious activity occurs. Take the following fictitious examples. An out-of-state motorist requests assistance for his disabled vehicle in a shopping mall near a major city in Colorado. The car is rented from the Minneapolis-St. Paul Airport. The driver says that he is attending a conference at the university located nearby but the security officer knows that school is on spring break and pretty much shut down. At the request of the security officer, he produces an international drivers' license that states that he is from London, England. The officer quietly calls for a nearby city police car to "stop by" and further inquires are made. The vehicle is shown to be rented from the airport and state and national computer checks do not show any wants or warrants for the driver. Although the person is rendered assistance, a number of postings are made to the regional fusion center to ascertain the motorist's identity and his purpose for visiting the United States. The center then makes inquires through a number of data banks including CPB and ICE.

The resources used by a fusion center would include such public databases as Lexis-Nexis, Google, ID Analytics, motor vehicle and driver files, criminal files, persons incarcerated, hate crimes, regional organized crime and drug task forces, sex offender classifications, and a variety of other databases. One resource is the Secure Automated Fast Event Tracking Network (SafetNet), which is a listing of subjects under investigation by a particular agency. The intent here is to prevent multiagencies from targeting the same suspect.

This raises many issues regarding privacy. The reality, however, is that credit card companies share all types of information for commercial interests. On a personal note, review your own credit report and see how much information has been collected about all your loans and credit cards. Computerized data banks today are used mainly to check a name or an investigative lead against outstanding warrants, crime and fraud behavior, and potential terrorist activity. Links for intelligence purposes are also made between organizations and individuals who may take part in criminal behaviors. Behaviors investigated could be frequent overseas flights to locations deemed centers of terrorist activity, transfer of funds between banks, use of fictitious identification, membership in or employment by certain organizations, purchase of one-way tickets, and use of cash. A related concept described by Lohr (2003) is data mining whereby travel trends and spending habits are used to target individuals for potential fraud or terrorism activity. This raises all kinds of questions regarding personal freedom. Persons reviewing their own credit activity often find incorrect information that needs to be corrected. Identity theft relies on a combination of electronic instructions and traditional paper larceny. As will be discussed, it is increasing at alarming rates.

Security and the Internet

The most notable advancement in technology in recent years is the Internet. As discussed by Grossman (1997), the Internet is nothing more than a number of computers linked together by networks. First created in the 1950s for defense research communication, the Internet then became a communications network for academic researchers and writers. By 1985, large private companies and colleges and universities had begun using the Internet for transferring messages and scientific material and for chats between interested parties. Concurrently, individual personal computers became inexpensive and started to be used for household and business applications. The general public was allowed to "subscribe" through service providers such as Compuserve and America Online (AOL), and the "you've-got-mail" culture was born for e-mail communications between individuals. By 1995, the Internet had become open and available for private and commercial ventures, which was further fueled by increased investment in so-called dot.com business enterprises for all kinds of goods and services, many of which collapsed in 2001.

Today there are billions of Internet users, and services continue to grow involving financial services, retail shopping via credit card or account, and education. Correspondingly, there has been the growth of social networking sites that allow people and organizations to share messages with a wide range of friends worldwide. However, the increased use of the Internet has given rise to related crimes including fraud, child pornography, computer stalking, and sales of illegal goods and services.

Legislative attempts continue to be made to place restrictions on the use of the Internet for criminal purposes. The most controversial of these issues continues to be child pornography and sexual predators targeting children. As outlined by Paladino (2003), amendments to the federal Communications Decency Act, passed by Congress in 1996, were enacted to forbid the transmission of "patently offensive" material to persons under the age of eighteen via interactive computer. That same year, the Child Pornography Protection Act was enacted to outlaw any visual depiction of a minor engaging in sexually explicit conduct. The intent of this law was to criminalize the distribution of virtual images of such conduct. In 1998, the Child On-Line Protection Act was passed to force commercial Web sites to take due diligence in ensuring that their subscribers were at least eighteen years of age. Later judicial review declared these three laws unconstitutional for violating the First Amendment and because of the vague definition of "obscene." However, certain types of cyber behaviors are illegal, such as communicating with a minor in an attempt to initiate a sexual liaison, which is outlawed in the Protection of Children from Sexual Predators Act, 2001. Nevertheless, as shown on Dateline NBC, many adults arrange liaisons with teenage victims through Internet interactions in chat rooms and common Internet Web sites.

As discussed by Schmalleger and Pittaro (2009) there are a wide gamut of nonsexual offenses committed through Internet such as illegal gambling, cyberstalking, cyberbullying, and larceny by identify theft. Identity theft, which is defined as the use of another person's identity for criminal purposes, has spawned a number of financial scams involving credit cards, online auctions, and other transactions. One that is very common is phishing, where a very official-like notice is sent to a target requesting a date of birth or social security number to address a problem with a bank account under one's name. Related is the Nigerian bank letter, whereby a target is asked by a victim of a troubled political or family estate to transfer millions of dollars out of the country. In return, the target will receive a portion of the proceeds. During these postings, personal banking account details are always requested. Despite the public warnings and general knowledge of these scams, many people continue to be victimized.

The Internet is the most widely used vehicle of communication between terrorist groups, who can use public access computers in libraries and cafes to relay information between cells. According to Henych (2003), U.S. colleges and universities are safe havens for this activity because public Internet access is available at student unions and libraries. The vast numbers of students at many institutions and the open Internet systems add complexity to this problem. There is the threat of a cyber-terrorist attack in which the Internet is used to hack into a secure system and cause damage to, for example, a water facility, airport, or electrical system.

Comprehensive International Security

From an organizational perspective, the most dramatic change in security services has been the creation of international security service corporations that offer comprehensive services to private companies and governments in the global economy. One example is Kroll Inc., which offers services in forensic accounting, crisis management, competitor analysis, and addresses risks such as industrial espionage, counterfeiting, computer fraud, identity fraud, and other financial crimes (Finnegan, 2009). Beau Dietl and Associates Investigative and Security Solutions, which was founded by a former New York City police detective, offers multinational corporations help in identifying global organized crime groups, investigating executives' backgrounds, tracing assets, controlling product fraud, and complying with national and international laws (Beau Dietl, 2004).

Concurrently, many private security companies in the United States have become subsidiaries or major holdings of international security conglomerates. For example Burns, Pinkerton, and Wells Fargo are part of Securitas International, headquartered in Sweden. The Wackenhut Corporation is also a subsidiary of Group 4 Falck A/S, also based in Sweden. These global security service operations employ thousands of guards, investigators, and analysts and offer a wide range of services all over the world and can be reviewed at www.securitasgroup.com. As will be discussed, private firms provide active military support in war-torn areas such as Iraq and Afghanistan.

THE POST-9/11 ERA

Domestic and international security must be viewed as a series of interlocking relationships on the federal, state, and local levels. The federal government, through its military forces, the CIA, FBI, Homeland Security, and other agencies, remains the first level for security by providing national and international intelligence gathering, funding, policy decisions, border defense, and emergency response. It is followed by state governments, which interact with federal agencies and provide leadership, equipment, training, and specialized personnel for local and county government and corporate units. Accordingly, most states have now created state homeland security organizations or antiterrorist units to coordinate state operations with the federal government.

On the next level, and perhaps the most important for daily operations, is a wide array of county, city, town, and village local law enforcement agencies and public authority police, private security firms, and citizen groups. Except for field operatives at the federal level, local security services personnel will most likely have contact with potential terrorist operatives or be in a position to provide intelligence.

As envisioned by the National Infrastructure Protection Plan (2009) there is also a need for increased cooperation and data sharing among public and private law enforcement and security agencies. The federal government and all state governments distribute information to police departments and the general public on security alerts. On the local and state levels, it is important that all security service providers begin to establish relationships for sharing information and listing resource assets that each agency could use in the event of a major event. Private sector companies and their security services are important stakeholders in these efforts. These topics will be fully explored in the subsequent chapters.

Summary

This chapter begins with the concept of security and security services and then presents a brief historical overview on the development of U.S. security services. The development of national security agencies actually began in the private sector and was eventually taken over by public bureaucracies. The various types of security operations that still exist—such as contract, internal, transportation, and executive protection—had been developed by the end of World War II. What adds to the complexity in addressing the issue of security is the wide range of public sector agencies that have full law enforcement powers but are titled "security."

The chapter reviewed the general development of current technology as it has been used in the field in an effort to trace the historical development of security practices. The contributions of radio and cellular communications, personal computers, the Internet, and CCTV cannot be understated as security planners rely on integrated systems to provide access and internal security. Biometric systems that perform eye, hand, face, or voice recognition for access are now the current generation of access tools for security planners.

Review Questions/Activities

1. How have changes in security affected your daily life? Have you recently used air transportation? If so, how were you screened at the airport?
2. Interview either a law enforcement or private security executive and discuss the relationship between police and security. Ask about the services that each provides.
3. Observe the technology used for security operations at your campus or at a nearby company or facility. To what extent has the entity adopted the security technology discussed in this chapter?
4. Interview a police or security service executive. Ask the person to review with you the changes that have

occurred in operations and technology over the past twenty years. What changes does the person foresee for the future?
5. As discussed in this chapter, a number of professional security organizations provide training and operational assistance. Based on those organizations that appear in this chapter, review through the Internet the range of activities that these groups provide. Ascertain what the requirements are to become an employee of the organization.

WebSearches

1. Create a list of security service agencies in your area, and classify each by the type of function or service that it performs, such as contract watch and guard, investigative, courier, and executive protection. Include in your listing whether they have any law enforcement powers. These agencies might include housing authority police, campus or university police, railroad police, water authority patrol, and so on. Furthermore, is the firm a holding or subsidiary of a national or international corporate group? This can be initiated by logging on to www.securitas.com, www.tyco.com, or www.group4 falck.com.

References

Bellis, Mary. 2003. "Selling the Cell Phone: History of Cellular Phones." Posted at http://inventors.about.com/library.weekly/ aa070899.htm. Accessed March 20, 2003.

Bureau of Justice Statistics. 2007. *Census of State and Local Law Enforcement Agencies—2004.* Washington, D.C.: United States Department of Justice.

Clifford, Mary. 2004. *Identifying and Exploring Security Essentials.* Upper Saddle River, N.J.: Prentice Hall.

Department of Homeland Security. 2002. "Homeland Security at a Glance." Accessed September 25, 2003 at www.dhs.gov.

Department of Homeland Security. 2009. "State and Local Fusion Centers." Web posted at http://www.dhs.gov/files/programs/gc_1156877184684.shtm. Accessed December 12, 2009.

Beau Dietl and Associates. 2004. "Beau Dietl and Associates Home Page." Posted at http://www.beaudietl.com. Accessed January 9, 2004.

Finnegan, William. 2009. The Secret Keeper: Jules Kroll and the World of Corporate Intelligence. *The New Yorker,* October 19, 2009.

Furchgott, Roy. 2003. "In a Single Swipe, a Wealth of Data (Beware of Thieves)" New York Times, March 13. Posted at www.magteck.com/media/news_articles.asp?sort. Accessed June 7, 2003.

Griffin, B. S., and C.T. Griffin. 1978. *Juvenile Delinquency in Perspective.* New York: Harper & Row.

Grossman, W. M. 1997. *Net.wars.* New York: New York University Press.

Henych, Mark. 2003. "Cyber Terrorism and Universities as a Potential Staging Ground." Paper presented at the International Association of Campus Law Enforcement Administrators, San Jose, Calif. June 2003.

Hess, Karen, and Henry M. Wrobleski. 1996. *Introduction to Private Security,* 4th ed. Minneapolis/St.Paul: West Publishing.

Lersch, K. M., ed. 2002. *Policing and Misconduct.* Upper Saddle River, N.J.: Prentice-Hall.

Lohr, Steve. 2003. "Data Expert Is Cautious about Misuse of Information." *The New York Times,* 25 March, C6.

McBride, R. B. 1994. "Critical Issues in Campus Policing." In J.W. Bizzack. *New Perspectives,* edited by Lexington, Ky: Autumn House, 268–288.

National Advisory Committee on Criminal Justice Standards and Goals. 1976. *Private Security: Report of the Task Force on Private Security.* Washington, D.C.: United States Department of Justice, Law Enforcement Assistance Administration.

National Infrastructure Protection Plan: Partnering to Enhance Protection and Resiliency. 2009. Washington, D.C.: United States Department of Homeland Security

Negroponte, Nicholas. 1995. *Being Digital.* New York: Alfred Kopf.

Paladino, Salvatore. 2003. "Public Policy and Internet Pornography Laws." Utica College of Syracuse University.

Pittman, David. 1974. "Drugs, Addiction and Crime." In *The Handbook on Criminology,* edited by Daniel Glasier. Chicago: Rand McNally, 209–232.

Poulin, K.C., and Charles P. Nemeth. 2005. Private Security and Public Safety. Upper Saddle River, NJ: Pearson Education.

Powell, John W. 1981. *Campus Security and Law Enforcement.* Boston: Butterworths.

Rosoff, Stephen M., Henry N. Pontell, and Robert H. Tillman. 2002. *Profit Without Honor: While-Collar Crime and the Looting of America.* Upper Saddle River, N.J.: Prentice-Hall.

Schmalleger, Frank, and Michael Pittaro. 2009. *Crimes of the Internet.* Upper Saddle River, N.J.: Pearson—Prentice-Hall.

Security Management. 2009. "2009 ASIS Exhibits." Vol. 53, No. 9, September 2009, 122.

Simonsen, C. E. 1998. *Private Security in America.* Upper Saddle River, N.J.: Prentice-Hall.

Thibault, Edward. A., Lawrence. Lynch, and R.B. McBride. 2001. *Proactive Police Management,* 5th ed. Upper Saddle River, N.J.: Prentice-Hall.

Utley, R. M. 2002. "Tales of the Texas Rangers." *American Heritage,* June/July: 40–47.

2

■ ■ ■

Legal Implications for the Security Function

KEY TERMS

civil law, common law, constitution, contract, jurisdiction, local law, negligence, ordinance, private law, procedural law, public law, reverse money laundering, *stare decisis*, statute, strict liability crime, substantive law, vicarious liability tort.

This chapter focuses on the nature of the U.S. legal system, the legal bases for the security function, and the implementation and administration of security policies. The discussion begins with an overview of the U.S. legal system, court structure, and the basic forms and sources of law. The discussion also considers the legal theories and bases for imposing civil or criminal liability on organizations that perform security services, legal requirements for the protection of customer or client information, laws governing the deployment of common security measures, and the public–private relationship in a security context.

U.S. LEGAL SYSTEM

Two different legal systems have developed over several centuries in Europe and North America: the civil law and common law systems. The civil law system is based on Roman law and the canons of the Roman Catholic Church (Terrill, 2009) and is characterized by adherence to a set of written laws or codes. The function of courts in a civil system is to determine whether a certain conduct violates the written code. If the conduct is not identified by the written language of the code setting forth a criminal sanction, then it is not a crime. For example, a hacker gains unauthorized access to a corporate network but does not destroy or take any data. The country's penal code provides that it is crime to access unlawfully a computer network and alter or remove data. Because the hacker did not alter or remove data, the court would determine that the hacker's conduct did not constitute a crime under the penal code.

Historically, countries on the continent of Europe—France, Italy, and Spain, for example—have been civil law countries. Explorers from those countries who settled in the Western Hemisphere established in those settlements the only laws and legal system they knew—the civil law system. Thus, Florida and Louisiana initially followed the traditions of the civil law system. Those states have since converted to the common law system.

The other major legal system is the common law system. This system is based on adherence to customs and traditions of the people (i.e., unwritten rules) and to court decisions. The common law system originated in England and was brought to the United States by colonists who settled in Plymouth, Massachusetts, and Jamestown, Virginia. Other countries originally part of the English Commonwealth—Canada, Australia, and New Zealand, for example—also follow the common law tradition. In early common law systems, decisions were grounded in the doctrine of *stare decisis*; that is, the court followed what other courts or legal bodies already had decided, whether it was the decision of another court made under similar circumstances or the decision of an executive such as a monarch.

As legislative bodies gained more prominence in common law systems, the primary authority of court decisions remained their guiding force. Courts still play the important role of determining whether a legislative act is constitutional, whether a regulation adopted by an administrative agency has been authorized by valid legislation, and whether, based on the court's interpretation of the statute or regulation, the particular conduct is prohibited. In fulfilling this role, courts in common law systems continue to refer to previous court decisions involving similar issues or factual situations—an interpretive concept commonly known as the rule of *stare decisis*.

As the provision of security services becomes more global in operation, attention must be given to the application of laws in foreign countries having different legal systems. A U.S. company that manufactures products in a foreign country and provides security for its employees and physical assets must be familiar with the legal system in that country, regulations pertaining to the performance of security services there, and the bases for civil and criminal liability arising from the provision of those services. Typically that kind of familiarity is acquired by retaining a U.S.-based law firm that has a branch office in the foreign country. The law firm that is retained should have the capacity to provide both counsel to managers in the United States and training for managers and employees in the foreign country.

FORMS AND SOURCES OF LAW

Within the U.S. common law system, we classify laws in several ways. Consideration of those classifications is helpful in understanding the purpose of laws and regulations that impact the security function.

Sources of Law

We can classify laws according to their source: constitutional, statutory, regulatory, and judicial. In the United States, the federal government and each of the states have a constitution that generally describes the powers and limitations of that government and the rights of its residents as well. The U.S. Constitution is the supreme law of the United States, and each state's constitution is the supreme law of that state, subject only to the superiority of the U.S. Constitution.

Constitutions differ from other forms of law in that their provisions originate with a legislative body and, at least in theory, are approved by the people. For example, the U.S. Constitution was drafted by a convention of delegates from each of the original colonies. That draft of the U.S. Constitution was approved by the Continental Congress acting under the Articles of Confederation and then submitted to the original states. Within each state, the decision whether to approve or reject the U.S. Constitution was submitted to a vote of its citizens. Similarly, the constitution of each state and amendments to it must be approved by the people of that state.

Federal and state constitutions authorize legislative bodies within each jurisdiction to enact laws. For example, Article I of the U.S. Constitution establishes the power of Congress to enact laws. A law enacted by legislative bodies at the federal or state level is commonly referred to as a *statute;* a law enacted by cities, towns, parishes, villages, and the like is usually referred to as a *local law* or an *ordinance.* Constitutions also authorize the executive body in each jurisdiction (president for the federal government, governor for each state, mayor for cities, etc.) to enforce the laws enacted by legislative bodies. Those executives frequently establish agencies or departments to carry out many of their detailed responsibilities. For example, over time, U.S. presidents have established agencies such as the Department of Defense, Department of State, and most recently, the Department of Homeland Security.

In the United States, executive and legislative bodies have delegated responsibility for the direct supervision of certain industries and the establishment of detailed rules and regulations governing the conduct of those industries to administrative agencies. The rules and regulations adopted by those agencies constitute another major source of law: administrative laws and regulations. For example, although Congress has enacted numerous laws pertaining to banking, regulations adopted by agencies such as the Department of Treasury, the Office of the Comptroller of the Currency, the Federal Deposit Insurance Commission, and the Federal Trade Commission govern the day-to-day activities of banking institutions. In some states, legislators have delegated the responsibility for the licensing of security companies and their employees to an appropriate administrative agency. Regulations adopted by administrative agencies have the force of law as long as the agency has not exceeded its legislative authority.

Although the U.S. Constitution is the supreme law of the land, U.S. Supreme Court decisions are the ultimate authority in interpreting the Constitution. The power of federal courts is established in Article III of the Constitution and was further strengthened by the U.S. Supreme Court in the 1803 case *Marbury v. Madison.* In that case, the court determined that Article III empowers federal courts to interpret the Constitution (i.e., to decide what the Constitution means), and that the Supreme Court has the final word on that meaning. Thus, the principal activity of courts at the federal and state levels is to interpret the meaning of federal and state constitutions, statutes, rules, and regulations in the context of disputes between states and localities, between branches of the government, and between citizens or business entities. Often the courts are asked to resolve issues of security and privacy that arise in various contexts (e.g., disputes between law enforcement and individuals, between security companies and individuals, and between individuals). Several of those issues are explored in this chapter.

Substantive or Procedural Law

Laws can also be classified as substantive or procedural. *Substantive law* defines the rights and obligations of individuals and organizations. Laws pertaining to contracts and torts are substantive because they state the rights of parties to contractual agreements or the standard of care that must be performed by individuals and the remedies that exist if the agreements or standards are not honored. *Procedural law* addresses the enforcement of legal rights (i.e., the rules for bringing lawsuits in court to enforce or protect a particular right). We consider substantive and procedural laws in relation to the security service function.

Public or Private Law

The third way to classify laws is as public or private. *Public law* encompasses laws that apply to governmental functions. For example, a law appropriating money for the government's fiscal budget is a public law because it establishes how public funds are to be spent. Criminal law also is public law because a criminal offense is an act committed against society (i.e., the public as a whole). *Private law* includes laws that apply to the conduct of individuals and businesses. For example, *contract law* is considered to be private law because it applies to agreements between individuals and/or business entities. *Tort law* is also considered to be private law. It provides a remedy of damages resulting from conduct committed by an individual or a business entity.

STRUCTURE OF U.S. COURT SYSTEMS

The U.S. federal government and each state have their own court systems. Additionally, the District of Columbia and each of the territories have their own court systems.

A three-tier system is the typical structure of the court system. Figure 2-1 depicts the basic federal court system, Figure 2-2 depicts the court system of a largely populated state (California), and Figure 2-3 depicts the court system of a small state (Rhode Island). Large or small, most government entities have a court structure that has a bottom tier of trial courts, which is the typical starting point for criminal and civil cases, an intermediate or appellate-level court to which all litigants may appeal a decision or verdict, and the top-level appellate court that usually hears only those appeals that it selects.

Within the federal court system, most civil and criminal cases are tried in the U.S. District Court. The country is divided into ninety-four federal judicial districts, each of which has its own court. Small states such as Vermont comprise an entire district. More populated states have

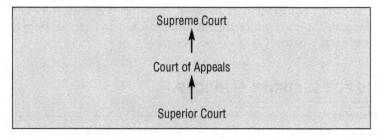

FIGURE 2-1   U.S. Court System

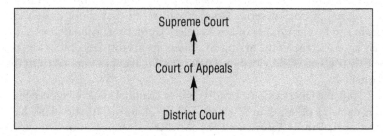

FIGURE 2-2   California Court System

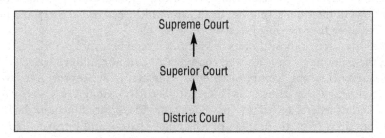

FIGURE 2-3   Rhode Island Court System

several districts. For example, California and New York have four federal judicial districts. The federal system has other courts that have limited jurisdiction, namely, the Court of International Trade and the Court of Federal Claims.

A decision of the federal district court or other trial court can be appealed to the U.S. Court of Appeals. This court is divided into thirteen circuits: the Federal Circuit is which hears appeals from the U.S. Court of International Trade and the U.S. Court of Federal Claims; the D.C. Circuit, which hears appeals from courts within the District of Columbia; and eleven numbered circuits, each of which hears appeals from the district courts in that circuit. For example, the First Circuit encompasses Maine, New Hampshire, Massachusetts, Rhode Island, and the territory of Puerto Rico; the Second Circuit encompasses Vermont, Connecticut, and New York.

The U.S. Supreme Court, composed of nine justices, is the highest court in the federal system. It hears direct appeals from the highest court of each state and from the U.S. Court of Appeals. Appeal to the U.S. Supreme Court is not an automatic right; the court selects those cases it wishes to hear by granting a writ of certiorari, which basically is an order directing the lower court to send a record of the proceedings before it to the Supreme Court.

The California court system is truly a three-tier system. All trials, whether involving family disputes, personal injury actions, probate matters, or criminal cases, are conducted in the Superior Court. Each county of the state has a superior court. Those of us old enough to remember the original television series *Dragnet* will recall that those cases were heard in "Superior Court in and for the County of Los Angeles." Upon conclusion of the trial, the unsuccessful party may appeal to the Court of Appeals. There are six districts of the Court of Appeals, and two of those districts are subdivided into divisions. Final appeals are taken to the Supreme Court of California.

In Rhode Island, the District Court handles minor criminal and civil proceedings (a minor civil suit involves damages of less than $10,000). Unlike California, Rhode Island has three trial courts: District Court, Family Court, and the Workers' Compensation Court. The Traffic Tribunal is a court of lesser jurisdiction. Appeals from the Traffic Tribunal are heard by the District Court. The Superior Court has dual authority over felony criminal cases and civil proceedings seeking more than $5,000 in damages, and it hears appeals from District Court decisions. The Supreme Court, which consists of five justices, hears appeals from the Superior Court, Family Court, and Workers' Compensation Court.

LEGAL BASIS FOR SECURITY SERVICES

The U.S. Constitution establishes the basis for the government's performance of security services. Article I, Section 8, of the Constitution empowers Congress to "provide for the common defence," "raise and support Armies," "provide and maintain a Navy," "make Rules for the Government and Regulation of the land and naval Forces," "provide for calling forth the Militia to execute the Laws of the Union," and "make all Laws which shall be necessary and proper for carrying into Execution the foregoing Powers."

Congress has exercised those powers by creating several branches of the armed forces or military (e.g., the army, navy, air force, and coast guard) and nonmilitary agencies dedicated to national security (i.e., the "common defence": the National Security Agency, Central Intelligence Agency, and Department of Homeland Security). Congress has also created or authorized numerous federal agencies to provide domestic security functions, including law enforcement functions (e.g., the Bureau of Alcohol, Tobacco, and Firearms [ATF] of the Department of Justice; the U.S. Secret Service [USSS] of the Department of Homeland

Security, which among other responsibilities performs executive protection at the federal level; the Federal Bureau of Investigation [FBI], which is the investigation arm of the Department of Justice; the U.S. Marshals Service of the Department of Justice; and the U.S. Postal Inspection Service [USPIS], which is the security and investigation arm of the U.S. Postal Service).

State constitutions likewise provide for the establishment of military (e.g., state national guard) and security and law enforcement agencies within each state. Those statutes generally provide the power to

- Carry firearms
- Detain and arrest
- Investigate
- Execute warrants
- Search and seize
- Offer and pay rewards for information

The legal basis for private sector security typically is not in a federal or state constitution or statute although some exceptions exist. For example, several states have mandated that insurance companies create special investigation units to combat false insurance applications and claims. The general purpose of those units is to protect company assets and the interests of policyholders. Additionally, federal and state laws or regulations mandate that various business entities perform specific security functions—examples are the Health Insurance Portability and Accountability Act of 1996 and the Gramm-Leach-Bliley Act of 1999, discussed later. The statutes or regulations of many states require private investigators who carry firearms to be licensed and impose minimum security standards for a range of professional and business activities. The federal government and most, if not all, states impose physical and other forms of security requirements on those who contract to provide services (e.g., defense contracts and construction work) for the government. In fact, most government contractors are required to adhere to the same security requirements as the government agency for which they work.

In the absence of a statutory or regulatory basis for security, however, the legal basis for private sector security services is derived from the common law right of private citizens and businesses to defend themselves and protect their property (Post and Kingsbury, 1977). In exercising this right, private sector individuals and businesses deploy security commensurate with the need to protect assets or minimize risk. The security function is performed by employees as part of business policy or operations or is outsourced to an independent contractor (e.g., Allied Barton or Securitas) or, as is the case in many instances, a combination of the two. In any event, the basis for such security is contractual, and a multitude of laws and court decisions exist to guide the performance of such contracts.

The legal basis for private sector security is also derived from a common law duty to protect the public from harm. The general rule is that an owner of a business or property has a legal duty to protect business patrons or persons at the business or on the property from harm that is reasonably foreseeable. If students residing in a dormitory have been assaulted by intruders, a similar assault in the future is reasonably foreseeable. The failure of the institution to employ security personnel or security devices that would effectively prevent such intrusions exposes it to civil liability for negligence. On the other hand, a restaurant has no duty to protect a patron from the sudden harm inflicted by another patron because the occurrence of such random act is not foreseeable.

CRIMINAL LIABILITY

Introduction to Criminal Liability

A crime is an act that in theory is committed against society as a whole. Because society or the people collectively are harmed, the government brings legal action against the perpetrator. The penalty imposed after a determination of guilt is designed to serve the legitimate needs of society: imprisonment in the case of serious crimes and fines or restitution in the case of minor offenses.

Crimes typically involve three elements: mens rea, or a guilty state of mind; actus reus, which is the guilty act; and some form of harm, either physical or economic. There are, however, exceptions. In the case of ultrahazardous activities or business activity that directly affects public health and welfare, criminal liability may be imposed even though the employee or business lacks a mens rea. Those crimes are commonly referred to as *strict liability crimes*. Criminal liability is imposed simply because the act was done. Examples of such activities include the manufacture of explosives, the labeling of food products and drugs, and the disposal of toxic waste. The conduct of security personnel typically does not involve strict liability crimes.

Government Employees

Within the public sector, law enforcement officials and other security personnel acting in a governmental capacity can be held criminally liable for willfully violating the constitutional rights of individuals (18 U.S.C. § 242). A recent federal appellate court decision illustrates this principle.

Government Employer

Criminal liability is not imposed on a government employer. In theory, crimes are acts committed on society as a whole (i.e., the government), and it would be incongruous to impose criminal liability on the government for the criminal conduct of its employees.

Mark White, a Gary, Indiana, police officer, also served as a security officer at a strip club. His responsibilities as a security officer were to maintain order and ensure that patrons and dancers acted in an orderly fashion. After a verbal altercation, White struck a dancer several times and threw her to the ground. Federal prosecutors charged White under 18 U.S.C. § 242 for violating the dancer's constitutional rights under color of law. White unsuccessfully claimed that he was acting as a private security officer. While working that night, White was wearing his badge and service gun, and when the dancer attempted to call the police on her cellular phone, White grabbed the phone from her hand and shouted, "I am the [expletive] police." The jury accurately concluded that White was acting as a police officer. He was convicted and sentenced to prison for twenty-seven months.—*United States v. White*, 2003.

Private Security Personnel

Criminal liability may also be imposed on private security employees. They are not given special recognition by the law. Thus, their acts are treated in the same manner as are the acts of any other private citizen. The following case is a good example.

> Defendant Bernier, a security officer at a nightclub, retrieved a shotgun from his boss to restrain a restless crowd outside the club. Bernier knew that the shotgun was loaded. He held the shotgun across his chest and used it to push the crowd away from the club entrance. As he continued to push, he accidentally discharged the gun and killed a person who was pushing near the entrance. Bernier was convicted of criminally negligent homicide.—*People v. Bernier,* 1994.

Does it make any difference whether the security guard was at the time an off-duty law enforcement officer? It depends on whether the officer was performing a law enforcement function at the time of the conduct. If the guard was, for example, escorting a combative customer outside the store for the purpose of making an arrest for disorderly conduct, the guard would be entitled to claim the same justification for the use of force as a police officer would. On the other hand, a guard who was not performing a law enforcement function can use only the same justification that anyone could claim in the arrest by a private citizen.

Criminal Liability of Private Security Supervisors and Employers

Supervisors of security personnel are liable criminally for the conduct of their employees only to the extent that they participate as a conspirator or are accessories in the criminal conduct. The basic rule is that the employer can be held criminally responsible for the conduct of employees if the criminal act was (1) performed as part of the usual and customary duties of the employee; and (2) was done for the benefit of the employer. Thus, in the example provided in *People v. Bernier,* the nightclub owner could also be charged with criminally negligent homicide because the shotgun was used as part of Bernier's responsibilities as a security guard, and the employer had provided the shotgun to Bernier.

TORT LIABILITY

Introduction to Tort Liability

The same conduct that constitutes a crime typically also constitutes a tort. A *tort* is a civil wrong committed against an individual or business for which the victim may sue to recover damages. There are three types of tortuous conduct: intentional ones, those involving negligence, and those for which liability may be imposed simply because they happened, as in the case of strict liability crimes.

Typical intentional torts involving the performance of security services include:

- **Assault and battery.** Threatening imminent physical harm (assault) and making physical contact with the victim (battery). *Example:* A retail store security employee deliberately and without justification grabs the arm of a customer and twists the customer's arm behind the back.
- **Conversion.** Taking another person's property and converting it to the perpetrator's own use. *Example:* An officer interviewing a complaining witness purposefully took a Mont Blanc pen belonging to the witness, left the premises of the witness, and continued to use the pen in the course of police business over the next several days.
- **Defamation.** Making false statements (libel, if written; slander, if spoken) designed to harm the victim's reputation. *Example:* A security officer publicly describes a store patron as "a drug dealer."

- **Trespass.** Deliberately entering private property without permission. *Example:* A law enforcement officer without justification forcibly opens the locked door of a residence and enters it.
- **False arrest.** Making an arrest without a warrant and without probable cause. *Example:* A security officer arrests the patron of a bar because of a personal grudge between the two. The arrest had nothing to do with any criminal conduct by the patron while at the bar.
- **False imprisonment.** Deliberately and unreasonably detaining an individual without justification. *Example:* A security officer in a retail store detains a customer for more than four hours despite the fact that the customer immediately produced a receipt for the merchandise that the guard suspected had been stolen.
- **Malicious prosecution.** Causing the commencement of a criminal proceeding against a person knowing that there is no probable cause for it. *Example:* Based on false information knowingly supplied by a security officer to the employer and forwarded by the employer to the police in revenge for abusive language used by the customer, the police filed a felony complaint alleging that the customer had stolen merchandise.

Constitutional and statutory torts are a subcategory of intentional tort. Federal and state laws impose civil liability on government employees and private individuals who violate the constitutional rights of persons. Such violations of rights protected by a constitution are referred to as *constitutional torts.* Federal and state laws also impose civil liability on public employees and private individuals who violate a duty created by that statute (statutory torts). The following are illustrations of these torts:

- **42 U.S.C. § 1983.** This federal law imposes civil liability for intentional violations of the constitutional, civil, or statutory rights of persons. Although the conduct must have been committed under color of federal law, conduct of private security service personnel can amount to a violation of this section, particularly when such personnel are off-duty police officers.
- **42 U.S.C. § 1320d-5.** This federal law (part of the Health Insurance Portability and Accountability Act of 1996) imposes a civil penalty of $100 per incident, or a total of $25,000 per person, for its violation, including violations of privacy and security rules pertaining to the transmission of patient information.

Negligence is the failure to exercise the level of care that a reasonable and prudent person would exercise under the circumstances, or simply, the failure to exercise reasonable care. It is a frequent basis for the imposition of liability on security service personnel and their employers. For example, an apartment complex hires an individual to serve as a security officer. The security employee receives a complaint of loud noise and obscene language at an apartment but fails to respond to that complaint. The employee receives a second message from a neighbor of the complainant's apartment 40 minutes later, indicating that the occupant of the apartment has been shot. The failure to respond to the original message, especially in the absence of any other complaints at that time that might have required the employee to make a judgment call about which complaint is the more urgent, could be considered a failure to exercise reasonable care (negligence). That failure could be a basis for imposing liability for damages on the employee and the owner of the complex.

Tort Liability of Public Sector Security Personnel and the Government

Civil liability may also be imposed on government employees, including security and law enforcement personnel, for statutory and intentional torts, as well as negligence, to the extent that the governmental entity has waived its sovereign immunity and allowed suits to be brought against it and its employees. The Federal Tort Claims Act provides that the United States may be sued for acts that, if committed by a private individual, would constitute a basis of tort liability (28 U.S.C. § 2674). Many states have likewise waived their sovereign immunity and allowed themselves to be sued for torts committed by employees in the course of their employment. As a practical matter, liability and the duty to pay damages typically is imposed on the governmental entity, not the employee individually.

Tort Liability of Private Sector Security Personnel

Private security personnel can be held personally liable for constitutional and intentional torts, as well as negligent acts committed in the course of performing their security functions. Liability of private security personnel is no different than the liability of a private individual. A private security service employee who drives the company's security vehicle while patrolling the company grounds may be held liable for an accident involving his or her operation of that vehicle as well as for conduct directly relating to the security function.

Tort Liability of Private Sector Supervisors and Employers

In addition to their exposure to criminal liability, private sector security supervisors and employers can be held responsible for their conduct and required to pay damages resulting from improper acts. Tort liability for negligence can be imposed directly upon the supervisor and/or employer for the following:

- Negligent hiring of security personnel, as illustrated by the following case:

> Puget Sound Protection (PSP) is a dealer in security services performed for ADT Security Systems. The contract with ADT required PSP to perform criminal background checks on employees who conducted door-to-door solicitations for ADT security systems. PSP hired a promotional representative without conducting a criminal background check. The representative had a criminal record, and PSP's general manager indicated that had he known of the criminal record, he would not have hired the representative. About two months after a door-to-door promotion at an owner's residence, the representative returned and raped the owner's daughter. The court held that the failure to conduct a criminal background check amounted to negligent hiring, but remanded the matter to the trial court for a determination of whether that negligence was a proximate cause of the rape.—*Rucshner v. ADT Security Systems, Inc.*, 2009.

- Negligent assignment or entrustment, for example, by providing a handgun to a security officer who has not been trained in the proper use and security of the device.
- Negligent training of security personnel, by failing to conduct training sessions required by law or regulation or to instruct on those functions essential to assigned tasks (*Miller v. Wal-Mart Stores, Inc.*, 1998).
- Negligent supervision of security activities, by failing, for example, to monitor or review the performance of a probationary hire.

Liability for negligent hiring, entrustment, training, and supervision, like all actions for negligence, requires proof (1) that the security provider owed a duty to the person injured to exercise reasonable care; (2) that the provider breached that duty by failing to exercise reasonable care in the hiring, entrustment, training, or supervision of the employee; (3) that the failure to exercise reasonable care was a cause of the injury; and (4) that the particular negligent act (e.g., negligent training) was a proximate cause of the injury. Additionally, liability may be imposed on the employer based on the legal doctrine of respondeat superior (i.e., the employer may be held liable for the negligent acts of an employee who was acting within the scope of the employer's authority and benefit of the employer). This type of tort liability is also known as *vicarious liability.* The following case illustrates this point.

Figueroa was a security officer employed by a private security company and assigned to work at Republic National Bank of New York in Manhattan. Acting contrary to specific orders to remain at his post in the bank lobby, Figueroa deliberately attacked the plaintiff, who was a security supervisor employed by the bank, at her workstation in the basement of the bank. The court held that because Figueroa had a long-standing grudge against the plaintiff and his conduct was in complete contravention of his responsibilities, he was not acting within the scope of his employment, and liability could not be imposed on his employer, the private security company.—*Dykes v. McRoberts Protective Agency, Inc.,* 1998.

As in the case of public sector liability, private sector employers can be held liable for the intentional torts, negligence, and constitutional torts of their employees committed within the scope of their employment. Consider the following cases.

Two corrections officers were employed as security personnel at Denny's Restaurant. After a member of an Asian American group complained about the delay in being seated, one of the officers escorted the complaining Asian American out of the restaurant and threatened to arrest him for disorderly conduct. A series of fights erupted outside the restaurant between the Asian American group and other restaurant patrons. A group of African Americans also waiting to be seated went outside to observe the argument. One of them went back inside and while describing the outside commotion, used an expletive. After the restaurant manager warned the African American group to be quiet or leave, the officers escorted them out of the restaurant. Members of both groups sued Denny's Restaurant and the security personnel for excluding them from the restaurant because of race in violation of 42 U.S.C. § 1983, a constitutional tort. The court held that the officers were acting in their official capacity as officers of the state when escorting the Asian Americans out of the restaurant and threatening to arrest them for disorderly conduct. Thus, Denny's could not be held liable for the official acts of government officers. The court also determined, however, that Denny's could be held liable for the conduct of the security personnel in escorting the African Americans out of the restaurant at the urging of the store manager because that conduct was within the scope of their employment as security personnel.—*Lizardo v. Denny's Inc.,* 2000.

Managers must be keenly aware of the legal repercussions of their conduct. In addition to the criminal liability that may be imposed on the business in the nature of a fine as a result of the manager's behavior, the business can also be held civilly liable and required to pay damages.

CONTRACT LIABILITY

Civil liability also can be imposed on security service personnel because of their failure to perform contractual responsibilities or for liability that is assumed by agreement of the parties. Consider the following case.

Simmons, a manufacturer of bedding products, entered into a contract with Pinkerton, a national company providing security services, for providing guard protection services at its regional distribution center twenty-four hours a day, seven days a week. The contract provided that Pinkerton would "ensure a professional, reliable and efficient effort to protect its client's property and personnel against security hazards." Pinkerton also accepted liability for all acts of negligence, fraud, or dishonesty on the part of its employees and represented that its employees were trained both in security and fire protection. Without investigating his background, Pinkerton hired William Hayne as a security officer. In addition to the fact that Hayne had lied on his employment application, Pinkerton failed to provide him with any fire protection training, which its own manuals indicated was mandatory for security personnel. A fire occurred, and Simmons sustained nearly $1 million in property damage as a result. Investigation revealed that the fire had been intentionally set and that Hayne and an office cleaner were the only persons present at the warehouse at the time of the fire. Hayne unsuccessfully attempted to extinguish the fire; he had attempted to use a reel fire hose but had not been trained to use the apparatus and was unable to do so. Simmons commenced an action against Pinkerton and recovered damages based on its violation of its responsibilities and promises under the contract.—*Simmons, Inc. v. Pinkerton's, Inc.*, 1985.

STATUTORY LIABILITY

We briefly alluded to the fact that security personnel and employers may be held liable for the failure to perform security functions mandated by statutory law. Congress has mandated the implementation of security safeguards for personal financial and health care information. Those enactments—the Gramm-Leach-Bliley Act of 1999 and the Health Insurance Portability and Accountability Act of 1996—additionally mandate compliance with the statutes and with regulations developed by governing agencies. Those compliance requirements are discussed in greater detail in Chapter 11. A variety of other security services may be mandated by state law. Those laws typically impose criminal and civil liability for a failure to perform or for negligent performance of the statutory duty.

LEGAL LIMITATIONS UPON PERFORMANCE OF THE SECURITY FUNCTION

A principal feature of the U.S. Constitution is the establishment of a system of checks and balances. The checks, or restraints, on government power are expressed in several amendments to the U.S. Constitution, mainly the first ten amendments known as the Bill of Rights. Most relevant from a security management perspective are the First, Fourth, Fifth, and Sixth Amendments. The First Amendment guarantees the freedom of speech, press, religion, association, and the right to petition for grievances. The Fourth Amendment prohibits the search and seizure of persons, property, and effects unless it is conducted reasonably, which typically means with a warrant issued by a neutral magistrate or judge based on the showing of probable cause or without a warrant if there is probable cause plus some other extenuating circumstance. The Fifth Amendment guarantees that no person can be compelled to be a witness against himself or herself, and the Sixth Amendment guarantees accused persons the assistance of counsel, thereby limiting the methods that law enforcement officers can employ to obtain a confession. Also, because these provisions of the Bill of Rights apply to the states, they serve as limitations on all law enforcement agencies—federal, state, or local—within the United States. Each state constitution also contains similar provisions limiting the performance of military and law enforcement functions in the state.

Although a thorough discussion of each of these constitutional protections is beyond the scope of this text, elaboration of some points is essential for security managers. First, the protections of the Bill of Rights constitute limitations on government agents and employees but not employees in the private sector. Thus, the Fourth Amendment does not prevent an employee of the United Parcel Service from opening and inspecting a package that is leaking a powdery substance. A shopping mall security employee does not need to read Miranda warnings to a store patron being interviewed regarding suspected shoplifting. That same mall security employee can disperse a crowd that has gathered in the mall because the freedom to assemble applies to public places, such as the sidewalk in front of a government building, but not to private property. However, malls occupy a unique place in constitutional law decision making; to the extent that a shopping mall becomes a forum for public meetings, the right of persons to assemble peacefully is protected by the Constitution. A related point is that private security personnel may, under certain circumstances, become agents of government officials. In that event, the private security personnel are subject to the same constitutional limitations as a government official.

In addition to constitutional limitations on the performance of security functions, there are instances when federal and state legislatures and regulatory agencies control the performance of public and private security functions. For example, federal law (18 U.S.C. § 2511) prohibits wiretapping by law enforcement *and* private persons without a warrant or a court order. Government security personnel have much broader powers to conduct wiretaps in national security matters. Those powers are set forth in the Foreign Intelligence Surveillance Act (50 U.S.C. §§ 1801–1811). Federal law also prohibits access to stored wire or electronic communications. As in the case of the Wiretap Act, it is a crime to access stored communications without compliance with the Electronic Communications Privacy Act (ECPA), which prescribes those situations when private or public sector security personnel can access such communications and what type of authorization is necessary to access them (see 18 U.S.C. §§ 2701–2712).

Employers have been able to conduct physical surveillance of employees for centuries. Technology, however, has significantly enhanced the ability to conduct surveillance, many times without the employee's knowledge. At the same time, the public has become increasingly protective of its privacy. Thus, whether employers in the public or private sector may engage in a particular method of surveillance involves weighing the employee's expectation of privacy and the employer's need to protect its assets and services.

The major methods of workplace surveillance are telephonic, video, and electronic. Phone systems can record the length, destination, and cost of employee phone calls. Some businesses maintain standards concerning the length of calls. For example, an airline could expect its operators to conclude a reservation within 2 minutes. The phone system could be utilized to measure not only employee performance but also company efficiency. Video surveillance of assembly-line production can likewise measure manufacturing efficiency and provide a record for quality assurance. Monitoring network use by employees is also pertinent to business operations. The maintenance of audit logs to ensure that access to proprietary information has been exercised only by authorized employees is essential to business operations and may be required by government regulators (e.g., the requirements of the HIPAA Security Rule).

As a general rule, public employees possess greater protection from surveillance because of the First, Fourth, and Fourteenth Amendments to the U.S. Constitution. Even in the public sector, however, employers can limit employees' expectation of privacy by informing them that certain activities will be monitored. For example, employers may post a banner on network computer screens informing employees that the computer is provided for business use and that employee use will be monitored.

Security managers must be cognizant, however, that most states also impose limitations on surveillance. For example, New York prohibits the use of hidden cameras in restrooms, changing rooms, and hotel rooms. California prohibits the use of cameras in employee restrooms or changing rooms unless the employer has obtained a court order.

The USA PATRIOT Act

Perhaps the single most significant legislation impacting public and private security is the Uniting and Strengthening America by Providing Appropriate Tools Required to Intercept and Obstruct Terrorism Act (USA PATRIOT Act, which has been abbreviated as USAPA). This legislation, enacted on October 26, 2001, in response to the 9/11 attacks on the World Trade Center and the Pentagon, consists of ten titles addressing a variety of issues related to terrorism and the funding of terrorists. Title I, Enhancing Domestic Security Against Terrorism, requires the director of the U.S. Secret Service Agency to develop a national network of electronic crime task forces patterned after the New York Electronic Crimes Task Force for the purpose of preventing, detecting, and investigating electronic crimes, including potential acts of terrorism against critical infrastructures and the financial payment systems. Additionally, Title I confers increased powers on the president to deal with acts of terrorism.

Title II, Enhanced Surveillance Procedures, grants expanded surveillance powers to the government for the principal purpose of combating terrorism. Some powers, however, extend to traditional domestic crimes. The more significant of those powers include the following:

- Authority for sneak-and-peek warrants; that is, warrants that authorize surreptitious entry and a search of premises without seizing anything and then delaying notice of the search to the occupant for a time period stated in the warrant.
- Use of pen registers and trap-and-trace devices (pen registers record outgoing address or number information, i.e., the address or number being contacted by the suspect, and trap-and-trace devices record incoming addresses or numbers) for electronic communications.
- Interception, with permission of the system owner, by law enforcement of communications between a computer system and the trespasser within the system.
- Authority of law enforcement to execute pen register, trap-and-trace, and access to stored communication warrants on nationwide basis.
- Cooperation and information sharing between law enforcement and foreign intelligence investigators.

In the foreign intelligence area, USAPA authorizes

- Roving surveillance where the target is likely to avoid identification.
- Foreign intelligence surveillance when gathering such intelligence is a significant reason but not the sole reason for the surveillance.
- The USA PATRIOT Act provided that many of these powers would sunset (expire) after a designated period of time. Congress has subsequently (Intelligence Reform and Terrorist Prevention Act of 2004, and USA PATRIOT Improvement and Reauthorization Act of 2005) either extended or eliminated the sunset provision for nearly every power.

Title III, International Money Laundering Abatement and Anti-Terrorist Financing Act of 2001, creates a new anti–money laundering strategy designed to curb traditional money laundering and what is commonly referred to as *reverse money laundering*—placing legitimate money in financial institutions and moving those funds from institution to institution in an effort to conceal their source and eventually to remove them from the financial stream to support criminal activity, including terrorism. The provisions of Title III that impact the performance of security services include the requirement that financial institutions establish anti–money laundering programs and a customer identification program designed to identify terrorists when accounts are opened and to perform enhanced due diligence with respect to financial transactions.

Title IV, Protecting the Border, focuses on increasing resources for investigating visa applicants, ensuring the integrity and security of visa documents, protecting the northern border of the United States, and preserving immigration benefits for victims of terrorism.

Title V, Removing Obstacles to Investigating Terrorism, includes provisions for using DNA to identify terrorists and other violent offenders, sharing information concerning terrorism activities obtained by law enforcement during surveillance or searches with foreign intelligence personnel, and extending Secret Service jurisdiction to the investigation of computer crimes, including those involving terrorism.

Title VI, Providing for Victims of Terrorism, Public Safety Officers, and Their Families, provides for the support of victims of terrorism, including public safety officers and their families.

Title VII, Increased Information Sharing for Critical Infrastructure Protection, consists of only one section, but it is a significant one. Title VII provides for expansion of the Regional Information Sharing System (RISS) to enable information sharing between federal, state, and local law enforcement to facilitate an effective response to terrorist attacks and activities.

Title VIII, Strengthening the Criminal Laws Against Terrorism, specifically defined several acts of terrorism (e.g., terrorist attacks against transportation systems) as criminal acts. Acts of terrorism are included as acts of racketeering activity, and there is no statute of limitations on the prosecution of crimes of terrorism.

Title IX, Improved Intelligence, includes acts of terrorism within the scope of foreign intelligence activities under the National Security Act and provides for sharing intelligence on terrorist activities among domestic and foreign intelligence agencies.

Title X, Miscellaneous, includes a number of miscellaneous provisions, including a study of the feasibility of using a biometric identifier scanning system at ports of entry, limits on the issuance of hazardous materials licenses, prohibitions on the admission of aliens who have engaged in money laundering, and contracting for the performance of security services at U.S. military installations.

The USA PATRIOT Act has had greatest impact in the area of investigations, particularly those concerning computer and electronic crimes. We will reconsider the act when we discuss the administration of security investigations.

Summary

Security administrators must consider a multitude of legal issues that define, mandate, or control the performance of security functions. Also, because the conduct of security personnel can result in the imposition of criminal and/or civil liability on the employer, the administrator of public or private security services performs unique risk-avoidance responsibilities that require appreciation for legal issues that impact risk and risk avoidance.

Review Questions/Activities

1. A company that produces toxic waste as a by-product employs security personnel whose duties, among others, are to ensure that no one accesses the drums of toxic waste. One night, one of the security employees removed a drum of toxic waste and dumped it in a nearby river. That dumping violated the Federal Toxic Substances Act, which imposes liability without regard to intent or lack of due care. What is the liability of the security employee who dumped the waste and of the director of security who employed and supervises the employee?

2. Under what circumstances can a law enforcement officer be held criminally responsible for the death of an individual?

3. What is the meaning of vicarious liability, and what must be shown to impose it on an employer?

4. If a company contracts with a private security firm to provide protection twenty-four hours a day, seven days a week for its facilities, can a third person injured as a result of the performance of services by the private firm sue the company for injuries sustained? What would be the theoretical basis for imposing liability on the company?

5. A security employee detained a store customer for 30 minutes because he believed that the customer had stolen merchandise. During the 30-minute detention, the customer repeatedly insisted that she had receipts for each of the items, and she complained about the security officer's rude treatment. The officer ultimately determined that all of the merchandise had been purchased and told the customer that she was free to leave. As the customer was leaving, the officer, in the presence of numerous store employees and customers, told the store manager that "I had to let the criminal go this time." Is the security employee liable for any harm to the patron? What about the liability of the store manager and the store itself?

6. An off-duty police officer installed a hidden camera in the storage area of the Wonderful Department Store where he works as a member of the security unit. The officer installed the camera because he heard that his girlfriend, who also worked at the store, had been flirting with another co-worker. The camera videotaped the girlfriend and co-worker engaging in a sexual act while on a work break, and the security officer delivered the tape to the store, which dismissed both participants. Could the dismissed employees recover damages from the off-duty policeman for violating their civil rights?

7. The security manager of APEX Security Service assigned Robert Jones, an APEX security department employee, to investigate an alarm at a building at APEX's manufacturing plant. The manager knew that Jones had been drinking alcoholic beverages and that it would be necessary for him to drive a security vehicle in order to perform the investigation. If Jones negligently operates the vehicle on one of the roads on the company's plant and strikes a pedestrian, can the security manager be held civilly liable for the injuries caused to the pedestrian? Could APEX be held liable?

8. The network security administrator of Hi-Tech Products suspected that one of his employees was downloading child pornography onto a company computer during work hours. The computer security administrator installed a "sniffer" on the network server to monitor traffic to and from the suspected employee's computer. After the administrator confirmed that there was a significant amount of traffic of image files to the suspect employee's computer, he conducted an after-hours search of the employee's computer. The search revealed that the employee possessed several megabytes of child pornography on the company computer's hard drive. Based on information supplied by the network administrator, Hi-Tech Products fired the employee. Did the network administrator properly conduct the surveillance and search of the employee's computer?

9. Consider that in the scenario in Question 8, the network administrator informed a federal law enforcement officer about the results of his network surveillance using the "sniffer," and the officer asked the administrator to conduct the search of the company computer's hard drive. Could the evidence seized by the network administrator and delivered to the officer be used in a criminal proceeding against the employee?

WebSearches

Many law-related Web sites can be used for legal research on security topics. The following Web search problems are designed to familiarize the student with the most common sites and the information that can be obtained from them.

1. Go to www.findlaw.com. Utilize the search mechanisms on that site to find an indictment or decision in a federal or state court that deals with the performance of security functions.
2. Go to Cornell Law School's Legal Information Institute's Web site at www4.law.cornell.edu. Using the search engine at that site, search the U.S. Code for a section that deals with the responsibilities of a health care provider to maintain the privacy of a patient's personal information.
3. Go to the Web site for the California court system at www.courtinfo.ca.gov. Using its search engine, find the most recent decision of the California Supreme Court that discusses the liability of an off-duty police officer for an assault of the customer of a store while the officer was employed by the store as a security officer.
4. Using one of your favorite Internet search engines, locate the Web site for the court system of another state that publishes decisions and has a search engine that allows for the keyword search of decisions. Locate a recent decision of this state that deals with the same legal issue presented in the previous problem.

References

Dykes v. McRoberts Protective Agency, Inc. 256 A.D.2d 2, 680 N.Y.S.2d 513 (N.Y. Supreme Ct., Appellate Division, 1st Dept., 1998).

Lizardo v. Denny's Inc., U.S. Dist. LEXIS 9785 (U.S. District Ct., Northern District of N.Y., 2000).

Miller v. Wal-Mart Stores, Inc., 219 Wis.2d 250, 580 N.W.2d 233 (Wisconsin Supreme Court, 1998).

People v. Bernier, 204 A.D.2d 732, 612 N.Y.S.2d 629 (N.Y. Supreme Ct., App. Div., 2nd Dept., 1994).

Post, Richard S., and Arthur A. Kingsbury. 1977. *Security Administration: An Introduction*, 3rd ed. Springfield, Ill: Charles C. Thomas.

Rucshner v. ADT Security Systems, Inc., 149 Wash. App. 665, 204 P.3d 271 (Wash. Ct. App., 2009).

Simmons, Inc. v. Pinkerton's, Inc., 762 F.2d 591 (U.S. Ct. of Appeals, 7th Cir., 1985).

Terrill, Richard J. 2009. *World Criminal Justice Systems: A Survey*, 7th ed. Cincinnati, Ohio: Anderson Publishing Co.

United States v. White, U.S. App. LEXIS 10868 (7th Cir., 2003).

3

■ ■ ■

Proactive Security Administration and Planning

KEY TERMS

client area, emergency planning, FEMA, gap analysis, law enforcement powers, leadership, long-range planning, manual of rules, operational policies, planning, resource support network, risk, security service typologies, strategic planning.

Proactive administration simply means anticipating events or issues before they become a major problem or critical event. The key to this is planning. Our planning model is based on first identifying the most pressing security problems faced by an agency or corporate entity and then applying human and technical resources to deal with the identified issues. Identifying these problems is achieved by short- and long-term planning, particularly after the identification of a risk. For security service planning, *risk* is defined as a situation or thing that can result in death, injuries, lawsuits, and the stoppages of services and production.

Planning must be viewed as a continuous process in which an organization analyzes its strengths, weaknesses, and challenges. To conduct planning, the following principles are important:

- Participation between all ranks of employees and "stakeholders" in the client area.
- Open lines of communication for both good and bad news including speaking one's mind without retaliation.
- Delegation of authority to employees and field supervisors when appropriate.
- Use of appropriate selection processes and compensation packages to attract and retain the best employees.
- Use of current technology with an acknowledgment of costs and limitations.
- Identification of support resources and services for dealing with major catastrophic events.

There are two main issues here. First, the security service organization must be able to have open lines of internal communication and communication with external groups;

second, a security service provider must be able to assess the extent to which the service can realistically address and respond to a wide range of potential risks and situations. For example, a city police department may be well prepared to address street crimes that occur in its community but may be totally unprepared to deal with mass casualties and evacuation that might occur if a freight train carrying hazardous materials derails in the center of town. Concurrently, a contract security service that provides access control services may be totally unprepared to provide guard services to a client facing a month-long labor dispute. While most banking institutions can address most frauds, many may be totally unprepared when assets begin disappearing from client accounts because of computer intrusions committed by an overseas competitor.

The extent to which a security service can address situations is based on agency size, mission, training, experience, and availability of resources. The proactive planning model used in this text considers all of these factors and focuses on planning and acknowledging limitations. It also acknowledges that although the agency may be prepared to deal with emergency first response, it needs to ally itself with a resource/support network to deal with major catastrophes and restoration of services.

A core concept related to this model is the identification of what we call the *client area*, which is defined as a geographic or agency entity for which services are provided. For a city police department, it would be people and businesses that reside in the municipal limits. For a large hospital, the client area might be defined as doctors, nurses, auxiliary staff, patients, and visitors who either work at or visit facilities owned by the hospital. The client area might include businesses and streets adjacent to hospital property. Very often, security services with public powers have de facto or "good-neighbor" working relationships with these security forces that provide emergency first response. Airport security forces deal not only with passengers and planes at the airport facility but also with the adjacent neighborhoods related to emergency landings and crashes, noise, traffic, and so on. Most complicated is the client area for a multinational corporation, which includes all persons and property working for or owned by the company around the world. The most immediate problems here include geographic and time–distance coordination and language barriers.

Related to the client area is the resource support network (RSN). This network is based on working relationships that have been forged between agency heads. For a large manufacturing corporation, the RSN might be police departments adjacent to its geographic location, county and state police agencies, and the county emergency management network. The network may be used not only for situations on a daily basis but also for major emergencies. It provides the framework for forging working relationships between the public and private sector law enforcement and security agencies. In some areas, this framework consists of agency heads having coffee to discuss issues to formal meetings on a monthly basis at which specific intelligence and training are presented. These active and sharing relationships break down barriers between public police and private sector security.

SECURITY SERVICE TYPOLOGIES

Based on the operational realities just described, we have devised the following four organizational planning models or typologies based on a security service's ability, experience, and authority to provide first response to emergency situations related to its client area and support network. Figure 3-1 summarizes these relationships based on two variables: resources and governmental powers.

RESOURCES	LEVEL II Maximum resources Limited powers 1,10	LEVEL IV Full powers Maximum resources 10,10
	LEVEL I Limited resources Limited powers 1,1	LEVEL III Limited resources Full powers 10,1
	GOVERNMENTAL POWER	

FIGURE 3-1   Security Services Planning Model

Level IV

The security service can deal with the vast majority of situations that occur in its client area and can be classified as a full-response organization. The service has personnel and resources that can be deployed in a short period of time and has very clear governmental enforcement and intervention powers. The service has an active working relationship with its resource support network, which is called on only for major events. Often it provides assistance, expertise, and resources to smaller agencies in the model. Examples of these full-response organizations include federal security agencies, state and large city or metropolitan police forces, and state public security operations that provide a wide range of protection services.

Level III

The service can deal with the majority of situations based on its client area and mission. It has full governmental powers but lacks certain resources and experience for specific major problems. For major situations, it relies on active assistance from other agencies in the resource support network. Small- to medium-size police forces, college and university police departments, and certain private security forces with powers would be categorized under this title.

Level II

Although the security service has a large amount of resources, it is limited in providing full services to its client area because it lacks governmental enforcement powers. It relies daily on the resource support network to deal with situations involving the need for arrest and use of other powers. Often this support network is called in to take over major crime investigations and emergency situations. Examples include private sector corporate security operations that often have more personnel and equipment than the neighboring municipality or town.

Level I

The security service has few personnel and available resources and does not exercise governmental powers. Thus, its resource support network often provides assistance on a frequent basis. Security services of this category include organizations that provide only watch and guard services.

Agency heads reviewing these typologies may flinch while reading these categories because they believe that their agency or unit can deal with most crises. Remember that these are typologies to be used for planning purposes and that all models have limitations. Even a Level IV agency will call in additional assistance during major catastrophic events.

GOVERNMENT POWER

Common to the four planning models presented is the issue of governmental power. As discussed in Chapter 2, federal, state, and local governments have various law enforcement and regulatory powers to provide for safety and security. In a discussion of security services, these powers would include the following:

1. Warrantless arrests based on probable cause for felony, misdemeanor, or petty offenses.
2. Execution of arrest and search warrants.
3. Issuance of motor vehicle summonses or citations on highways.
4. Stoppage of motor vehicle and commercial land traffic on railroads and waterways.
5. Evacuation of people from population centers.
6. Custodial intervention powers for those persons who pose a danger to themselves and others.
7. Use of deadly physical force and ability to carry firearms.
8. Issuance and use of nonlethal weapons such as conducted energy devices (Taser), oleocapsecum spray, and baton.

While these powers may seem fairly clear, their use and execution are very complex and governed by statutes and agency practice and policies. For example, in certain states, state police officers have statewide powers for all offenses while municipal police officers have powers only in their immediate county and may go into another county for an arrest situation only if they possess a warrant. In other states, a municipal police officer may make an arrest for any felony or misdemeanor based on probable cause anywhere in the state. However, most departments frown on off-duty arrests outside the immediate geographical jurisdiction unless there is a life-threatening incident.

In certain states, the extent of police power is based on the type of offense, the jurisdiction, and the authority of the agency. Traffic offenses illustrate this complexity. In some states, traffic summonses can be issued only by a police officer employed in the geographical area where the offense occurred.

All states have designated various levels of authority to their law enforcement agents. The following model describes these arrangements.

Full Police

State law enforcement powers are available to personnel in all areas at any time. Federal officers have nationwide authority; and state powers are often granted to enhance federal investigative efforts and assist state and local police forces. Officers are armed on the basis of their authority.

Police Limited

General law enforcement powers are limited to the performance of official duties related to the person's position or only on properties owned by the public or private entity. These powers are often delegated generally to public safety employees employed by operating authorities such as housing, transportation, and nuclear/electric power services. Federal officers use police power only when they perform specific duties related to an agency mission. Some agencies might place limits on arrest powers or the ability to carry authorized weapons or issue traffic summonses. Personnel may or may not be authorized to carry firearms but may be allowed to carry other weapons such as a baton or law enforcement–level pepper spray.

None

Employees in this category do not exercise official police powers. They may take actions such as making an arrest or holding a person in custody under common law or specific powers granted to citizens. These personnel generally perform their duties unarmed.

DISCUSSION OF POWER

In many states, full or limited law enforcement powers may be delegated by statute to private institutions. In the late 1800s, railroad police officers were given public police powers in many states to protect property and passengers. The main reason for this was the inability of states and municipalities to extend police protection to what was at times a far-flung enterprise that crossed city and county jurisdictions. That tradition continues today as railroad police continue to be granted police authority by the superintendent of state police because there is a continuing "state interest" for granting authority. A "state interest" implies that the government believes that police powers are necessary for a private entity because the state does not wish to allocate resources to protect a specific client area or the client group is better served by its own protection service.

The practice of state interest is common on college and university campuses and at private hospitals. In many states, the superintendent of state police or the county sheriff has the power to delegate police power to security personnel employed by private colleges and universities. Often the officer has police power on college property in the county where the college is located or in counties where the college owns property. In some localities, the city or town also grants police power to these personnel to obtain available backup response for situations caused by college students in downtown bars and housing facilities.

It is not surprising that hiring controls and practices are related to the extent of law enforcement powers. In the public sector, police and security personnel are selected through written examinations, oral interviews, physical agility testing, medical testing, and certain background information. In states that delegate powers to private officers, personnel must complete designated training programs that are on the same level with courses for police officers. Certification or granting warrant powers depends on completing mandated training and maintaining a "clean" record. The current problem nationally is with minimum model security organizations in the private sector with no law enforcement powers. Often these are contract or small company watch and guard agencies. Security officers are paid minimum wages with no benefits and may not be subject to character checks and training.

For emergency situations, federal and state governments have the power to order emergency evacuations or to declare a state of emergency and issue executive orders about using private property, establishing public curfews, and suspending constitutional rights. Presidential decision directive (PDD) 39, originally issued in 1992 and amended in 1999, and updated under the National Response Framework (2008) establishes the federal response plan for disaster relief and terrorist events. Among other duties, it gives the Federal Emergency Management Administration (FEMA) the responsibility for organizing the federal response plan for preparedness, planning, and disaster assistance. The FBI is empowered to be in charge of criminal investigation activities related to a terrorist attack.

PLANNING IN GENERAL

There are many textbook definitions of planning. For our purposes in dealing with security matters, *planning* is defined as the process of organizing security service resources to deal with immediate and long-range security concerns and issues and to address and mitigate potential emergency situations. *Immediate security services* are the day-to-day services that must be provided to maintain a safe and secure environment. *Potential emergency situations* are those that are life threatening and totally disruptive to the work of an agency or company that might, under certain circumstances, occur in the existing environment. More formal definitions appear in every management textbook, and each has certain commonalities, as discussed in Thibault, Lynch, and McBride (2004):

1. Plans are created to deal with the future and address real-life issues. In other words, what does the organization wish to do and how does it wish to get there? Additionally, planning describes how the organization will deal with immediate and long-term challenges.

2. Plans organize people and departments into subunits, groups, or entities to deal with daily tasks and work assignments. For security service management, these are categorized into line, administrative, and auxiliary assignments. Line personnel, such as patrol officers and investigators, deal with the crime calls, investigations, and requests for security services. Auxiliary members, such as dispatchers, car mechanics, and clerks, provide support for line functions. Overall policy and direction are provided by administrative sections that can facilitate planning; legal, internal review, and financial assistance. The goal for immediate plans is to provide some form of consistency for daily operations and to define the roles and expectations for each member of the unit.

3. Agency plans identify and monitor general objectives and the methods by which the objectives can be achieved. Very often the objectives reflect current public policy or security situations caused by the external environment. Based on current events, a security service located at a busy seaport must address the potential for arms smuggling, transport of nuclear devices, human smuggling, and persons coming on ships with illegal passports and visas.

4. Work assignments are described and categorized by order of importance. Most security providers are concerned with day-to-day services such as protecting people, property, and other company assets; who does what; and how to become part of the agency's operational plan.

5. The organization's budget is based on planning. The budget includes planned income and disbursement of funds for personnel, equipment, and travel. The difference between income and disbursement is either a profit or loss. In the public sector, tax monies provide the basic funding for an agency; in the private sector, funding may be based on company allocations and service contracts based on the company's overall economic life (i.e., profit). In public services, the administrator prepares a budget, which estimates operational costs and available funds. Each security service agency has its own plan for budgeting. The budget is generally for a fiscal year, which is an organization's business year. For most federal agencies, the budget year is from July 1 to June 30; in the private sector, the budget year can begin on January 1 and end December 31 or begin on another specific date and end twelve months later.

6. Planning is viewed as a continuous process and is based on immediate data, intuition, and ever-changing national and world events. Data for security information is provided by crime records, service calls, field reports, information obtained from agencies in the resource support network, state and national crime reports, and trends reported in professional business journals.

7. Finally, and of great importance, planning defines the mission, values, and vision of the organization. *Mission* defines why the organization exists and what it plans to do for clients or the community. A Web review of the mission statements for many security service organizations determined that their mission is to provide quality services to clients or members of the community. Organizational values are the common beliefs

that an organization fosters for all its members and puts into operational practice every day. Such values might include behaving ethically, protecting citizen rights, appreciating diversity, being fair, and providing professional services. Related to values is the vision statement for the organization. The vision statement describes fundamental desired goal or states what the organization wishes to achieve. For example, one housing security department has placed on its patrol cars and brochures, "We will be a model public safety organization in partnership with the community we serve"; a university campus has this vision statement, "This community belongs to all of us." Both values and vision should be clear and realistic and understood by all members of the organization after organization-wide discussion and debate. Too often, in conducting department reviews, the authors have found that values and mission statements appear in manuals and brochures but are never understood or adopted by line or supervisory staff in the organization.

TYPES OF PLANS

Operational Plans

Operational plans exist in many forms. In the public sector, they are often referred to as the *manual of rules*. The specific operational guidelines may be related to various other policy documents such as collective bargaining agreements and local codes and regulations. In private sector organizations, they are referred to as *operational policies*. Regardless of title, operational plans generally describe how daily tasks are to be conducted and the work rules to which members must adhere. They also describe organizational ranks, the authority of each rank, and the legal processes that affect the organization. Overall, an operational plan is a comprehensive document that describes the organization's vision and its expectations of employees. A review of various plans for a wide range of security service agencies might include the following:

Item	Function
Mission, vision, and values	Describes goals and general expectations for employees based on the mission and vision of the organization.
Organization and authority	Presents organizational chart and a brief description of the chain of command and job duties for each position. In addition to describing the internal chain of command, this section describes to whom the unit and the director of chief security officers reports. We have found this to be a problem in corporations and public sector units for which security is not the main service being provided (other services include education, hospital services, and environmental safety).
Time and attendance	Describes report-to-duty procedures, shifts assignments and requests for vacation or personal time, calling in sick, and so on. In unionized organizations, these will be governed by contractual work rules.
Equipment and weapons	Details uniforms, equipment, and types of weapons authorized to be carried. Often includes use of force and deadly physical force.

(Continued)

(Continued)

Item	Function
Computer use	Outlines rules for computer use by employees and prohibitions against illegal or personal use.
Complaint investigation	Outlines how complaints are taken from dissatisfied clients or those complaining of illegal use of governmental powers such as excessive force; includes forms for this purpose and procedures to follow up on and resolve complaints.
Media relations	Presents the general rules for responding to media inquiries for information including who acts as organization's spokesperson.
Ethics	Defines professional behavior for all employees both on and off duty.
General	Describes the general range of duties for all employees such as patrol, communications, investigations, and crime analysis.
Emergency	Describes building evacuations, personnel mobilizations, and death notifications.

For security services conducting patrol operations, the operational plan should include patrol post designations, emergency response procedures, use of force by department members, detention and arraignment procedures for prisoners, and the use of specialized equipment. An example of an operational plan pertaining to notification for hazardous conditions, suspicious packages, and other potentially hazardous conditions is given in Figure 3-2. In this example, taken from Tufts University (2010), the plan contains the general policy, definitions, procedures, responsibilities, and possible actions to take. The operational plan not only defines general reaction and responsibilities but also serves as a resource for training and incident review.

Short-Term Planning

Short-term plans address work situations that may not be covered in the duty manual or procedural changes that occur because of court rulings, agency policy changes, and new information obtained from research studies. In recent years, security service departments have had to devise short-term plans to deal with computer crime cases and secure electronic evidence because these procedures are still being developed in many cases. Short-term planning also deals with scheduled events such as parades, demonstrations, athletic activities, and major business conventions. Planning for them includes logistics, staffing, threat analysis, and threat countermeasures that may have to be employed. Eventually, if a plan seems to work over a period of time and is used on a frequent basis, it may become a "standard procedure" and then become part of the general operational plan.

GENERAL PLANNING PROCESS

We have defined operational and short-term plans. Now we discuss the process that they involve. Also, what kind of planning is used for long-term issues or strategic planning? The main difference between these plans and the concept of strategic planning is the time factor in terms

TUFTS UNIVERSITY
DEPARTMENT OF PUBLIC SAFETY

GENERAL DIRECTIVE

EFFECTIVE DATE:	NUMBER:	AMENDS/SUPERSEDES:
10/25/01	GD01-011	

SUBJECT:	SECTION
Hasardous Conditions Response	2-33

Commentary

This policy is intended to provide guidance in responding to a notification of a hazardous condition, suspicious package, biological contamination, chemical spill, gas leak/strange odor, or other questionable substance. Notification of appropriate personnel should be timely; however it should not hinder or interfere in any way with immediate life safety tasks such as administering CPR/First Responder or duties related to safe building evacuation.

1. **Policy**

    By using established procedure, a potentially dangerous situation such as those listed above, can be handled with the least amount of risk and minimal panic. **In all cases, the safety of building occupants and responding personnel will be of primary importance.**

2. **Procedure**

    A. Public Safety personnel working dispatch will, upon receipt of notification of any of the above situations notify the shift supervisor and sector officers of the reported condition. The dispatcher shall also do the following:

    1. Obtain pertinent information about the caller and the exact location and status of the hazard.
    2. Instruct the caller to refrain from opening any suspicious packages or investigating a questionable substance or odor.
    3. Calmly instruct the caller to leave the room or area where the hazard is located, and to instruct others to do the same.
    4. **Contact/inform the Station Commander, Director of Public Safety.**
    5. **Contact/inform the Environmental Health & Safety Office if additional resources, expertise and/or support are needed.**

    B. Unless advised of a course of action to take by the Director or the Station Commander, the shift supervisor will use all available information to determine if the building should be evacuated. Supervisors are reminded that thorough investigative techniques will help to place the event in the appropriate perspective thereby helping to ensure safety, and avoid panic and overreaction. If, after a thorough investigation of the reported incident it is determined that the building should be evacuated, the shift supervisor will instruct the dispatcher to contact the local fire department.

FIGURE 3-2 **Example of an Operational Plan**

Among the facts that should be considered in deciding whether or not to evacuate the building are:

1. The safety of the building occupants.
2. The source and strength of information about the hazard or condition. Including information from persons at the location.
3. Whether it is the first report, or have there been repeated incidents of this nature.
4. The number of occupants and the type of occupancy.
5. Whether there has been any unusual activity on campus such as protests or demonstrations.
6. Whether scheduled campus activity such as exams may be a motive to cause evacuation of a building.

C. If the condition or hazard exists in a building or area in which a public event is in progress, the shift supervisor will notify the person in charge of the event. The decision to evacuate the building will remain with the shift supervisor. Should a condition or hazard exist in a residence hall or academic building, every effort to notify occupants will be made. Under certain circumstances, the fire alarm can be used to evacuate the building except in situations where there is a reported gas leak. In these instances, alternative means of notification such as knocking on doors may be the safest method of evacuation.

   The Office of Residential Life will be notified during business hours if the building is an occupied residence hall. After normal business hours the on-call administrator will be notified. If the building is an academic, administrative or athletic facility, the department heads will be notified.

   If a residence hall must be evacuated for a lengthy period of time, students can be temporarily housed in Cohen Auditorium, Gancher Center, and Campus Center etc.

D. If a building is evacuated, the following shall occur:

1. Occupants should be assembled in established fire evacuation assembly areas, but at least 100 yards away from the building or area.
2. Once the building has been evacuated, all exterior perimeter areas will be secured.
3. The Director or his designee shall establish a command post and determine if the FBI, State Police and/or Department of Public Health should be notified.
4. The decision for occupants to re-enter the building or area will be made by the Director or his designee. Designee shall include shift supervisors.
5. The shift supervisor will ensure that all proper documentation of the event is accomplished. This includes a CAD entry into ARMS, as well as a full detailed incident report including who was notified and what actions were taken.

FIGURE 3-2   Continued

Source: Courtesy of Tufts University Department of Public Safety.

of immediate versus long term. Planning is often seen as an abstract art but it must be a method for reviewing actual issues. The following is a composite of a planning process (Thibault, Lynch, and McBride, 2004: 387–390):

1. Defining issues or identifying problems is perhaps the most difficult part of planning. The issue here is whether the problem is something that has to be addressed by policy makers or by a unit head. In issue or problem identification, it is important to have data that show the extent of the problem. "People being mugged in parking lots" for a corporate security unit has to be broken down by the usual questions of where, when, why, and how many.

2. Determining current status and future objectives—the resources or support systems the organization has and the future resources that might be needed—includes gathering data

in relation to the problem. For example, an agency wishing to reduce street crime would review crime reports, intelligence information, and actual observations obtained from surveillance units or cameras.

3. Developing courses of action involves planning to take action by dealing with questions such as these: What do we want to do? How much time and money are we willing to spend? Often there is an organizational imperative to simply solve the problem and either make it go away or keep it under reasonable constraints. Action items include developing new procedures and programs or introducing new equipment.

4. Implementing the plan occurs after a decision is made to take a course of action. It is given a rank in relationship to other organizational priorities. "Obtaining concurrences" means obtaining the agreement of all who are involved with the plan such as line officers, investigators, and upper-level managers.

5. Evaluating and reconsidering involves measuring actual performance in comparison to desired performance. In other words, ask how the plan worked, what did not work, and what new issues emerged.

STRATEGIC PLANNING

Strategic planning is a misused management tool because it is often confused with short- and long-term planning and sometimes risk analysis. Citing a definition by Paul Forbes in his *Handbook for Strategic Planning,* King (2002) states that *strategic planning* is the continuous process of evaluating the nature of a business or service, identifying long-range objectives, identifying goals, developing strategies to reach the goals, and allocating resources to carry out the strategies. The key is that planning is undertaken by upper-level management and policy makers to review the organization's basic business and predict how the organization fits into the "future big picture" in terms of long-range client needs, population and workforce changes, changes in technology, and anticipated competition.

The main difference between strategic and long-term planning is that the latter assumes that the external environment will essentially remain stable for the next three to six years. Strategic planning, however, considers the internal and external environments of the organization. In organization theory, the internal environment encompasses all people, units, and procedures within the organization, and the external environment includes all forces outside the organization. Another key element of strategic planning is that the organization makes disciplined decisions regarding the core of its business or service delivery plan.

CASE STUDY IN PLANNING

Security supervisors at a major shopping mall noticed an increase in vehicle thefts during the winter months. Using simple data analysis, they found that 90 percent of the vehicles had been stolen between the hours of 4:30 P.M. and 9:00 P.M. Most of the vehicles were luxury cars or Toyota Camrys. Except for patrol cars, the department did not have any surveillance equipment for the parking lots, especially the shadowed areas.

The county sheriff's department did, however, have such equipment for drug surveillances and lent a hi-tech surveillance van with one deputy to the department. Based on theft complaints, most of the vehicles were being stolen from the north side of the mall, which was adjacent to expressway ramps.

Three mall officers and the sheriff's deputy were assigned to conduct surveillance and, hopefully, intercept the car thieves. Within two days into the detail, the task force struck gold. A dark Buick was observed on camera making too many passes in and out of the parking area. It suddenly came to a stop in front of a BMW and within minutes two men were out working the door and eventually the ignition system. They were apprehended just as they got the engine running. The suspect vehicle managed to elude the dragnet but was eventually stopped by patrol units at the expressway ramp.

Based on this experience and further evaluation, the mall planned to increase lighting in the parking lots and start a "driver assistance" jeep patrol to assist drivers with their cars. It was decided to use this customer assistance approach as a way of making more field inquiries for people who seemed to be having trouble starting cars. Patrol personnel were also trained on how to look for carjackers, and the sheriff's department began sharing more up-to-date data on car theft rings.

For this discussion, we realize that many security service units may be part of a larger organization or political entity. Too often, planning is not undertaken until upper-level management or the political leadership undertakes an overall review of functions and services. Because planning is a continuous process, the unit or department in a large organization should conduct strategic planning on its own for a number of reasons. Strategic planning demonstrates dynamic management, and the information obtained through it can be immediately used for operational plan changes and budget forecasting. It is also good to be ahead of the game in the planning function because all too often "forced" assignments can appear from an organization's leadership at a moment's notice and often involve some kind of crisis.

Steps in the Strategic Planning Process

As described by King (2002), the strategic planning process basically has six steps:

1. **Planning to plan.** As with short-term planning, this is the difficult step. It starts by asking the question, What are we going to do in the future based on what we do, what we know, and what our competitors are up to? Answering these questions involves everyone in the organization and all stakeholders. For planning purposes, stakeholders include service clients, visitors, customers, resource support networkers, and intradepartment units that the security service usually deals with on daily issues as well as organization and community leaders.

2. **Values scan.** This step reviews the organization's current values to ascertain whether to retain, change, or discard them. Values are operational and ethical traits that define the organization, such as honesty, upholding constitutional rights, fairness, ethical behavior both on and off duty, and forging working relationships with the client/community.

3. **Mission reformation.** Based on the overall strategic planning exercise, this step determines the need to change the way that the organization conducts business or undertakes operations.

4. **SWOT analysis.** SWOT stands for *strengths, weaknesses, opportunities,* and *threats. Strengths* are those programs, procedures, and equipment that contribute to the agency or department mission in a positive way. *Weaknesses* are the same items that undermine the agency's daily operations. *Opportunities* are defined as economic, political, or social changes that could affect the very nature of the business in a positive way. *Threats* are internal and external variables that might negatively affect the operations of the department both in the immediate and long-term future. Threats can be anything that could have a

negative impact, such as weather, a dramatic decrease in agency funding, unusual criminal activity, and lawsuits for personnel actions.

The information for SWOT analysis is obtained from a number of sources such as agency or department reports, interviews with clients, small group and focus discussions, questionnaires, and telephone interviews. It also comes from reviews of state, national, and international trends in employment, crimes, technology, and so on. Obviously, the information gathered from risk management is very important. In conducting SWOT exercises, managers immediately realize that the information they obtain may not be factual but perceptional. Very often, clients and stakeholder express beliefs about safety that are unfounded but are "true" because there are bits of information commonly held. An example is, "Everyone knows you never go into the parking lots at night because employees get mugged!"

5. **Future action plans.** Based on the preceding steps, action plans are developed to make fundamental changes to the organization.
6. **Contingency plans.** This is the scary part of planning. What happens if expectations suddenly change or a new opportunity arises that throws the organization and plan off-balance?

PLANNING IN ACTION

CENTRAL STATE HOSPITAL

The director of police at Central State Hospital realized after a staff meeting that the organization's environment would be radically changed in the not-so-distant future. Several factors caused him to realize this. A recent newspaper article reported that two small community hospitals might close within the next two years because of their inability to compete and make money because of rising costs. This meant that more patients would be coming to Central State. Another factor was an unfounded report from a corrections officer that the State Division of Prisons would transfer all psychiatric patients to Central State by the end of the year. The third, which had been the main topic of the meeting, was a national labor union's plan to unionize hospital nurses.

While the public safety department was well staffed and equipped, the director could see in her crystal ball that security service operations would be changing because the parent organization was changing. The director created a strategic planning task force under the direction of a deputy chief and assigned patrol officers, supervisors, and clerical staff to the group. They were charged with reviewing all phases of their current operation and predicting what changes would be coming from the external environment.

The group began discussions and inquiries based on known and rumored information. They found that while their mission (providing quality law enforcement and protection services) and vision ("We will be the model for hospital public safety services in the Northwest United States") would not be changing, the following findings would impact operations:

1. It was true that the prison would be sending psychiatric patients but only for short-term emergency care. Thus, it would be necessary to train officers and staff on emergency situations involving these patients.
2. While the community hospitals would indeed be closing, it might be possible that Central State would take over these properties for specialized or emergency care. This raised all kinds of questions regarding staffing and coordination for what would be essentially satellite operations.
3. The nurses union would probably become a reality, and sentiments were also expressed that the police staff might also be unionized to improve working conditions and

salaries. Thus, management, including the security service unit, would have to operate in a unionized environment.

4. As these discussions were continuing, the hospital attorney announced that all staff, including police, would have to become familiar with the regulations regarding the Health Insurance Portability and Accountability Act (HIPAA). HIPAA regulations which went into effect in 2003, require that all health care organizations initiate procedures for the protection of patient information. This includes training all staff and reviewing electronic data procedures. It was also recommended that the department create an electronic data unit to deal with computer offenses and potential HIPAA complaints. (A further discussion of HIPAA is presented in Chapter 11.)

5. The department should initiate a customer feedback program. In essence, this is a short survey that asks patients, staff, and visitors who needed services what they felt about the service they received, the attentiveness of the staff, and the quickness of the response.

As a result of the strategic planning exercise, the group created a report or "blueprint" that considered all of these factors and made recommendations for additional staffing, training, and equipment. While by no means perfect, it provided the organization a plan for the next five years.

Gap Analysis

One technique that can be used in security planning is called gap analysis. In its basic format, gap represents the difference between a benchmark, standard, or desired goal and what actually occurs or the present status. (Strategic Planning, n.d) Planners then define the impediments or resources needed to fill the gap in order to achieve the desired outcome. Business enterprises use this method as a means of presenting desired outcomes for marketing and reorganization.

As part of the strategic planning process, a review team would look at various issues and determine what is needed to achieve the desired goals. For example, at the medical facility, the review teams addressed the issue of equipping officers with Tasers:

Goal—Equip all security personnel with Tasers.

Current Status—There has been a 20 percent increase in officers using physical force to subdue combative individuals; officers are not equipped with Tasers to deal with combative individuals; public police must be called for assistance and there is often delay in responding; three members injured during the past six months, resulting in nine sick days.

Impediments—Need for senior management approval; funding needs to be defined for training and equipment; review impact on liability insurance; state legal requirements that must be met.

The "impediments" identified are items that need to be resolved in order for the plan to go forward. For planning purposes these would be charted and a timetable created for resolution of each item in order of priority.

ROLE OF LEADERSHIP

Leadership is a core element in planning. Although there are many definitions of the term *leadership*, we define it as the ability to get things done under a variety of circumstances. Leadership perhaps can be explained as serving in a variety of roles depending on what is going on, sometimes called *situational leadership for decision making.* Without a crisis, most proactive administrators are able to consult with a number of various groups before making a decision that affects the unit or the organization. In times of a crisis, proactive administrators have to be decisive because they must make decisions that impact the life or death of employees or clients and the future of the organization.

The person who is responsible for any one of the plans discussed in this chapter must have the requisite authority in the organizational structure. Regardless of titles, he or she has to take the lead, marshal resources, and set goals and timetables for completing the plan. If anything, he or she has to "rally the troops," showing why the planning project is important not only to the organization but also to each individual. This is true even in military and semimilitary bureaucracies, which operate on a highly defined set of relationships and expectations. Case studies in public administration and business management programs point to the fact that failure to inspire often leads to project failure or incompletion and, sometimes, sabotage. Proactive administrators, then, have good interpersonal skills, meaning the ability to work with people and share information. Above all, they are out in front and willing to take risks and responsibility for success and failure. A review of resumes of security service executives that we know indicate that all have in common progressive formal education and training either by the agency/company or through professional associations such as ASIS. If anything, they realize that leadership requires the necessary analytical tools and information to make "right" decisions.

Security service administrators do not live in a vacuum. Regardless of model type, they often report to someone or some entity. In a private sector organization that has a security service unit, the chief administrator (e.g., the vice president, director, or chief) will report to an upper-level vice president or the president. In a public bureaucracy, the same is true, or the head reports to an elected official. Private sector security service firms, such as watch and guard units, report to their customers. Thus, there is always the client area, which consists of taxpayers, customers, vendors, and so on. Planning, accordingly, becomes a more important event because the chief administrator has to sell the program in terms of how the security services can contribute to the mission of the organization in terms of employee protection, loss recovery, or personal safety for clients. One of the authors attended a meeting of the heads of university, parks and recreation, and environmental security services in one state to discuss employee relations issues. As the meeting progressed, they all agreed that they were the "stepchildren" of their parent organizations because none of their organizations were in the primary business of law enforcement and security. The meeting had to continually refocus on the daily operational demands imposed by the primary mission of the organization, not on the mission of the security services unit. In private firms, selling services is real in terms of anticipating costs, providing quality services, staying ahead of the competition, and making a profit. If customers or clients are unhappy, they find someone else!

Summary

In this chapter we presented the proactive security planning model, which is based on consultations with a wide range of publics including employees and stakeholders; reviews of technology, resources, and support; and identification of the client area and resource support network.

Four security service typologies were presented based on the agency resources and governmental powers. We must emphasize that these are models for agency classifications and planning purposes. All agencies must rely on outside assistance in major emergencies. We then presented an overview on short- and long-term planning, strategic planning, and leadership.

Review Questions/Activities

1. Analyze four agencies in your area, and fit them into one of the four security service typologies presented. You may wish to discuss your finding with an agency representative. To measure strengths and weaknesses, present a number of situations and ascertain how the agency would respond to them. Examples might include a barricaded suspect with hostages, a small plane crash, and a computer virus that destroys the entire computing system.

2. From area security service agencies, obtain samples of short- and long-term plans that are not classified or confidential.

3. Apply the strategic planning model to yourself in terms of your career or educational aspirations.

4. Select a major agency or organization in your community that has a security service to protect human and material assets. Define their client area as discussed in the text.

5. For the agencies or organizations presented in Question 1, to whom does the unit report? What is the client area? Then review the mission, vision, and value statement and see whether they fit the general description provided in this chapter.

WebSearches

1. With the guidance of your instructor, search the Web for a strategic plan created by a private or public sector organization. To what extend did the organization use the concepts described in this chapter such as values, mission, SWOT and Gap?

2. Using your favorite Internet search engine, search the Web for resources on planning for the security of physical premises. List the five sites that you found most informative and briefly describe why you placed them on your list.

References

King, John. 2002. "Strategic Planning." Presentation to Executive Training Institute, International Association of Campus Law Enforcement Administrators, Orlando, Florida, November 7, 2003.

Thibault, Edward A., Lawrence Lynch, and R. B. McBride. 2004. *Proactive Police Management,* 6th ed. Upper Saddle River, N.J.: Prentice-Hall.

4

■ ■ ■

Risk Mitigation through Security

KEY TERMS

assets, cost-benefit analysis, countermeasure, enterprise risk management (ERM), enterprise security risk management (ESRM), risk, risk assessment, risk management, risk mitigation, threat, vulnerability.

You might recall the television ad, "The greatest risk is not taking one." A 2001 version of the ad by insurance giant American International Group (AIG) has been captured on You Tube and can be found at http://www.youtube.com/watch?v=At6F0M4bSP8. AIG subsequently became a victim of the 2008 financial crisis and a participant in the government bailout program. Testimony before the U.S. Senate revealed that a bailout became necessary because AIG "took unmonitored and unnecessary risks" and "made huge numbers of irresponsible bets" (Dennis, 2009). The lesson, for AIG and all of us, is clear: Risk management is vital to the economic health, perhaps survival, of a business enterprise. So, what is risk and what is security's role in a company's risk management? Those are the questions the current chapter focuses on.

The concept of risk can be defined in several ways. ASIS International's General Security Risk Assessment Guideline (2003) defines risk as "the potential for an unwanted outcome resulting from an incident, event, or occurrence, as determined by its likelihood and the associated consequences." Davidson (2009) defines security risk as the "possibility of loss resulting from a threat, security incident, or event" and Vellani (2007) defines risk as "the possibility of asset loss, damage, or destruction as a result of a threat exploiting a specific vulnerability." Risk, thus, deals with possibilities, the possibilities that some event will occur that could cause damage to a business.

Risk may be classified, or subdivided, in many ways: financial, credit, operational, reputational, and security, to name just a few. Most businesses are exposed to multiple forms of risk and some forms of risk may be more important than others, depending on the nature of a particular business. In the case of Google, the risk of theft of proprietary information is paramount. For an online merchant, the risk of a denial of service attack that could disable its Web site, or the risk of a database security breach, may be paramount. Investment banks, for example, Lehman Brothers, failed in 2008 because they failed to manage their core business—financial risk. Other businesses and homeowners sustained devastating losses because they failed to manage their own financial and credit risks.

It is not possible to eliminate all risks; the essential task is to effectively manage, or mitigate, risk to a level that is essential to a company's profit margins or a public agency's reputation and operation. Because risk comes in many forms, an effective risk management strategy seeks to address exposure to risk globally (i.e., across the organization). This strategy is referred to as *enterprise risk management* (ERM). Enterprise security risk management (ESRM) is a subset of ERM. According to Davidson (2009), ESRM "encompasses the more traditional security risks, such as asset protection, as well as broader security issues, such as safety, IT security, and brand integrity." Johnson and Spivey (2008) define ESRM as "[t]he component of an enterprise risk management model focused on the security perspective for identification, assessment, and mitigation of those events that impact an organization's ability to achieve its business goals and objectives." This chapter focuses on enterprise security risk management.

Enterprise security risk management involves four phased processes. The first phase is risk assessment, which is "the process of assessing security-related risks from internal and external threats to an entity, its assets, or personnel" (ASIS International, 2003: 5). The second phase is risk prioritization—the process of determining which assets are most valuable and at risk, thus, most in need of protective countermeasures. The third phase is risk mitigation, which is "the effort to reduce loss of life and property by lessening the impact of disasters" (FEMA, 2009). The final phase is risk operationalization—the process of putting the risk mitigation plan into operation.

The risk management process is illustrated as follows:

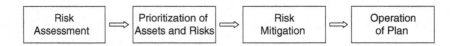

| Risk Assessment | ⟹ | Prioritization of Assets and Risks | ⟹ | Risk Mitigation | ⟹ | Operation of Plan |

PHASE I: RISK ASSESSMENT

The initial phase of risk management is the process of risk assessment. We utilize the following scenario to illustrate this process. A fictitious firm that we call Canal City Paychecks asked a security-consulting firm to conduct a site review/survey. Canal City was in the business of preparing weekly paychecks and tax forms for a number of small regional firms. It employed more than 100 people. Approximately 75 percent of the employees worked at computer terminals taking in client information, creating accounts, and creating pay documents and tax forms. The security for the building, located in a suburban industrial park near an airport, consisted of traditional key-locked doors and automatic fire and intrusion alarms turned on at night. The owner was initially concerned about burglars at night but later confided that the spouse of an employee showed up one morning to confront her husband about an alleged love affair that was going on at a local hotel. There was a nasty confrontation in the parking lot, and police were called to break it up.

The consultant's review team first asked for the firm's security policies and overall plan, employee handbooks, and a general idea of what the company would look like in the next five to ten years. Although there was no security plan, the employee handbook did have some language about civility, confidentiality, and general work rules. The firm's strategic plan outlined strong growth potential for the business and the likelihood that it would have to move from the current location within the next 5 to 10 years.

The team spent about two days at the firm, conducted interviews with key management personnel and some employees, and spent some time with the local police and fire department. The team also reviewed the building's external lighting and door security at night and in the morning and interviewed the night cleaners before they left. It also reviewed all businesses in the immediate area.

Taking all this information into account, the team asked upper-level management, including the director of security, the following initial questions:

1. We notice that most of your client payroll and tax records are transmitted to you electronically. What would happen if you lost electric power and your computer system shut down? If your building caught fire or was hit by a plane, do you have another location to go to? Are your electronic records stored in a backup site?
2. Do you have a computer-use policy? Several of the employees were seen working video games during the visit. There are no provisions in the employee handbook governing the use of computers. How are these computers monitored?
3. What background checks are performed on prospective employees?
4. You say that you are thinking about CCTV in the parking lots. How many incidents have occurred? Who would monitor the cameras?
5. You have more than 150 computers tied to your mainframe. Who is responsible for computer and network security? What monitoring functions are performed related to outside attacks? What monitoring for insider attacks is conducted on individual employees?
6. Do you realize that you are in a designated floodplain and that this area is prone to flooding every fifteen years?
7. It appears that people can enter your building at will. Have you considered a reception area at the front door? Do you have an employee/visitor entrance protocol?

The owner was, at first, concerned with external security rather than the overall picture. The review team, however, was engaged in *risk assessment*—"the process of assessing security-related risks from internal and external threats to an entity, its assets, or personnel" (ASIS International, 2003). A typical enterprise security risk assessment encompasses the following process:

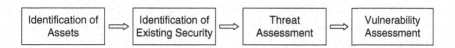

A risk assessment can be conducted by a third-party vendor like the security consulting firm in the scenario described above, or internally by the entity itself. Regardless of the method used, the following concerns are addressed in a typical risk assessment:

- **What are the company's assets?** The first step in risk assessment is the identification of the entity's assets. *Assets* can be defined as people, equipment, property, business information, and professional or business reputation. For Canal City Paychecks, people include employees, visitors, vendors, and clients. The equipment and property include buildings, computers, and all communications and support equipment. For this enterprise, client and employee information and software applications are the core of its business operation. What would happen if client information is destroyed, tampered with, or given to a third party for fraudulent use? To be most effective, management and employees throughout the enterprise must participate in the process of identifying assets and in placing a value on the assets. Diverse functional units within the company may identify assets not identified by others and may have a different impression of an asset's value.
- **What policies or procedures are in place to secure or protect those assets?** In order to assess risk, it is important to understand what security policies already exist and how assets currently are protected. What policies currently are in effect? How are they enforced? Who

has ownership of the responsibility to enforce the policies? What types of security measures (e.g., perimeter fencing, access controls, CCTV, surveillance cameras inside the facility, and alarm systems) are currently employed? How many security personnel are employed? Are they employed full or part time? What equipment do they have at their disposal, for example, flashlights, batons, cell phones, pagers, and night vision goggles, to enhance their ability to provide security?

- **How are these assets vulnerable?** In other words, how can assets be accessed, altered, destroyed, or damaged? Vulnerabilities range, for example, from the catastrophic destruction of the main production building by a tornado to the hacking of a database on a computer network containing the personal financial information of clients to the midnight reading by a janitor of a research design proposal left open on an employee's desk. A *vulnerability* thus is distinguishable from a threat; vulnerabilities encompass "weaknesses or gaps in a security program that can be exploited by threats to gain unauthorized access to an asset" (Vellani, 2007). Vulnerabilities generally fall into three categories: physical, technical, and operational. Physical vulnerabilities include, for example, a broken CCTV camera lens, a malfunctioning alarm, and access doors without locks. Technical vulnerabilities include, for example, weak password access control and out-of-date antivirus protection software. Operational vulnerabilities encompass matters such as the lack of a computer-use policy, lack of training for security personnel, and inadequate internal controls that enable the booking of fictitious sales, and thus, fraudulent financial reporting.

- **What are the threats to the assets?** A *threat* is a "[n]atural or man-made occurrence, individual, entity, or action that has or indicates the potential to harm life, information, operations, the environment, and/or property" (DHS NIPP, 2009: 33). During a risk assessment, managers and employees are asked to identify the threats that may occur and result in damage or loss. Threats may exist from an external source or they may be internal. An employee's abuse of the computer network by unwittingly downloading software that corrupts the network and destroys data is an example of an internal threat. The occurrence of a flood or other natural disaster is an example of an external threat.

- **What is the probability that a threat will occur?** The critical element in risk assessment is the determination or assessment of the probability that the threat will occur. The probability, for example, that a flood will occur is much different for the business plant located at the top of a mountain than for the plant at the base. The likelihood of a flood is much lower for the business located in Blythe, California, than for the business situated on the frontage of the James River in Richmond, Virginia. Probability can be based on empirical data (e.g., the frequency of flooding of the James River) or, in some instances, must be based on hunches. Probability analysis typically includes local and national data and comparisons with similar institutions; national and international crime and emergency event trends and industry trends are also used. Frequently, the assessment leaders create threat scenarios and ask employees their assessment of the likelihood of an occurrence and what would happen in best- and worst-case scenarios.

PHASE II: PRIORITIZATION OF ASSETS AND RISKS

Risk may be defined using the formula:

$$Risk = Threat + Vulnerability$$

Once assets and risks to the enterprise have been identified and assessed, they must be prioritized. As stated earlier, not all risks can be eliminated. Further, some risks may be too costly to address and mitigate. Likewise, the value of certain assets may be so minimal that mitigation of them makes little sense financially despite a high level of risk.

- **What assets are the most valuable? What do we need to protect "at all costs?"** There are certain assets so critical to the mission of the company that they must be protected "at all costs," that is, regardless of the vulnerability and threat level to those assets. For example, the CEO of a large financial institution will likely have a security detail that serves as a bodyguard while on travel from headquarters. A file clerk will not have that same level of protection. The formula for a new pharmaceutical product that has been developed by the research and development group will be protected "at all cost" if that product, when available on the market, will significantly affect the company's revenue and reputation. In the case of Canal City Paychecks, the most valued assets could be client payroll information and software technologies critical to performance of the business plan.
- **What is our liability if such events occur?** This is the nightmare of questions that includes both legal and fiscal liability. If an event occurs and we fail to provide a service, could our clients file a criminal or civil action in a state or federal court? How will such an event affect our insurance rates? For example, what is the liability of Canal City Paychecks if an employee, in violation of company policy, takes the personal information of a client's employees and sells that information to identity fraudsters who subsequently use the information to obtain credit cards and purchase goods totaling $90,000 with the counterfeit cards? Assuming that the monetary loss is $90,000 or more, is there greater loss by the damage to the company's business reputation when the employee's acts are publicized in the national media?
- **What do we do to get back to business or restore services if an event occurs?** Very often risk management leaves out this part of the equation. Although this point will be discussed in the chapter on emergency management, business and service scenarios should include replacement costs, downtime, borrowing cash on a temporary basis, and having backup sites in which to resume business. Assume, for example, that a major ice storm causes a power outage that lasts six days and the Canal City Paychecks lacked access to an emergency generator. How does the company get back to business in time to process the payroll of its clients in a timely manner?
- **What is the effect on our business and leadership reputation?** This goes back to asking the basic core questions: What do we do, how do we do it, and what happens if we do not perform? In some cases, the answer is clear: Customers or clients simply walk and the business folds! In other situations, management responsible for failing to plan for the event is asked to resign. We know of many public sector officials who were replaced because they did not have a clue on how to respond to the rash of anthrax threats that occurred after September 11. Figure 4–1 is a risk assessment matrix of selected threats to assets of Canal City Paychecks.

During this phase, a value must be placed on assets and probabilities or possibilities assigned to threats and vulnerabilities. It is a rare occurrence that the value of an asset to the organization will be equal to the quantification of the risk. On the assumption that the value level of an asset can be equated to the value of a vulnerability and the probability of a threat occurring, a matrix can be developed that portrays the basis for analyzing and prioritizing assets and risk, as shown in Figure 4-2.

Using the risk matrix model (Figure 4-2), the information asset has a high asset value and the asset has a high vulnerability. If the possibility of threat occurrence was very high, the risk

Asset	Priority	Type of Risk	Vulnerability	Recovery Requirement	Action Plan
Building	Essential	Burglary—old locks	Vulnerable	Immediate	Install biometric control
Building	Nonessential	near airport—data theft	Vulnerable	Immediate	Install biometric control
Parking lot	Nonessential	Personnel safety	Vulnerable	Delayed	Improved lighting
Personnel	Essential	Access to client data	Vulnerable	Immediate	Training
Information	Critical	Theft of client data	Vulnerable	Immediate	Database access controls
Equipment	Critical	Computer network intrusion	Vulnerable	Immediate	Install hardware and software firewalls

FIGURE 4-1   Paychecks Risk Assessment Matrix

(9) A–HIGH T–HIGH V–HIGH	(8) A–HIGH T–HIGH V–MEDIUM	(8) A–HIGH T–MEDIUM V–HIGH	(8) A–MEDIUM T–HIGH V–HIGH	(7) A–HIGH T–MEDIUM V–MEDIUM	(7) A–MEDIUM T–MEDIUM V–HIGH
(7) A–MEDIUM A–HIGH V–MEDIUM	(7) A–HIGH T–HIGH V–LOW	(7) A–HIGH T–LOW V–HIGH	(7) A–LOW T–HIGH V–HIGH	(6) A–MEDIUM T–MEDIUM V–MEDIUM	(6) A–HIGH T–MEDIUM V–LOW
(6) A–HIGH T–LOW V–MEDIUM	(6) A–MEDIUM T–HIGH V–LOW	(6) A–MEDIUM T–LOW V–HIGH	(6) A–LOW T–MEDIUM V–HIGH	(6) A–LOW T–HIGH V–MEDIUM	(5) A–HIGH T–LOW V–LOW
(5) A–LOW T–HIGH V–LOW	(5) A–LOW T–LOW V–HIGH	(5) A–MEDIUM T–MEDIUM V–LOW	(5) A–MEDIUM T–LOW V–MEDIUM	(5) A–LOW T–MEDIUM V–MEDIUM	(4) A–MEDIUM T–LOW V–LOW
(4) A–LOW T–MEDIUM V–LOW		(4) A–LOW T–LOW V–MEDIUM			(3) A–LOW T–LOW V–LOW

FIGURE 4–2   Risk Matrix Model

Legend: A—Asset Value   HIGH—3

  T—Threat Probability   MEDIUM—2

  V—Vulnerability   LOW—1

level for that information would be at its highest–9. On the other hand, if Canal City's parking lot has a low asset value, and though vulnerable (let's say medium level of vulnerability), the probability of a threat is very lot, the risk level for the parking lot would be 4. Once the risk level is determined, the company can proceed to devise a plan to mitigate the risk.

PHASE III: RISK MITIGATION

Once assets have been identified and prioritized and the same has been accomplished for risks (threats and vulnerabilities), the entity must determine how each risk can be reduced or eliminated through the implementation of countermeasures, the cost of implementing the countermeasures, and the relative benefit to the entity (e.g., the value of protecting a critical asset) by implementing a particular countermeasure. Upon deciding whether to implement particular countermeasures, the entity must then implement them. This process is known as risk mitigation, and may be illustrated as follows:

Identification of Countermeasures

Countermeasures are defined by Vellani (2007) as "measures that include policies and procedures, physical security equipment and protection systems, and security personnel" and that are designed to mitigate risk. DHS NIPP (2009) refers to countermeasures as "risk management actions" and defines those actions as "measures designed to prevent, deter, and mitigate the threat; reduce vulnerability to an attack or other disaster; minimize consequences; and enable timely, efficient response and restoration in a post-event situation." In essence, a countermeasure is any type of action that may be used to deter, prevent, or mitigate the occurrence of a threat or vulnerability.

During the risk mitigation phase, security personnel must identify a variety of potential countermeasures that could be used for each risk presented to company assets, perform a cost-benefit analysis with respect to each of the alternatives, and determine how each countermeasure will be implemented.

Cost-Benefit Analysis

When several alternative countermeasures have been identified, the process of selection begins. Typically, whether countermeasures will be selected or not depends on a cost-benefit analysis. Costs for each alternative countermeasure should be identified for personnel, implementing the operational change, buying a piece of equipment, training personnel, and, in some cases, doing nothing! This discussion also must take into account the mission and values of the organization and the culture of the institution. For example, right now, requiring all employees and students to wear identification cards on the outside of their clothing would not work at the majority of colleges and universities in the United States. However, this is standard practice at most government agencies and corporate headquarters.

Risk managers often assign qualitative values in terms of a ratio. Take, for example, Canal City Paychecks. The external reviewers recommended hiring a computer security specialist which, based on regional salaries, would cost $125,000 plus about $45,000 in fringe benefits. This total cost of $170,000 was matched to a figure of $1.5 million that it would cost to restore the company's computer system if an external attack were to occur. This cost included restoration time, replacement of parts, insurance payments, and a number of other costs. For every dollar spent on this new security position, the company would save approximately $9 in recovery costs.

Often decision making in a risk assessment exercise cannot be measured in dollars and cents. After the series of school shootings that occurred between 1996 and 2000, many school districts initiated safety programs, hired additional security staff, and deployed metal detectors at access points. In turn, many police departments began armed intruder response training exercises. Although the national rate of school violence has declined and statistics show that schools are very safe places in comparison with adjoining neighborhoods, parents and teachers demanded these safety procedures no matter the cost or the likelihood that violence would occur. In the pharmaceutical industry, the formula for an innovative product may be so valuable to the company's viability that security measures to protect against unauthorized access may be implemented regardless of cost. In such case, the benefit derived from protecting the proprietary nature of the formula has nearly an unlimited value. Thus, cost is not a concern.

Developing Countermeasures

Having selected the countermeasure, it must be developed (e.g., a security policy) or implemented (e.g., acquiring and installing a surveillance camera and metal detector). If a decision is made to acquire surveillance technology as a countermeasure to the threat of loss of sensitive information, ASIS International (2007: 19) suggest several action items:

- Regularly inspect telecommunications equipment, cables, and terminals for technical surveillance compromises using equipment, methodologies, and personnel capable of detecting current threats.
- Offices and meeting rooms should be regularly inspected for technical surveillance vulnerabilities on a random basis and also immediately prior to any sensitive or proprietary discussions.
- Use credible and trusted service providers for technical countermeasures support. Be sure to perform a thorough screening process before engaging a particular vendor.
- Perform periodic scans for unauthorized wireless network devices, regardless of whether a wireless network is installed.

Thus viewed, the implementation of a countermeasure involves much more than its initial installation, and costs of ongoing maintenance and monitoring must be factored into the cost-benefit analysis.

PHASE IV: THE OPERATIONS PHASE OF RISK MANAGEMENT

The final phase of enterprise security risk management is the implementation and operationalization of the risk management plan. Someone must take ownership of the ESRM plan. Davidson (2009) reports that one company, Diebold, Inc., placed the responsibility for the risk assessment in the hands of three vice presidents of functional areas. Once the initial review was completed, groups were formed to review the "subset" of risks. The company's board of directors created a Governance Risk and Compliance Oversight Board to perform general supervision of risk management and compliance on a global basis.

In other companies or public agencies the functional vice presidents themselves may assume responsibility for management of the plan. Such functional vice presidents often have titles such as Chief Risk Officer (CRO), Chief Security Officer (CSO), and/or Chief Information Security Officer (CISO). In many respects, risk management from the perspective of the C-suite signifies the importance of risk throughout the enterprise and demonstrates a buy-in at the highest level of the company. Often management of various portions of the enterprise security risk plan is delegated to subgroups within the organization. Although one might assume that because security risks are the focus, management of the plan must be assigned to the *security* department. That usually is not the case. Security personnel are always engaged in the operation of the plan, but input and collaboration is often sought from other operational units, such as internal audit, human resources, legal, sales, and production. Furthermore, a company or agency may have more than one security function—for example, a department that focuses on physical security and a separate department that focuses on computer or information security. In an enterprise-wide security risk management process, all security operations and other critical or related functional areas will be engaged in the process of operating the plan.

Summary

Whether or not required by law or regulation, the implementation of an enterprise security risk management plan is essential to the viability of any organization. The typical plan encompasses four phases: risk assessment, risk analysis and prioritization, risk mitigation, and risk management.

The effective implementation of ESRM is led by top management with the engagement of functional areas throughout the enterprise related to security of the organization and protection of its assets.

Review Questions/Activities

1. Conduct a general risk assessment of your residence or apartment. What are the assets in your apartment? What potential external threats are present? What kind of locks and alarms do you have on your doors and windows? What internal vulnerabilities are there? Do you smoke? Do you have insurance that would cover a fire that wipes out all of your belongings? Is your residence a basement apartment susceptible to flooding?

2. Select a major corporation that operates on a global scale. Identify the major assets of that company, its potential vulnerabilities, and its external threats.

Suggest countermeasures that could be utilized to protect the assets from loss or damage resulting from the vulnerabilities and threats.

3. Select a public agency in the United States. After research designed to glean as much information essential to ESRM, do the nature of assets, vulnerabilities, and threats differ from those you found in the case of the global corporation in the previous activity? Are the ESRM issues and processes different for the public agency? For example, would a public agency apply a cost-benefit analysis in a different manner?

Web Searches

1. Access the publication of the U.S. General Accounting Office pertaining to information on security risk assessment that is available at http://www.gao.gov/special.pubs/ai99139.pdf. After reviewing the document, prepare a brief paper describing the process and methodology of conducting a risk assessment.

2. Access http://library.ahima.org/xpedio/groups/public/documents/ahima/pub_bok1_021089.html and review the risk-analysis guidelines presented at

this site. After reviewing the guidelines, determine whether the process for conducting a risk assessment is any different for governmental or private health care facilities.

3. Using your favorite Internet search engine, locate three enterprise risk assessment policies, plans, or guidelines. Compare and contrast the differences in these plans with respect to the identification of the four-phase process described in this chapter.

References

ASIS International. 2003. *General Security Risk Assessment Guideline.* Arlington, VA: ASIS International.

ASIS International. 2007. *Information Asset Protection Guideline.* Arlington, VA: ASIS International.

Davidson, Mary. July 2009. "Managing Risk across the Enterprise." *Security Management,* Vol. 53, No. 7.

Dennis, Brady. 2009. "Bernanke Blasts AIG for 'Irresponsible Bets' That Led to Bailouts." *Washington Post,* March 4, 2009, p. D01.

Federal Emergency Management Agency [FEMA]. Website, last accessed on December 15, 2009 at www.fema.gov/government/mitigation.shtm#1

Johnson, Michael P., and Spivey, Jeff M. January 2008. "ERM and the Security Professional." *Risk Management,* Vol. 52, No. 1.

Vellani, Karim. 2007. *Strategic Security Management: A Risk Assessment Guide for Decision Makers.* Burlington, MA: Butterworth-Heinemann.

United States Department of Homeland Security. 2009. *National Infrastructure Protection Plan.* Available at: www.dhs.gov/xlibrary/assets/NIPP_Plan.pdf [DHS NIPP]

5

■ ■ ■

Securing Assets—Humans and Property

KEY TERMS

access control,   central monitoring,   contract vs. proprietary,   crime prevention through environmental design,   health care facility,   internal access control,   layering, perimeter,   workplace violence.

Most recently we were involved in the construction of a new building that would house our academic department. Included in the construction was a 125-person-capacity auditorium, classrooms with the latest educational technology, two computer classrooms, faculty offices, a student lounge, a seminar conference room, and two project laboratories. The laboratories would be used for research with area and private sector security as well as provide room for evidence lockers. The question that naturally came up was, what will be the security program for this facility?

Some advocated for a fortress area but realized that college academic buildings have to be somewhat open for academic, administrative, and social activities. What was needed was a secure area that would meet federal and state security requirements for cyber security and identity protection management research. The secure area would be accessible only to those personnel undertaking projects.

The security plan called for the area to be accessible by card and biometric thumb reader and monitored by a series of CCTV cameras scanning the secure area. A security plan was developed which would also need to tie into the campus fire alarm systems. Computers had to be integrated with the campus server but the laboratory computers needed to be secured. In the event of an emergency, the doors would have to be released to allow occupants to escape. A security officer would have to be appointed who would be responsible for authentication of identities and issuance of credentials. The access system would have to be tied into the main campus alarm system.

This project forced planners to address a number of operational questions, which in turn, led to other questions. These form the focus of this chapter. An organization's assets are varied, and the threats are endless. Workplace violence, employee safety, terrorism, natural and man-made disasters, burglary, and employee theft are just a few of the issues that security service policy makers have to deal with. Often individuals and organizations install security devices and programs for the sake of appearance. For the example given at the beginning, an intrusion alarm in many homes does nothing for the perimeter of the property and pool areas. Thus, the issues that always remain for planners are target protection and the amount the person concerned is willing to pay for personnel and equipment.

PERIMETER SECURITY

Starting with walled fortifications, humans have used the concept of perimeter security for safety. Until the development of artillery powered by gunpowder, the idea of the walled city or a castle with well-stocked garrisons and an endless water supply provided the ideal response for safety from outlaws and invading armies. Inside the perimeter were secure areas for the ruler's family quarters and the court treasury as well as food, livestock, and other valuable items. This concept continued with the development of industrialized societies. In all areas of commerce and personal life, money, jewelry, and other valuables were protected by secured doors, safes, and, sometimes, armed guards. Eventually, owners of factories and workplaces installed security measures to protect production facilities and warehouses. The arrival of the Information Age, which is presented in Chapter 6, clearly shows that information is now an important target that requires measures other than locks and alarms.

The concept for the fortified business or home has stayed with us as exemplified by plant security, physical and electronic fencing, gated communities, and so on. The goals are to keep certain people from entering, allowing access for certain people depending on time and date, and monitoring the whereabouts of employees and making life miserable for anyone who tries to enter a building or area without authorization. These goals are summarized by Simonsen (1998: 244), who speaks about the five D's of perimeter security: deter, detect, delay, deny, and destroy.

If it were a simple task, most businesses would be able to fortify their perimeters and keep out wrongdoers. The reality is that most organizations, except prisons and nuclear plant facilities, need public access to make money or provide services. Thus, a balance must be struck between access, control, and customer service.

The number of programs and equipment used for perimeter security are endless as demonstrated by former Communist states that used every device to keep their citizens from leaving the country and outsiders from entering. Cutting down trees; building wall and guard towers; installing fences, lights, electronic listening devices, and concertina wire (thin cut barbed wire); and utilizing motor patrols, checkpoints, and "shoot to kill zones" along a perimeter route are just a few of the procedures formerly used in eastern Europe and currently between the border of North Korea and South Korea. Since 9/11, debate continues on how to secure borders in the United States using some of these measures and electronic screening. For example, for seaport security, gamma ray equipment is being used to examine or x-ray the contents of ship containers for humans, contraband, and nuclear material for weapons. The images that emerge are then matched with the container manifest. If something does not match, customs officers open and examine the container.

Perimeter Access Control

Most organizations begin a perimeter security program with some form of controlled access to their premises (i.e., facility, building, or area) starting with main entranceways and back entrances and fire escapes. The extent to which measures are employed depends on the type of assets to be secured, the need for public access, the risks or threats that the organization faces, and the institution's willingness to create and implement access control procedures. For our discussion, access to premises can be classified according to the following categories used for threat assessment (U.S. Department of Homeland Security, 2005):

- **Restricted.** Access is available only to employees with security clearances through one control point. Premises are patrolled by security service personnel who are armed and have orders to shoot to kill intruders or persons trying to escape. The facility, building, or area is fenced, alarmed, and monitored by CCTV. There is designated parking within 300 feet or more from the area or building. Aircraft are prohibited from flying or landing anywhere near the premises.
- **Controlled.** Premises are fenced and alarmed and are patrolled by security around the clock. Premises are open to visitors who have been cleared by security personnel for specific business purposes and must be escorted while they are in the building, facility, or area. There are controlled entrances and designated parking areas. Employees have various levels of security clearances depending on their rank, title, and job description.
- **Limited.** Security patrols conduct general monitoring during business hours, and visitors are logged in at designated entrances. Employees and visitors might be required to wear identification tags at all times. There are designated parking areas and controlled access entrance for visitors. Premises are locked, alarmed, and patrolled during nonbusiness hours.
- **Moderate.** There is open access during business hours, but the premises are generally locked and patrolled during nonbusiness hours. Entry areas are unprotected.
- **Unlimited.** Access is open at all times. Entry areas are not protected.

Security planners often refer to the concept of *layering,* which means placing security devices and impediments between something of value and an offender. The most common example is the bank vault full of money and values. Between the vault and the external environment are doors, guards, electronic access control points, and eventually, access to the vault itself. Layering is a useful concept for protecting assets in a defined area, but it becomes difficult to practice it for mobile assets, and in areas that require open customer access and information technology.

External access for restricted, controlled, and limited premises may require the use of locks and keys, card access/detection, and "hands-on" or electronic searches of carry-in and carryout items. Electronic alarms, CCTVs, thermal imaging devices, and motion detector devices can be used in remote and nonbusiness areas. From a management perspective, there is a need to implement central monitoring of all areas. As Vinsik (2009) discusses, an integrated security program includes a number of security issues such as screening of employees, identification and authentication, security for IT operations, and a number of other functions.

A key element is not simply installing equipment but creating and enforcing access control procedures and rules. What this means is that the organization defines the rules for entry and internal operations in order to provide for a secure and safe environment and holds everyone to the same standard. At the same time, the organization has to weigh the issue of undue hardship on its customers and visitors. This happens all the time at airports, rock concerts, hospitals, and just about every major organization. In one day while visiting student interns at three sites, the authors were required to sign in at all locations, receive visitor passes, and, in two cases, go through electronic screening for weapons and be escorted at all times. All three organizations had signs that stated that visitors would be searched and screened—in another words, visitors were put on notice! The main concern at two locations was people bringing weapons and bombs into public facilities. The concern at the third location—a psychiatric center for correctional services—was self-evident in terms of keeping the inmates in and stopping contraband from coming into the facility. In many locations, certain governmental organizations such as the

Transportation Security Administration (TSA) and Customs and Border Protection (CBP) have a monopoly of services with national security practices. Airports and border checkpoints are good examples. If you do not like being searched, do not go near the control points. On the other hand, a shopping center has to be totally user-friendly or customers will not come.

TO GUARD OR NOT TO GUARD

A sudden rise in robberies in the Midwest several years ago prompted many banks to redeploy the familiar armed guard in the front lobby as a means of deterrence. Most burglars and robbers do not want the additional task of confronting a person who is armed with a gun as they are trying to steal money. Based on conservative calculations that appear in Chapter 10, it takes about 5.5 people to staff one post twenty-four hours a day, seven days a week, 365 days of the year. In addition to the costs for salary, there are issues regarding uniforms, equipment, and benefits. In high traffic areas, uniformed security service personnel are very useful in conveying an immediate public message that security is present and they can answer questions and give directions. How many guards are needed depends on the number of fixed access points or the anticipated number of calls for service. Calls for service is used as an indicator of the number of personnel needed.

Whether or not the officer is a member of the organization or a contract service provider is also discussed in the next section.

A major issue involving the use of security personnel is whether personnel should be armed. Returning to our discussion of security service agencies in Chapter 3, Level III and Level IV agency personnel must be armed because they have governmental powers, and there is an expectation that they may have to use physical and deadly physical force to protect themselves and others while enforcing these statutes. For Levels I and II, the answer is based on the type of target or area that is being protected, the potential for deadly force or possession of weapons by employees and visitors, and whether arming will deter unlawful activity. Thus, the following questions must be addressed:

1. What level of emergency response does the organization require? Let's take the call of shots fired, person down. Is a quick response required, or can outside agencies respond quickly?
2. Do security service personnel have law enforcement powers? If there is an expectation that members will be making arrests, protecting large sums of money, and stopping vehicles, they should be armed.
3. What do we have that criminals want? To protect money and precious valuables (e.g., jewels, art, and artifacts) and high-risk areas, arming personnel is necessary to deter and repel attacks. If the facility is a nuclear plant, strategic dam, or electric plant, perimeter guards should be armed. If the facility or area simply requires Level I personnel, they may not be required to be armed.

CONTRACT VS. PROPRIETARY AGENCIES

Determining whether to use contract agencies or proprietary (in-house) personnel for security services remains an issue for planners. This debate often occurs in Level I organizations that need security personnel for perimeter or limited internal protection. This issue has been debated since the creation of security service organizations in the nineteenth century and continues to the present. Citing a comprehensive 1971 Rand Report review on this issue, Green (1981) suggested that contract agencies are dollar-for-dollar less expensive in terms of direct and administrative costs. The vendor, in essence, assumes the management function and is required to conduct personnel selection and provide equipment and training. There is also increased flexibility in terms of removing personnel who are not performing satisfactorily. The client is thus charged a fee per officer or technician times the number of hours or days required. The contract vendor pays the officers approximately two-thirds the hourly or daily rate and keeps the rest for profit. Other benefits from contract agencies include mere flexibility in staffing, which enables the organization to change its staffing needs by contract with a provider without resorting to layoffs or emergency hiring. As discussed in Chapter 10, agency or union hiring and termination rules are other issues. Firing a unionized security service officer is indeed more complex and difficult than firing a nonunionized officer because formal procedures require due process regarding formal notice and hearing.

While national and regional contract guard agencies are available to provide these services, municipal and county police departments often provide security services on a contract basis that includes a formal arrangement with the police department or police union or an informal arrangement with an officer (Reiss, 1988). There are many variations of these arrangements around the country. What is often not clear is who is responsible when an officer must take action and use official powers. What happens if an officer is injured during an off-duty security detail? Is the officer, the department, or the security client responsible for lost wages and medical bills? Other issues are the number of hours of overtime personnel may work and in what types of venues. Most departments do not want their sworn personnel working security at bars and strip clubs or providing executive protection to unsavory characters. Thus, departments that use the formal contract model issue work permits and define compensation rates as well as liability issues related to the use of force, false arrest, and medical matters.

The main issue with contract agencies comes down to this axiom: You get what you pay for! As is most often the case, most contract personnel are paid minimum wages with no benefits. That is why costs are so low. Hiring and training standards are kept to the minimum state requirement. If there are no state standards, there are few or no hiring requirements and training! Turnover—the number of employees who leave the agency within a year—is generally very high because contract personnel look for other opportunities with benefits. Our experience has shown that contract agencies cut expenses to make their profit line. A recent audit conducted by one state comptroller's office found that contract agencies supplying services to public facilities, including nuclear power plants, were not able to maintain staffing levels and did not provide requisite training. They also failed to conduct personnel background investigations.

The main issues that arise with contract personnel have to do with quality. Security service personnel who are hired and trained by the organization, in theory, will give it greater services attention and loyalty. Personnel get to know the organization, its members, and its mission. Ideally, there is less turnover for proprietary personnel, who are better paid and have benefits and a career ladder. We use the term *in theory* because the issues of quality are often dictated by regional economic realities. In areas that have expensive housing and living costs (e.g., Boston, Metro New York, New Jersey, Washington, D.C., Los Angeles, San Francisco, and San Jose) turnover for security service personnel may be high with both contract and proprietary security services because their salaries and benefits are not high enough to afford housing and other costs.

Using our model for services in Chapter 3, the following are questions that have to be answered on whether to use a contract service or develop a proprietary system.

What do you want the security staff to do? If a list of tasks goes beyond simple deterrence or staffing a post to providing information to visitors and keeping people out of certain areas, in-house staff should be considered. This means that there is a need for higher hiring standards and special training and that negative consequences could occur if a person fails to perform assigned tasks.

Will the force be using governmental powers? Except for special event situations using outside police, it is important for an organization to have its own security personnel whom it selects and trains, and who should be well versed in organizational goals and mission and have detailed background information about employees, clients, and visitors as needed.

Will the force be armed? It is important for the agency to have its own personnel who are selected and trained. Personnel who are working in high-density areas, such as college campuses, hospitals, and public buildings should be highly trained and know when to use force, including deadly physical force.

INTERNAL ACCESS CONTROLS

Internal access control is the total of procedures and practices by which employees, clients, and the general public are allowed access to all areas of a building or facility. Some organizations have high-security areas that could include vaults, computer banks, experimental research areas, executive suites, records areas, and operations centers. Employee rank or title in the organization can define who goes where at a given date and time. As a side note, we really emphasize background checks for security service employees because they have access to the entire "kingdom." As discussed in Chapter 4, locks and keys followed by card access are the most common security applications used. Newer facilities use magnetic or proximity readers to monitor and control employee movements. High-risk areas may have CCTV monitors and a guard to control access.

Centralized vs. Decentralized Monitoring

Access to high security areas and internal movements in them should have centralized monitoring by CCTV and computers in a central communications center. For example, a biological research facility with high security needs would monitor a researcher's movements from entering the building until leaving through the use of a card proximity reader. The researcher's movements in and out of the various laboratories and research areas are controlled and monitored. If the researcher attempts to use a card to enter a denied area, the CCTV will identify and make her a computer entry; and security personnel or management may inquire as to her intentions. Not all facilities wish to have this much monitoring, in which case traditional locks and keys or stand-alone card access locks might provide access to nonsecure areas and employee offices.

A note of caution on centralized monitoring: While hardware designers can make bells and whistles to alert patrols if there is a security breach, it may be impossible for one person to monitor CCTV units, alarm systems, patrol units, and answer the phone at the same time. A detailed job analysis with traffic and volume considerations has to be completed in order to provide proper staffing. Unfortunately, the increase of CCTV systems has created an illusion that someone is monitoring the screens all the time and can send patrol personnel to respond to suspicious persons or incidents. What CCTV actually does is to provide tapes for playback of events over a period of time and to focus on a certain area if there is high crime activity. Figure 5-1 portrays the typical computer and monitoring equipment utilized for CCTV monitoring of a medium-size corporate facility.

How Much Does This Cost?

We wish that we could give precise quotes for all of the equipment illustrated but that would be impossible. Equipment costs are based on type of unit, wiring, location, number of junction boxes, and general weather conditions (especially for outside alarms and cameras). In one security

FIGURE 5-1 Using an updated CCTV system, a security officer monitors multiple screens for a hotel..
Source: Alvis Upitis/Getty Images.

contract, the director of public safety at a leading engineering school estimated that it would cost about $4,000 per doorway to install alarms and monitoring devices in laboratories. Unless a security service unit provides an extensive research and planning unit, it is important to obtain the services of an equipment consultant to address application and equipment costs. The following are some basic factors that should be considered in hiring both a consultant and eventually an equipment vendor:

- **Vendor track record.** Determine what work the company has performed in the last several years. This means reviewing proposals from several sources as opposed to "friends" who are in the business. Federal and state organizations have detailed purchasing procedures, which require public notice and competitive bidding. The same process applies to consultants.
- **Client satisfaction with the vendor.** This requires making both phone calls and visits to facilities to review the vendor's work.
- **History of the consultant and company.** As with other technological firms, mergers, acquisitions, and bankruptcies are part of the security technology industry. Thus, a firm with a long-established national record gets higher marks than a new operation. Administrators must be wary of the consultant who seems to recommend only one company for equipment and supplies. This may indicate a "sweetheart" relationship.
- **Service and maintenance.** As with anything else, it is important to have a service or maintenance contract on the installed equipment.

RULES AND REGULATIONS AND ACTUAL PRACTICE

As with perimeter access, rules and regulations define employee movement and behavior. The main internal threats to an organization by employees are misconduct and mistakes. Employee misconduct encompasses a wide range of behaviors, from violations of rules and regulations to outright criminal behavior.

The often-heard notion is that security practice starts at the top. Thus, executives and policy makers have to abide by the same rules and procedures as do middle managers, line employees, and support staff. If a new employee has to go through various checkpoints or use a proximity card for access or wear an identification card at all times, all members of the organization must do the same thing. The case studies that discuss security breakdowns in an organization can be tied to personal shortcomings or lax daily practice in security procedures.

In some cases, certain behaviors on the job become part of the culture as illustrated in Frank McCourt's book *Tis*. Recalling his work on the New York docks after World War II, McCourt wrote that it was okay to take things from the ships as long as you could carry it home! In one major company, security audits found that most equipment were leaving the premises between 9 A.M. and 5 P.M. and from areas that had excellent perimeter security. Some of the issues are not so clear-cut and become part of everyday practice.

Consider the following cases:

Joe, a repair technician, routinely takes home tools from the company shop and uses them for his weekend business in fixing computers and audiovisual equipment. He has permission from the supervisor with the warning not to lose anything.

Janice, an executive secretary, uses the company's computer system to book vacations for a selected clientele. When confronted with this, she defended her actions by saying that she did it during her lunch period.

Walter, a security supervisor, is allowed to take the company car home. He routinely transports his daughter to and from the college she attends three hours from home.

Running football pools and sports programs as well as conducting various forms of personal business often becomes part of the unwritten rules of the workplace. In some cases, employees often mimic the behavior of supervisors and management.

An audit of internal security controls begins with a candid discussion of work rules and practices and what is acceptable and not. What often happens in the preceding scenarios is that the employees are disciplined or fired for an activity that everyone apparently is doing. Following this discussion is a review of external and internal security strengths and weaknesses by random checks or having consultants test an organization's security system. For example, airport security agents are tested by auditors who try to enter with fake but very authentic-looking handguns and other contraband.

SECURITY PLANNING/CRIME PREVENTION THROUGH ENVIRONMENTAL DESIGN

In the late 1970s two important developments in security occurred. First, there was a sudden movement to install locks and alarms and window protection gates without due concern for employee and customer access and aesthetic appearance. Many applications involved retrofitting, which is very costly. As contractors drilled and installed wire and cable, all kinds of impediments and walls were discovered that were not on the blueprints. As this took place, urban planners and architects were beginning to consider security issues with building design and placement as well as exterior issues such as lighting, trees and shrubbery, and playground areas. This started a movement called *crime prevention through environmental design* (CPTED) that captured the attention of many planners who were trying to reduce crime on urban streets and in housing projects. The leaders of this movement, Oscar Newman, Jane Jacobs, and others, saw that security could be provided not only by locks, alarms, and guards but also by designing and planning the access control points. The term *defensive space* came into common security planning usage (National Advisory Committee, 1976). The second development affected the concept of crime prevention, which, in essence, was based on the philosophy that individuals needed to be responsible for their own property and be willing to notify and assist law enforcement and security. This was the genesis for such programs as Neighborhood Watch, McGruff the Crime Dog, and Operation Identification.

CPTED ideally starts before buildings or areas are built. It involves a group of architects, contractors, purchasing officers, and security service planners. The group then maps the terrain and visualizes motor and foot traffic in an effort to minimize the number of access points and "pull" people toward those designated points with paths, walkways, signs, and natural barriers. It then assesses whether risks are present and to what extent will "target hardening" occur. Will there be a need for weapons screening? To what extent will CCTV be used for monitoring internal and perimeter points? Planners also work with a variety of stakeholders who include executives, employee groups, and event service clients. CPTED emphasizes both security procedures and enforcement of rules and regulations. This is very apparent for applications in school security. Planners review not only building and space configurations but also visitor conduct codes and ways to assess possible threats from visitors or employees (Poulin and Nemeth, 2005). In programs and audits on "safer schools by design," planners also engage students in identifying and resolving school safety issues.

Crime prevention programs continue to be presented in various ways. Many communities still use Operation Identification and Neighborhood Watch under the auspices of community policing. Operation Identification assists crime prevention officers to detect serial numbers etched on items of value, such as bikes and computer equipment, for easy identification and recovery if they are stolen. A group of residents in a Neighborhood Watch basically watches the area and one another and notifies the police of suspicious persons and drug trafficking or other illegal activity.

There are a number of new, innovative programs. Personal safety information and crime alerts can be "flashed" over computer networks by e-mail. As evidenced by the WebSearches at the end of chapters, many agencies have established home pages to present news and security information. One of the main complaints about such home pages is that they are often not updated in a timely manner. A more traditional yet effective program is simple personal safety training, in which security service personnel present topics to employees and residents. At the authors' campus, a recent seminar on workplace violence attracted many employees.

Lighting

One of CPTED concerns is lighting. It is perhaps the most inexpensive resource used in security operations at night. The key to lighting is creating enough lumens for security service personnel to observe people and activities and deter someone from committing an offense.

Lighting equipment is classified as incandescent, gaseous discharge, or quartz. Incandescent lighting is commonly used in homes and businesses and provides instant illumination when activated. Mercury vapor and sodium vapor are examples of gaseous discharge lighting; they are used in streets, parking lots, bridges, and athletic arenas. They are more cost-efficient and produce less heat than incandescent lamps. Their shortcoming is that it takes time for them to relight after a power shutdown. A quartz lamp produces very bright light and can be used for high-risk areas. The type and numbers of lighting units are based on their intended use. Common streetlight patterns are spread either in symmetrical or asymmetrical patterns, depending on the range of the area to be lighted. Special perimeter applications might use floodlights or searchlights to focus on a specific area and produce visual glare to make the intruder uncomfortable.

SECURITY SERVICE OF SPECIAL POPULATIONS AND SITUATIONS

This section discusses some of the unique variables that security service administrators must address for what we call special populations and situations. The first two—workplace violence and fire safety—are situational threats that are common to all organizations. Special attention is then given to colleges and universities and medical health facilities, laboratories, airports, and shopping malls/retail facilities.

Workplace Violence

The term *workplace violence* became popular with a rash of killings of supervisors by employees in postal facilities in the mid-1980s. Through extensive media coverage, the term became associated with employees suddenly going berserk and killing supervisors and/or fellow employees, and finally themselves. While there is no exact definition, operationally it encompasses a wide range of violent and nonviolent crimes occurring in and out of the workplace including murder, robbery, assault, sexual assault, stalking, harassment, and larceny. The term defies an exact definition because it is so broad. Thomas Ryan (2003) underscores the problems with definition and data collection: "If you take it to the nth degree, George Custer was the victim of workplace violence."

The National Victims Crime Survey asked respondents whether they had been victimized either at work or while going to and from the workplace. Responses indicated that there were 1.7 million violent work victimizations between 1993 and 1999, consisting of 1.3 million simple assaults, 325,000 aggravated assaults (involving a weapon or serious physical injury), 36,500 rapes and sexual assault, 70,000 robberies, and 900 homicides. According to the data, workplace violence accounted for 18 percent of all violent crimes during this period (Bureau of Justice Statistics, 2004). Most workers who are killed in accidents and robberies work in high-risk occupations (e.g., police officer, corrections officer, private security worker, taxi driver, and bartender). In another survey reported by the U.S. Department of Labor (2006), nearly 5 percent of the 7.1 million private and public organizations reported an incident of workplace violence within a twelve-month period prior to completing the survey. Approximately half of the reported incidents occurred in state and local government work sites. This can be attributed to workplaces in high crime areas or dealing with unstable or violent persons. In the private sector, establishments that produced goods reported a higher percentage of co-worker workplace violence. For service sector establishments, workplace violence tended to be done by criminals and customers and persons involved in a domestic violence dispute.

The report noted that workplace violence had a negative impact on the workforce in terms of workers compensation and insurance costs, days off for injuries, and property damages. Of the establishments reporting incidents of workplace violence, almost 9 percent did not have a workplace violence prevention program or policy.

Rather than strictly focus on data and definitions, Ryan (2003) suggests two courses of action. For high-risk occupations, employers have to take steps to reduce crimes against their employees, especially those who work alone with easy access to cash, such as taxi drivers and convenience store clerks. These steps include using frequent patrols, CCTV monitoring, protective screening, personal panic alarms, and removing signs and ads from windows so that patrols and passersby can see inside in addition to prohibiting employees from working alone. Other risk factors to consider are the degree of public access to the workplace and degree of security needed. These efforts include electronic access to worker areas and the deployment of security guards. Another practice is reviewing security history or trends for the specific workplace or region. Typical prevention measures might include extra security personnel during periods of time when there is a high volume of cash.

The other classification involves potentially violent situations that fall outside of the normal workplace or service delivery mode. Police officers, prison workers, and employees in psychiatric hospitals are trained to deal with workplace violence. Students at a college do not expect to be taken hostage during Sociology 101, which meets Monday, Wednesday, and Friday at 9:30 A.M. According to the authors' experience, the leading types of workplace violence are domestic disputes (e.g., a spouse or ex comes into a workplace setting to settle things), employee disputes by those who have been terminated or disciplined, and situations in which the person has failed in pursuit of a goal, such as a promotion and terminal degree. Hess and Wrobleski (1996: 627) discuss the causes of workplace violence, which they find is fueled by increased access to firearms and "toxic workplace conditions" of the Information Age that include complex work rules, raiding pension funds, lack of job security, and lack of procedures for resolving disputes between an organization and its client population.

There are no fool-proof methods to deal with workplace violence. In addition to regular security practices and policies, many organizations have begun to establish threat assessment committees to increase communication between managers, security service providers, and human resource professionals when an employee or a client starts to act out or makes a threat. The variables that these teams consider include the behavior or act itself, the likely causes for it, and the potential that a threat might occur. If there is some basis to the threat, specific courses of action can be recommended such as a warning, counseling, increased security measures, termination from the workplace, or criminal action.

Many states have enacted law requiring employers to create workplace violence policies and conduct employee training on workplace violence related to work-specific information and what to do in the event of an emergency. This information includes evaluating risks related to the work site. As discussed in Chapter 4, risk evaluation includes a review of past incidents, employee surveys of actual or potential workplace violence incidents, and security surveys. Those tasks that are related to "high risk" include:

Exchange of money

Delivery of passengers, goods, or services

Mobile workplace assignments or assignment in high crime settings

Working with unstable or volatile persons in health care, social service, or criminal justice settings

Working alone or late at night.

A workplace violence policy or training program would include information regarding the above and how employees can report incidents or, if dealing with co-workers, how to deal with situations.

On the other side of spectrum, certain states, such as Ohio and Florida, passed laws that allow employees to carry concealed weapons in the workplace. The Ohio statute allows weapons except in day care centers, government buildings, airports, and bars. In Ohio, employers, however, have the option of posting notices that weapons are banned on their premises. In Florida, weapons can be brought to work but, in most cases, they must be kept in locked vehicles unless there is a federal or state law prohibiting firearms for security reasons. To view trends of this nature, please review www.workviolence.news.

Fire Safety

An often overlooked issue in protecting organizational assets is fire prevention. The events of 9/11 at the World Trade Center in New York demonstrated how fragile modern buildings can become when airplanes collide with them. The cause of most fire-related injuries and fatalities is toxic smoke generated by carpets, furniture, and other building materials made of synthetic substances. In contrast, a defective sprinkler system that is accidentally or maliciously activated can cause millions of dollars of damage. The National Fire Protection Association (2009) reports that in 2008 there were 1,451,500 fires that were responded to by public fire departments. Approximately 40 percent of these fires took place in structures mostly in residential properties. There were 3,320 civilian fire deaths; about 83 percent occurred in homes.

Fire alarm systems and response plans must be an integral part of an organization's security program. Most fire alarm systems consist of smoke and heat detectors that emit a signal when activated. Ideally, the detector is connected to an alarm panel, which in turn is tied into a fire station or a central monitoring station. Some alarm systems are stand-alone panels unique to one building that require review by first responders to obtain the location of the signal because smoke and flame might not be visible. Newer systems can use CCTV which also sounds an alert if there is a sudden appearance of heat and flames. Another important element is a fire suppression or sprinkler system. In basic operations, a sprinkler system is a series of waterheads connected to a waterline. The sprinkler is activated if there is a sudden surge of heat or smoke.

Calling the fire department is another issue. Many small communities are served by volunteer agencies. Many communities have difficulty in fire department staffing during the day because many volunteers commute to work at a distance from their residences and there has been a decline in voluntarism for hazardous tasks. Thus, response time may vary, depending on the time and day. Because of this reality, many organizations have agreements with volunteer departments to have security service personnel visually confirm a fire before the station dispatches equipment.

According to the Governors Task Force (2000), the overall plan for fire safety must address the following:

1. Building construction must be in compliance with the state fire code. State fire codes detail regulations for construction and for the installation of alarms and sprinklers and exit signs.
2. Organizations must have either a program of state-mandated inspections or a self-inspection system to identify code violations and/or maintenance problems. These inspection programs must include a minimum number of fire drills per year.
3. All organizations must have rules that address fire safety–related issues pertaining to their line of business. This includes having special rules and regulations for high-risk materials

on premises, such as oxygen portals in hospitals. For example, most colleges prohibit the use of candles, space heaters, and certain kinds of appliances in residence hall rooms. Persons who set off alarms maliciously may be prosecuted criminally or face dismissal from the institution.

4. Buildings must be equipped with the proper type of fire extinguishers.
5. Fire safety should be part of annual training and orientation for employees, especially as to evacuation routes and plans for assisting disabled staff and patients.

As part of a proactive fire safety program, many agencies have initiated tabletop and actual drills using fire equipment to address fire safety issues particular to the building type and location. Exercises of this nature provide security and fire planners a knowledge of building layouts. Discussing a drill in a high-rise building in Dallas, Texas, Phelps (2009) reports that responders were not able to immediately locate stairwells to bring equipments to the sixth floor. This was an important issue that had to be corrected for future responses.

Summary

This chapter reviewed the basic concepts related to perimeter security and the challenges that many organizations face in protecting their employees, customers, and visitors. As discussed, internal organizational policies and appropriate technology are an important part of the security planning process.

Review Questions/Activities

1. Review either a national or regional incident of workplace violence. What were the causes of the incident? What was the response from security services personnel? Were there telltale signs before the incident?
2. Contact the state or regional fire coordinators office and review fire statistics for the past two years. Have deaths due to fire incidents increased or decreased?
3. Review the perimeter security on your campus and rate five major buildings according to the perimeter access control classifications presented in this chapter. To what extent does CPTED occur either within the immediate areas or in these facilities?
4. Interview a security services manager and ask the following questions. What are the advantages and disadvantages of contract versus proprietary security officers? Under what circumstances should security services personnel be armed?

WebSearches

1. Access Security Management at www.securityman-agement.com. Review a recent article for 2010 that deal with physical security. Prepare a brief review of the article and how it applies to this important topic.
2. Using your favorite search engine, type "work-place violence professional associations" and review the many titles and sources on this topic as they relate to specific occupations. Under the direction of your instructor, select one occupation and review how it perceives and responds to this issue.
3. Access the National Fire Prevention Association at www.NFPA.Org and review recent articles or features from their journal or Web site. What are the concerns expressed by the authors on fire safety?

References

Bureauof Justice Statistics. 2004. "Crime Characteristics." Posted at http://www.ojp.usdoj.gov/bjs/cvict. Accessed January 7, 2004.

Governors Task Force. 2000. *Report of the New York State Governors' Task Force on Campus Fire Safety.* Albany, N.Y.: Executive Chamber.

Green, Gion. 1981. *Introduction to Security,* 3rd ed. Boston: Butterworths.

Hess, Karen, and Harry Wrobleski. 1996. *Introduction to Private Security.* Minneapolis/St. Paul: West.

National Advisory Committee on Criminal Justice Standards and Goals. 1976. *Private Security: Report of the Task Force on Private Security.* Washington, D.C.: US Department of Justice.

National Fire Protection Association. 2009. "Fire Loss in the U.S. 2008." Posted at http://www.nfpa.org/assets/files/PDF/OS.fireloss.pdf. Accessed December 1, 2009.

Phelps, E. Floyd. (October 2009). *Exercising Is Good For Everyone.* Security Management. Posted at http://www.securitymanagement.com/article/exercising-good-everyone-006222

Poulin, K.C., and Charles Nemeth. 2005. *Private Security and Public Safety.* Upper Saddle River, N.J.: Pearson Prentice-Hall.

Reiss, Albert J. 1988. *Private Employment of Public Police.* Washington, D.C.: National Institute of Justice.

Ryan, Thomas. 2003. "Workplace Violence." Lecture at State University of New York Command School, Albany, New York, January 6.

Simonsen, Clifford E. 1998. *Private Security in America.* Upper Saddle River, N.J.: Prentice-Hall.

United States Department of Homeland Security, 2005. *Campus Preparedness and Assessment.* Washington, DC: United States Department of Homeland Security, Ofice of State and County Government Coordination and Preparedness.

United States Department of Labor—News, Bureau of Labor Statistics, October 27, 2006. *Survey of Workplace Violence Prevention, 2005.* Washington, DC: Bureau of Labor Statistics

Vinsik, Steve. 2009. "The Search for an Integrated Security Environment." *GSN: Government Security News.* July 2009, Vol. 7, No. 8, pp. 1, 15

6

■ ■ ■

Securing Critical Assets— Information and Intellectual Property

KEY TERMS

accuracy, authenticity, availability, biometrics, confidentiality, countermeasure, encryption, firewall, intellectual property, local area network, logic bomb, megabyte, personal digital assistant, server, social engineering, spyware, steganography, trade secret, Trojan horse, USB, virtual private network, virus, wide area network, worm.

IT'S THE INFORMATION AGE

Two decades before the current millennium, the world entered what has been described as the Information Age (Toffler, 1987). The growth has been amazing. By 1992, revenue from U.S. sales of personal computers was higher than the revenue from sales of supercomputers, mainframe computers, midrange computers, and workstations combined. More than 132 million personal computers were sold worldwide during 2002 (Plunkett Research, 2003).

During the 1990s, the Internet became the preferred information marketplace in the United States. By December 2000, 164 million Americans accessed Web sites (Nielson, 2000). During June 2003, 177.5 million (almost 60 percent) of Americans had access to the Internet and 122.4 million were active Internet users at home (Nielson, 2003). More than 9 billion searches were performed utilizing Internet search engines in April 2010 (Nielson, 2010). *E-commerce* and *e-business* have become household terms; the annual amount of e-commerce in the United States grew to $45 billion in 2002 (Ecommercetimes, 2003), and it was projected that e-business, called *B2B*, would surpass $721 billion in 2003 (eMarketer.com, 2003). Today students share information through instant messaging and social networking sites. Between January 2009 and January 2010, U.S. visitors to Facebook increased by 96.5 percent (a total exceeding 57 million) and U.S. visitors to Twitter increased by 800 percent (ClickZ, 2010). It is projected that by 2014, nearly two-thirds of all Internet users, or 164.9 million Americans, will be regular users of social networking (eMarketer.com, 2010). This thirst for information has enabled peer-to-peer information-sharing technologies such as MP3, the technology that many people currently use for downloading and sharing audio and video files, and a significant leap in the number of devices that facilitate such technologies.

In addition to the Internet, business organizations and government agencies, including law enforcement agencies, have established local area networks (LANs) for communication within a limited physical area. Local police officers patrol in cars equipped with laptop computers that have wireless access to criminal record databases. Multinational businesses deploy wide area networks (WANs) for internal communication between domestic and foreign units. Employees telecommute from home utilizing virtual private networks and "camp out" at airports between flights accessing corporate networks with wireless connections. The next iteration, at least in the corporate world, likely will be cloud computing, which involves the delivery of data and software applications from a third-party vendor located off-site that shares its resources through Web-application and Web services. An example would be data and applications provided on request from Google.

During this millennium, developments in technology will advance network connectivity and provide access to multiple Internets whenever and wherever desired. Mega- and gigabytes of data will be stored on devices as small as watches and rings. A *megabyte* is approximately 1 million bytes. One letter or number takes less than three bytes. This chapter has just over 100,000 bytes, and this is one of 14 chapters. So the entire textbook is more than 1 megabyte in length. Retailers now sell USB drives that are less than the size of an adult thumb that have a capacity to store 16 gigabytes of data, or 16,000 copies of this textbook.

Digital information can be distributed via computer workstations, personal desktops, laptops, wireless PDAs, and smartphones. Previously, we described the PDA in some detail. The focus now, however, is on a variety of smart phones—I-phone, Blackberry, Droid, Palm Pre, to name a few, that provide wireless access to the Internet, e-mail, text messaging, and company networks. Who knows what devices and technology will be available ten years from now?

The importance and value of information and information technologies to government agencies and private sector businesses were highlighted in the days and months following the terrorist attacks on September 11, 2001. Banks and other financial institutions in lower Manhattan near the World Trade Center were unable to process electronic fund transfers because network servers were inoperable and all redundant servers were located in the area impacted by the attacks. Government officials realized that several federal agencies had relevant information that foreigners in the United States on expired visas were attending flight school to learn how to fly commercial jets but were not interested in learning how to perform takeoffs and landings. These agencies had information but did not utilize it.

Since 9/11, the formation of the Department of Homeland Security was the result of the recognized need to gather, share, and filter information into useful knowledge; develop technologies that will protect information systems and infrastructures, and enable sharing and analysis of information in databases that historically have not talked with each other. These needs remain the focus of legislation, regulation, and boardroom discussions.

It is important to remember, however, that digital or electronic data are not the only forms of information. People retain information in their heads, and the more experience an employee has, the more information he can apply to the benefit of the employer. This information asset is commonly known as *intellectual capital*. Although much information today is communicated, transmitted, or stored in digital form, business organizations and government agencies continue to generate information on paper or have documents of various types stored in filing cabinets. Information also is stored in audio and video nondigital formats. Because information is a valuable asset to an organization or agency, the security of information assets is integral to the development of risk-management strategies and the development and implementation of enterprise-wide security policies.

INFORMATION SECURITY

Information security is the process of ensuring the *availability, accuracy, authenticity,* and *confidentiality* of information. Another term used to describe the same process is *information assurance.*

Availability means that information must be obtainable by members of an organization who need to use it when and where they need it, for transacting business and providing services. Otherwise, information has little value to an organization. For example, an organization engaged in e-commerce or e-business will not survive if its Web site cannot be accessed by customers or strategic partners or if the specific information that the customer needs cannot be located easily.

Accuracy involves two concepts: First, information quality does not improve over time, and, thus, information in its original form must be free from errors or mistakes, and second, information must have integrity (i.e., there must be some assurance that it has not been corrupted, degraded, or modified in some unauthorized manner) (Pitkin, 2000).

Authenticity means that the information is what it purports to be (i.e., in the form as indicated by the creator or sender) and that the creator or sender is who he or she purports to be. One of the classic online securities fraud cases occurred when the fraudster "spoofed" (made a counterfeit copy of) the bloomberg.com Web site and posted inaccurate stock information on the counterfeit site. When the market for that stock increased, the fraudster sold at the higher price, netting considerable gains from the unsuspecting and trusting investor.

Lastly, *confidentiality* means that information must be available only to those individuals who are authorized to possess, view, or transmit it. If a competitor can access trade secrets, a company will quickly lose its competitive advantage and the value of that information to it.

Numerous proactive measures can be employed to ensure the availability, accuracy, authenticity, and confidentiality of information. From a risk-management standpoint, the most important measure is the establishment of an effective information security policy that can be employed throughout the organization.

INFORMATION SECURITY POLICIES AND PROCEDURES

The first step in the process of information security is to establish, implement, and maintain a comprehensive information security policy for the organization. Establishment of an information security policy involves a four-step process: (1) identification and valuation of information assets, (2) identification and assessment of threats to the enterprise and to information assets, (3) identification and assessment of vulnerabilities, and (4) a determination of countermeasures that have been and should be deployed, including a cost-benefit analysis of the feasibility of implementing the countermeasures.

Information and Its Value

Information is a major asset, if not *the* major asset, in public and private sector organizations. Information assets can be categorized in many ways. Customer lists, accounts receivable statements and records, payroll documents, tax documents, legal documents, criminal records, intelligence records, investigation files, and employee manuals are information assets common to any business or security service organization. Those assets may be written on paper, recorded on audiotape or videotape, or stored digitally.

Information also exists in other forms. People are an important information asset. An engineer developing the design for a new product retains information concerning that design in his mind. The chemist who was part of the expert team that developed the formula for Viagra retains information concerning the formula and the scientific process, both of which are of value to the employer and competitors. Employees who have worked for a business or government agency for several years possess information assets that typically have greater value than those of newly hired employees. Organizations frequently outsource essential services, including security, and the selection of the contract supplier of those services should be based on the experience and skill (intellectual capital) that the contractor can provide. The employees of that contractor have access to information owned by the organization that hired it. All forms of an organization's information must be protected or secured.

The initial step in formulating an organization-wide information security policy is the identification of all information assets and prioritization of those assets in terms of their value to the organization. All employees should be engaged in the process of identification. Once all information assets have been identified, department heads or an employee team assigned to the task should place a value on each of the assets in terms of the organization's mission and business plan.

Many organizations, public and private sector, possess information assets unique to their business or governmental responsibility: trade secrets, such as the formula for a wrinkle-reducing facial lotion, classified military or intelligence documents, and wiretap evidence to be used in an organized crime investigation. Because of its unique nature and its critical relationship to the organization's business plan or strategic mission, such information has special value to the organization. For example, the formula for Viagra is critical to pharmaceutical manufacturer Pfizer's business plan. Similarly, foreign intelligence obtained by the U.S. government through the use of Echelon satellite technology is critical to preventing terrorist attacks.

Intellectual property is a specialized type of information. Although definitions vary, *intellectual property* includes trade secrets, copyrighted material (e.g., books, television productions, movies, and musical performance), patented products (inventions), and trademarks (logos on merchandise). Recently, federal law has defined the term *trade secret* broadly to include business and technical information that the owner has taken reasonable precautions to keep secret. Thus, the source code for software, a specialized customer list, or a unique process for data mining would qualify as trade secrets. In the public sector, this type of information is referred to as *classified,* or *proprietary, information.* From a management perspective, securing this type of information requires more than locking it up; the information must be used, which means that access to it must be controlled. We discuss measures designed to protect information later in this chapter when we consider countermeasures.

THREATS TO INFORMATION

There are two general categories of threats to information, physical and technological, and each of those categories includes subcategories, as indicated in the following chart:

Physical Threats	Technological Threats
Human error	Human error
Malicious/criminal acts	Malicious/criminal acts
Natural disasters	System failures

Physical Threats to Information

Technology has had a dual impact on physical threats: Because of the preoccupation with technology, it is easy to forget that physical threats to information remain and that information continues to exist in physical as well as digital forms.

HUMAN ERROR   The principal threats to information caused by human error are inadvertent disclosure and destruction of information. Employees routinely leave important documents on their desks when they leave work. The information on those documents is easily accessible by the custodial staff or—worse—a contracted custodial service employee. Given the rate of economic espionage, undercover janitorial employees working for a competitor business or government can steal proprietary information and copy or photograph the documents while employees are away from workstations or after hours.

Other inadvertent disclosures can result when file cabinets are not locked, when trade secret documents are left in the copier, when documents remain active on the computer screen or are forwarded to an incorrect address, and when PDAs are absentmindedly left at a hotel after a business trip. Employees also destroy information by tossing documents in the trash, inadvertently deleting files, and even deleting portions of a document. A formula can be altered significantly merely by altering a couple of characters or numbers.

MALICIOUS ACTS   Information is susceptible to a variety of malicious acts from a variety of sources. Intellectual property is the favorite target of business competitors, foreign governments, and ordinary thieves who plan to sell trade secrets to those competitors or foreign governments. For the past several years, the theft of intellectual property has been the type of security attack that has resulted in the greatest financial loss to U.S. businesses and public agencies (Computer Security Institute 2009). The survey respondents in the CSI study (2009) report losses in the tens of millions USD from the theft of intellectual property. Payroll documents contain personal employee information (e.g., social security numbers, mother's maiden name, and date of birth). That information is targeted by identity thieves who intend to sell the identification information to others or who plan to use it to commit other crimes—for example, to apply for a credit card in the employee's name.

Because identity fraud is used in combination with a number of other criminal acts, it has become the number one economic crime. The Federal Trade Commission received more than 80,000 reports of identity theft in 2001 (National Center for the Victims of Crime, 2003). Business transaction records also are a target of information thieves, especially records of online transactions maintained in a database.

Nearly all purchases on the Internet are conducted by use of a credit card. Merchants typically maintain digital or paper records of credit card transaction information such as the cardholder's name, account number, and expiration date. Furthermore, merchants employ third-party marketing and customer relation firms to identify consumer trends and regional disparities in purchasing practices. Frequently, transactional information, including credit card data, is shared with those third-party businesses, and such information is accessible on the network databases of those companies. Thieves do not need the actual card to conduct purchases on the World Wide Web—just the cardholder's name and the account number and expiration date. Other necessary information can be obtained elsewhere, if needed.

Another major threat is the theft of laptops. A typical business traveler stores gigabytes of the company's digital information on her or his laptop. A thief can acquire a treasure trove of information simply by stealing the laptop. Typical locations of thefts are airports and hotel rooms in foreign countries. Laptop thefts were the third most frequent type of attack reported during 2008 (CSI, 2009).

Theft can, and often does, occur from the inside. As noted in statistical surveys discussed previously, more than half of computer and noncomputer crimes are committed by insiders. Employees steal intellectual property and sell it to the highest bidder. Employees in the payroll department may purloin personal identification information to sell to outsiders, and employees who process business transactions use and misuse information for the purpose of stealing from the company. Historically, employees have been considered the major source of economic crimes (Ferraro, 2000: 139).

Theft is not the only malicious act posing a physical threat to the loss or destruction of information. Acts of sabotage perpetrated by political or hate groups (depending on the nature of business) or acts conducted during labor disputes present significant physical threats to the security of information.

It also is important to remember that in this day and age, an organization's information is not restricted to its physical plant. Employees telecommute, retaining information on desktop computers or laptops in their homes. Employees travel, taking information in their laptops, PDAs, smartphones, compact disks, and other portable storage devices. The same physical threats that apply to the organization's work environment also exist, although perhaps in different degrees, to the telecommuter's home or the traveling employee's hotel room.

NATURAL DISASTERS   Documents in paper or on tape or disk form can suffer the same damage from natural disasters as the buildings and equipment where the documents are housed. Natural disasters such as fires, tornadoes, and floods threaten the accuracy and availability of information in hard copy as well as digital form. Lightning strikes that cause power surges can endanger information stored on hard drives.

Technological Threats to Information

Technology is a double-edged sword: It has elevated the importance of information as an asset, and it has enabled significant threats to the security of information. Technology has enabled organizations to store information more economically and to share it with employees, business partners, and customers with ease and speed. More businesses engage in e-commerce or e-business each month, and government agencies are actively engaged in e-government transactions.

HUMAN ERROR   Digital information is prone to a variety of threats resulting from human error. Employees can enter incorrect information, cause unintended keystroke entries (e.g., by laying a book on the keyboard), inadvertently delete a document, shut down the computer without saving the document active on the screen, e-mail a sensitive document to the wrong address, and forget to shut down the computer when leaving work for the day. This list of human failures is endless.

MALICIOUS ACTS   Malicious technology-related acts can be further subdivided into three categories: misuse or abuse of networks by employees, malicious attacks on an organization's network, and acts directed toward an organization's Web site.

Numerous surveys conducted each year seek to identify the types of attacks sustained by public and private sector organizations and attempt to identify trends. Although the results of those surveys may not accurately reflect technology threats to a specific organization, they do provide a starting point in the threat assessment process.

Perhaps the most widely recognized and referenced survey is the CSI Computer Crime and Security Survey. Each year the Computer Security Institute (CSI) conducts a computer crime and security survey. Respondents include public and private sector organizations and, within each sector, organizations of different size, and within the private sector, different industry types, including nonprofit organizations such as colleges and universities.

The 2008 CSI survey reveals startling statistical results. Although nearly all of the survey respondents use antivirus software (97 percent), firewalls (94 percent), anti-spyware software (80 percent), and intrusion detection systems (69 percent), as well as other security technologies, 46 percent of the respondents acknowledged unauthorized use of their computer systems within the past year, 44 percent reported employee abuse of network access, and 29 percent reported unauthorized access to the network by employees. Virus attacks were experienced by 50 percent of respondents, denial of service attacks by 21 percent, and system penetrations by 13 percent. Theft of proprietary information continues to be a leading type of financial loss resulting from attacks to computer or network systems, with the average loss amounting to approximately $250,000 over the past year by those who responded to the survey.

HARDWARE AND SYSTEM FAILURES Computer hardware and software can misfunction at any time. In large organizations where computers are connected to a network, a malfunction of one computer is unlikely to threaten the network. When information has been saved on network servers, the crash of a hard drive or failure of a motherboard probably would harm information only on the computer that is not saved to the network. In these instances in which the majority of data is saved on the employee's personal computer or laptop, however, the hardware failure can be a major threat to information residing in that computer.

The much bigger threat is hardware or application software failure. Network servers store database files with gigabytes of information that are critical to business operations. *Servers* are computers that store much larger quantities of data than do desktop or personal computers. The failure of a server can result from hardware malfunction or from software interoperability issues. Large businesses operate networks with a multitude of application programs. Some programs may be commercial but from a variety of producers (Microsoft, Sun, Adobe, Corel, etc.), and other programs may be unique to the organization and developed by programmers at the organization. As vulnerabilities to existing programs are disclosed, the producers of the program issue security patches, which are revisions or additions to the existing code designed to plug a security hole in the software. Occasionally, the revision or patch prevents the software from working with other programs designed by the company or other software producers. The network failure results when the organization implements the patch without testing its compatibility with existing programs.

Misuse or Abuse of Networks

Employees misuse or abuse organizational networks in four major ways: (1) violating privileges by accessing information without authority, (2) downloading and/or distributing pornography, including child pornography, (3) accessing information for the purpose of engaging in economic espionage, and (4) intentionally destroying data.

Most organizations have acceptable use policies controlling their networks and the Internet and whether employees can use the organization's Internet access for personal e-mail or instant messaging or to surf the Internet for personal reasons, for example, shopping. Many organizations further restrict employee access to certain areas of the network; for example, the database containing payroll information. Obviously, there is no reason for every employee to have access to the organization's payroll information of all employees. Employees routinely misuse or abuse those privileges. For example, in one case, an employee who was upset that a co-worker had terminated their relationship accessed the co-worker's e-mail account and sent messages from it. The most frequent misuse of network privileges is employee downloads and/or distribution of pornography.

For organizations whose trade secrets are a valuable commodity, the threat that thieves will engage an insider in espionage is very real. Many recent cases of espionage that involve technology either as the subject of the theft or the medium of the theft are conspiracies that include an inside employee as one of the co-conspirators. Remember that double-edged sword description of technology? The need to employ an insider is fostered by technology. If employees do not have authorized access to the area of the network where digital copies of trade secrets are stored, they are nevertheless in a better position to gain access to it than an outsider performing some sort of a brute force attack.

Once an employee gains access to the trade secret, technology enables its transmission beyond the organization's safety net. The employee can encrypt (code) the file containing the secret data or hide the file in an image-utilizing steganography. *Encryption* is the application of cryptography to code a message in a cipher code (i.e., scrambling the data). The scrambled message is then forwarded to the co-conspirator, who has the key to decrypt the message. *Steganography* programs enable an employee to hide a file inside an image without distorting the appearance of the image (e.g., a picture of the employee's children) to the naked eye. The employee then e-mails the picture to the co-conspirator with a message that reads, "Hey, take a look at this recent picture of the kids." The co-conspirator has the password that allows access to the hidden file. Worse yet, the employee could encrypt the file hidden by steganography. The threat is real: Encryption and steganography programs are available as free downloads from the Internet.

The threat that employees will destroy data by misuse or abuse of the network also exists. Employees typically are instructed not to bring software programs or games from home to use on their networked computers. Such programs can contain viruses or other forms of malware, or bad software, which can corrupt the employee's computer as well as the organization's network. The impact of the virus could damage a file, destroy all files on a database, and even bring the network to its knees.

Malicious Attacks on Networks

According to the 2008 CSI study, 47 percent of the survey respondents had experienced at least one security incident or system attack during the previous year. Most of the survey respondents believed that independent hackers and disgruntled employees were the source of the attacks. A smaller percentage of respondents identified business competitors, foreign corporations, and foreign governments as likely sources of those attacks.

Attackers commit network intrusions and system penetrations as part of a scheme to commit a variety of cyber crimes, including credit card fraud, identity fraud, and economic espionage. Others attack systems to acquire information that can later be used to extort money from the system's owner. The attack on the database of CD Universe and the theft of thousands of credit card account numbers is a perfect example. The hacker, identified as Maxim, attempted to extort money from CD Universe by threatening to release the account numbers if CD Universe failed to pay him $100,000. When CD Universe refused to pay, Maxim posted the numbers on a Web site. Fortunately, the site quickly was located and taken offline.

Other offenders simply seek the theft or destruction of data or systems as their objective. Some of these attackers employ a malicious code; others engage in social engineering to gain access to the network or system. *Social engineering* is the use of "influence and persuasion to deceive people by convincing them that the social engineer is someone he is not, or by manipulation. As a result, the social engineer is able to take advantage of people to obtain information with or without the use of technology" (Mitnick and Simon, 2002). A typical method is a phone call to an employee from an individual who identifies herself as the security consultant employed by the company to repair holes in the company's network. The imposter says that she has identified the employee's computer as part of the problem and needs to repair the network authorization (i.e., the user ID and password for the computer). The "helpful" employee then provides the "consultant" with his user ID and password, thereby enabling the hacker to gain access to the network.

The most frequent types of attacks are by viruses and worms. A *virus* is a string of malicious software (hence, "malware") that attaches to a program or file. Once the host computer has been infected and the program activated, the virus spreads throughout the network. Legendary examples of viruses are the Melissa virus and the I Love You virus. A *worm* is a type of virus that replicates itself when it infects the host. By replicating quickly, the worm can consume the entire storage capacity of the computer or network and render them catatonic. The Blaster and Welchia worms infected numerous computer network systems during the summer of 2003, shutting down the Maryland Department of Motor Vehicles network and paralyzing the networks of numerous colleges and universities.

Other attack devices are the Trojan horse and logic bomb. A *Trojan horse* is a form of malware that, once installed in the host, enables its owner to take control of the host. An owner who can gain control of a network of many computers can then use that host network as the launching pad for a distributed denial of service attack, which typically is a simultaneous attack by hundreds or thousands of computers on a Web site.

The *logic bomb* is the favorite device of disgruntled employees. An employee suspects that he is about to be terminated from employment. Angry and bitter, he installs malicious code written much like a virus but with an added feature. The code is designed to execute on the happening of an event; for example, the removal of the employee's user ID from the network, on a specific date (e.g., Friday the thirteenth), or on a specific instruction.

Attacks on Web Sites

The two major threats to organizations that utilize the Internet for e-commerce, e-business, e-government, or simply Web presence are (1) the interruption of business and (2) the loss of reputation. The specific threat to business interruption is a distributed denial of service (DDoS) attack on the organization's online servers. The most damaging attack occurred in February 2000 when a fifteen-year-old from Montreal, Canada, known as Mafiaboy, attacked major Web sites such as ebay.com, CNN.com, amazon.com, Yahoo!, Excite, and E-Trade. A detailed account of this DDoS attack is presented in Richard Power's book, *Tangled Web: Tales of Digital Crime from the Shadows of Cyberspace* (2000).

The specific threat to the loss of reputation is the defacement of a Web site. Although defacements do not cause direct damage to the site, they signal that the site is not secure. Attackers frequently deface Web sites to send a political message. Recently, *The New York Times* Web site was subjected to a defacement, as were fbi.gov, whitehouse.gov, and dhs.gov sites.

VULNERABILITY ASSESSMENT

Vulnerabilities are conditions or weaknesses in security that could be exploited by a threat. Because threats can be physical or technological in nature, there are physical and technological vulnerabilities. The absence of motion sensors, a guard watch, or other security measures during evening hours leaves the organization's facility vulnerable to unauthorized physical access and its information vulnerable to theft. The lack of access controls and policies for regular security maintenance of software renders digital information, including intellectual property, vulnerable to unauthorized access internally by a conspiratorial employee and externally by a malicious hacker.

It is essential to identify and assess vulnerabilities on a routine basis. Unfortunately, many vulnerabilities are never identified until they have been exploited. For example, most security gaps in software programs are unknown until exploited by a virus or worm. Once exposed, countermeasures in the form of security patches are developed to eliminate or mitigate the vulnerability.

The identification of vulnerabilities is an organization-wide process. The initial step is to identify all known vulnerabilities. All departments in the organization should be engaged in that process; individuals within each department typically are familiar with known weaknesses. Moreover, engaging employees in a team approach to identifying vulnerabilities is an excellent way to heighten employee awareness of these vulnerabilities.

The second step is to assess the importance of the vulnerability. It simply is not possible to mitigate every vulnerability. For example, if a particular threat is virtually nonexistent, the vulnerability to that threat should not be assessed as critical. Also, even though a threat may be likely, it may not make economic sense to eliminate the vulnerability to it if the threat is not likely to cause the loss of money or reputation.

COUNTERMEASURES

Countermeasures are policies and activities that address identified vulnerabilities in an effort to prevent or mitigate threats. Countermeasures can consist of physical tasks and objects or policies and procedures. Some countermeasures can be implemented with minimal cost; others can consume major chunks of a budget. Certain countermeasures must be employed regardless of cost.

Although the identification and selection of countermeasures are unique to each organization because such measures are designed to address its specific and vulnerabilities, the following are widely accepted countermeasures common to most organizations:

- Enterprise-wide information security policy that includes
  - Access controls for physical access to the facility and areas within the facility, as well as computer access to information
  - Acceptable use of policies regarding computers, networks, Internet, e-mail, instant messaging, etc.
  - Protection of information while employees are away from work stations—for example, the use of locked file cabinets and clean desk policies
  - System to monitor network traffic and use
  - Incident response plan
  - Business interruption plan
  - Disaster recovery plan
  - Designation of security staff responsible for maintenance and enforcement of policy
  - Effective disciplinary standards and procedures for violations of policy
- Employee awareness and training programs
- Confidentiality and noncompete agreements that employees must sign
- Process for the referral of security incidents to law enforcement

- Physical security
- Network and computer security hardware and software, including
  - Firewalls
  - Antivirus software
  - Intrusion detection systems
  - Encryption
  - Redundant servers and systems
- Biometrics to authenticate access privileges
  - Photo ID cards
  - Finger or handprint scans
  - Voice identification devices
  - Facial recognition

USE OF COST-BENEFIT ANALYSIS TO RANK INFORMATION SECURITY NEEDS

The final stage in the development of an enterprise-wide information security policy is establishing the priority of security needs and countermeasures. An organization can identify any number of countermeasures. Most organizations, however, do not have a limitless supply of cash to employ all of them. Likewise, most organizations do not have the desire or *organizational will* to do so. At this point, management must perform a cost-benefit analysis and make a critical decision. Does the organization spend a specific amount on a new and aggressive marketing plan designed to increase revenue or a portion of that amount on a security plan that is designed to save costs? Critical to that decision is management analysis of which countermeasures must be employed at any cost and which should be employed because the benefits of security outweigh the cost.

The benefits of security are measured by the value that an information asset represents to the organization because it is not subject to destruction or loss. This value is difficult to calculate and, for the management team of most organizations, is not an easy concept to understand. Benefits are calculated by assessing the value of the particular information asset, how much of that value is exposed to risk, and the extent of risk to which the asset is exposed (Whitman and Mattord, 2003). By way of illustration, consider a large pharmaceutical company that has developed a miracle drug to cure cancer and has received regulatory approval to sell the drug. Because there is no existing competition in the market, the formula for that drug is the company's primary asset; that is, the asset that differentiates the company as a small local research company from its potential as a major multinational drug manufacturer. Because of the critical need for total secrecy, the entire value of the asset is exposed to risk, and without controls on the access to information, both internal and external, most of the asset's value as a secret is exposed to risk. In this instance, because of the "priceless" value of the asset, the company will be willing to absorb considerable costs in the deployment of state-of-the-art biometric and software controls to protect the information.

PROTECTING INFORMATION AND SENSITIVE DATA

Once the information security policy has been devised, management must implement and maintain it. We discuss various administrative measures for the protection of information throughout this text. A brief overview of security technologies is appropriate here.

ACCESS CONTROLS   The most commonly used method of access control is a *password*, a series of characters that provides the user access to a computer, network, or to certain areas of a network. Password characters may be letters or numbers; to be most effective, they should be a combination of letters and numbers. There was a time when the most common password in use was "password." Hackers knew that, which rendered that word useless.

Other passwords of little use are the user's first or last name, name of the organization, and words in common use. A skilled hacker can utilize a software program known as a *password cracker* that essentially performs a dictionary search of potential passwords. The most effective password, therefore, is a lengthy random combination of letters and numbers.

FIREWALLS   A *firewall* is the equivalent of a perimeter fence or wall around the network or computer. It can consist of hardware or software or both. The home computer user typically employs firewall software on her personal computer. Some firewall software programs are available as free downloads; others can be purchased for less than $50. Organizations with computer networks of reasonable size typically employ hardware and software. Firewalls can be configured to limit access to the network, limit traffic within it, restrict certain file types, and restrict specified sources. Firewalls serve as the computer traffic cop, limiting access and traffic from inside the organization to the outside.

ANTIVIRUS SOFTWARE   The use of antivirus software is essential to protect computers and networks. Antivirus software blocks the infection of a network or a nonnetworked computer by an internal or external virus or worm attack. Most antivirus software allow the user to configure the computer or network to block infected files from the network or to quarantine them if accepted.

SPYWARE   Spyware is the software that enables a network administrator or user to determine the types of surveillance or monitoring technologies in use on a particular computer or network. The benefit of spyware is that it can identify the use of a Trojan horse that may be employed on a networked computer.

ENCRYPTION   We previously discussed the malicious use of encryption by hackers. Encryption can also be used to protect information. Financial institutions that transmit cash by electronic fund transfers encrypt the data for transmission. Organizations engaged in e-commerce or e-business utilize encryption for business transactions. The common encryption programs utilized for Internet transactions are Secure Sockets Layer and Secure Electronic Transaction. The most common program used for encrypted e-mail communications is Pretty Good Privacy.

VIRTUAL PRIVATE NETWORK   A virtual private network is a secure connection between remote users or networks. This type of network operates much like an encrypted tunnel, allowing information to be transmitted securely from a telecommuter to the main office.

BIOMETRICS   A biometric device captures human characteristics such as a fingerprint, voice pattern, or handwriting. Biometric technologies can be used to control access to information, for example, a fingerprint scan on a laptop, just as they can be used to control physical access to a building.

Summary

The availability of personal computers and laptops and the accessibility to the Internet for e-commerce, e-business, and the communication of information by average consumers have significantly increased the value of information to organizations. To have value, information must be available, accurate, authentic, and, when appropriate, confidential. The increased value of information has signaled the need for risk management strategies to secure that information.

An essential risk management objective is the development and implementation of an enterprise-wide information security policy. The development and implementation of that policy involves a continuous process that includes the identification of information assets; the identification and assessment of threats to those assets and the vulnerability of the information; and the identification and deployment of countermeasures that can be used to secure the information, given, of course, a cost-benefit risk analysis of those countermeasures. The most important aspect of information security strategies is that they must be adopted and their use urged by top management.

Review Questions/Activities

1. Describe the information assets possessed by security service agencies and methods that could be utilized to secure those assets.
2. What countermeasures could be employed to curtail the incidents of identity fraud resulting from the theft of identification information from databases of online merchants, third-party consultants, or affiliated companies?
3. Studies reveal that credit card fraud for online transactions is between eight and eleven times higher than for physical transactions. What reasons exist for this difference?
4. Describe the difference between encryption and steganography. How do these technologies contribute to the concept that technology is a two-edged sword; that is, it can be utilized to secure data to prevent crime and to hide data to facilitate the commission of crime.
5. Describe how social engineering can be utilized to obtain physical access to a building or technological access to a network database containing classified information.
6. Your organization's budget for security programs and equipment this year is $200,000. A recent information security study at your organization indicates that recommended countermeasures to combat the organization's vulnerability to attacks will cost $1.4 million. As the administrator of your security unit, what factors would you consider in deciding which of the recommended countermeasures to purchase and implement?
7. Ask your classmates what types of passwords they use. For example, how long is the password, is it all letters or a combination of letters and numbers, is it based on an address or favorite sports team, and so on? What implications for security are suggested by their responses?
8. Should spyware be able to detect whether law enforcement agents are monitoring the use of your computer?

WebSearches

1. Access the Web site of *Information Security* magazine at www.searchsecurity.com and locate a recent article that discusses best practices or policies in information security.
2. Access the Web site www.securityfocus.com, and locate an article that discusses a recent virus or worm that has been circulated on the Internet and the degree of danger that it poses to computer or network users.
3. Access the Web site for the security association formerly known as the American Society for Industrial Security, now ASIS International, at www.asisonline.org. After reviewing the various resources at that site, access that association's premier magazine,

Security Management, and locate the monthly column Legal Reporter in the current issue. Discuss one of the cases reported in the column.

4. Access the International Association of Professional Security Consultants at www.iapsc.org. After reviewing the various resources at this site, locate one of the best-practices guidelines adopted by IAPSC and summarize the best practices suggested in that resource.

References

ClickZ. 2010. "Facebook Doubles Audience Year-on-Year, MySpace Continues Decline". Accessed on May 25, 2010, at www.clickz.com/3636504.

Computer Security Institute. 2009. *Computer Crime and Security Survey 2008*. Accessed on October 12, 2009, at *www.gocsi.com*.

Ecommercetimes. 2003. "U.S. E-Commerce Topped $45 Billion in 2002." Accessed October 5, 2003, from *www.ecommercetimes.com/perl/story/20840.html*.

eMarketer.com. 2003. "Worldwide B2B E-Commerce to Surpass $1 Trillion By Year's End." Accessed October 4, 2003, from *www.emarketer.com/news/article.php? 1002125*.

eMarketer.com. 2010. "Social Network Demographics and Usage." Accessed May 24, 2010, from www.emarketer.com/Reports/All/emarketer_2000644.aspx.

Ferraro, Eugene F. 2000. *Undercover Investigations in the Workplace*. Boston: Butterworth-Heinemann.

Mitnick, Kevin D., and William L. Simon. 2002. *The Art of Deception*. Indianapolis, Ind.: Wiley Publishing.

National Center for the Victims of Crime. 2003. "Identity Theft Statistics." Accessed on September 16, 2003, from www.ncvc.org.

Nielson/Net Ratings. 2000. "December 2000 Internet Usage Stats." Accessed June 21, 2004, from *www.clickz.com/stats/big_picture/traffic_patterns/article.php/ 5931_568191*.

Nielson/Net Ratings. 2003. "Canada and U.S. Internet Usage." Accessed June 21, 2004, from *www.clickz.com/stats/big_picture/traffic_patterns/article.php/ 5931_2237901*.

Nielson/Net Ratings. 2010. "Top 10 U.S. Search Providers, Home and Work." Accessed May 25, 2010, from http://en-us.nielsen.com/rankings/insights/rankings/internet.

Pitkin, Donald. 2000. *Information Security: Policies and Procedure*. Upper Saddle River, N.J.: Prentice-Hall.

Plunkett Research. 2003. "Computers, Software and Information Technology Trends & Market Analysis." Accessed October 4, 2003, from *www.plunkettresearch.com/technology/infotech_trends.htm*.

Power, Richard. 2000. *Tangled Web: Tales of Digital Crime from the Shadows of Cyberspace*. Indianapolis, Ind.: Que.

Toffler, Alvin. 1987. *The Third Wave*. New York: Random House.

Whitman, Michael E., and Herbert J Mattord. 2003. *Principles of Information Security*. Boston: Thomson Course Technology.

7

∎ ∎ ∎

Security Issues
in Specific Areas

KEY TERMS

**Clery Act, general aviation, hate crime, health care facility, mass prevention/
prophylaxis plans, mass transit, Real-ID, recreation, RFID, school resource officer,
shrinkage, TSA.**

This chapter reviews security administration concerns and issues related to a selected group of
industries and other areas in the United States. These areas include colleges and universities,
schools, hospitals, laboratories, transportation, malls and retail, ports, mass transit, and trucking.
The reader will note that each area has unique characteristics that pose challenges for security
service professionals in providing for a safe and secure environment.

COLLEGE AND UNIVERSITY SECURITY

More than 4,000 colleges and universities in the United States provide educational, research, and
social activities for students, area residents, and visitors. Security and law enforcement services
are provided by campus security or police departments. These departments have either full police
powers or just common law powers depending on the type and mission of institution. In their
survey of campus departments for calendar years 2004–2005, the United States Department of
Justice reported that nearly 93 percent of responding public institutions had sworn officers that
were armed. Nearly 67 percent of both private and public institutions used armed officers, the
survey reported. The study included agencies serving four-year U.S. universities and colleges with
an enrollment of 2,500 or more and those serving two-year public colleges with an enrollment of
10,000 or more.

From a security service standpoint, colleges and universities need to be viewed as independent cities with daily visitors and residents that are supplied with food, lodging, parking, and a
wide range of social services. As with any city, campuses experience a microcosm of all violent
and property crime offenses. New challenges also include relationship violence, fraud cases, cyber
crime, and identity theft. According to the Campus Law Enforcement Survey for 2004–2005,
campuses average sixty-two reports of violent crime per 1,000 students (2009).

The campus environment is very challenging in that security service personnel are dealing
with a client population that primarily ranges from eighteen to twenty-four years of age and is

taught to question everything. The management of most colleges and universities is based on a business–shared decision-making model whereby most academic, personnel, and operational decisions must go through a series of committee reviews.

Numbers can be deceiving. While a college may list its enrollment as 10,000 students, security planners often deal with the same number of staff and guests on any given day. Game day for football and basketball at major Division I schools often draws thousands of spectators in addition to hundreds of area law enforcement personnel for perimeter and traffic control. College and university law enforcement departments run the entire gamut of security service organizational models presented in Chapter 3. The extent of their powers and operating capacity is determined by institutional size and whether they are public or private institutions. For example, the forty-member department at the University of Wisconsin would be considered a Level III agency based on its size and operational capabilities, which include dog and horse patrols. On the other hand, many community colleges and small liberal arts institutions either contract for security services or have in-house departments that mirror a Level I arrangement. An issue that some campuses departments face is the arming of police and security personnel, which is often regulated by the state and determined by the college president or board of trustees. According to the Campus Law Enforcement survey for 2004–2005 of 750 institutions, 74 percent of the campuses surveyed employed sworn law enforcement officers with full arrest power. Approximately 67 percent of the agencies had armed officers.

A number of federal and state regulations impact college and university security operations. The most noted is the federal Jeanne Clery Disclosure of Campus Security Policy and Campus Crime Statistics Act (Clery Act), which was originally enacted in 1990 and has been revised several times under its current title. The Clery Act is named for a student who was murdered in her residence hall room in 1986. Her parents used an out-of-court settlement to establish Security on Campus, which was instrumental in the passage of this and similar state laws on campus safety. Updates on the Campus Crime Act and campus safety in general can be obtained by visiting the Security on Campus Web site at www.securityoncampus.org. In summary, the Act requires all colleges and universities to publish statistics on certain crimes on campus, adjoining roadways, and properties owned by the educational institution, and report security practices in general and in residence halls (Security on Campus, 2004). Particular attention is paid to listing various offices where students can report crimes. Also, the campus has to report how it will notify the campus community of serious crimes. Further amendments to the Clery Act in the past three years require the publication of policies on the following:

- The admission of registered sex offenders on campus
- Protocols for the investigation of missing college students
- Reporting violent felony offenses to both campus law enforcement and local police

Most recently, the U.S. Department of Education announced that it will require colleges report on fire safety.

As discussed in many publications on campus crime, the most pressing issue facing campus departments is student alcohol and drug abuse, which is the underlying cause of many offenses. A number of cases involving students who have been killed or injured from drinking too much or using drugs have been well publicized. Some of these incidents occur while the students are pledging fraternities and sororities or trying out for sports teams. Most schools have programs from educational activities to zero tolerance, but they seem to have had little impact on drinking either on or off campus.

Hate crime on campus is another area of concern for campus security officials. A hate crime occurs when a crime is committed on the basis of race, religion, ethnicity/national origin, disability, or sexual orientation. As outlined by Hogan (2003), the Civil Rights Act of 1969 was enacted to protect individuals from violence on the basis of race, religion, national origin, and color. Later amendments to the Act and new federal statutes include sexual orientation, disability, and gender. Sentencing or crime category enhancements (misdemeanor to felony status) for prosecution purposes were added by many states to their criminal codes, and the majority of campuses have some form of hate crime language in their campus disciplinary codes. Most incidents that occur are in the form of criminal mischief (graffiti) and harassment by phone or computer. Accordingly, most schools have response protocols to deal with the investigation and victim needs (see International Association of Campus Law Enforcement Administrators, 1993). Not surprisingly, security service personnel have been called to respond to incidents that are deemed by some students to be a hate crime but are actually only in bad taste or a First Amendment constitutional right issue (e.g., hanging a Nazi flag in a dorm room).

Many colleges and universities in the Gulf Coast areas were affected by hurricanes Katrina and Rita, particularly Tulane University, Louisiana State University, and Loyola. These and other schools had to deal with the destruction of classrooms and long-term shutdown of facilities, and in some cases, the layoff of employees. This highlighted the importance of having emergency action plans to deal with major catastrophic incidents as will be discussed in Chapter 9.

Pandemic viruses are another area of concern. The question being addressed today is how campuses will operate if large number of faculty and students are taken down by the viruses such as the N1H1. This is of particular concern as college-age persons are very susceptible to this virus. Thus emergency plans have to deal with the potential of shortening the academic calendar or going to Internet-based classes if the campus must shut down operations.

Active Shooter Events and Response

The murder of 36 students at Virginia Polytechnic Institute and State University (Virginia Tech) on April 17, 2007, also had a profound impact on college and university security. In the early morning hours, senior student Seung Hu Cho murdered two students at a residence hall. Cho was described by fellow students as a "loner." He had acquired several handguns through legitimate means at a Virginia gun shop. While police were investigating this incident, he entered a science building about two hours later and began a shooting spree that killed thirty-two students and himself. There was an immediate response by campus and area police when the shooting started.

The Virginia Tech murders were the worst homicide event in the history of American higher education. An intensive review was conducted by Virginia Governor's Review Panel on the background to the shootings, the personal history of Cho, and the public safety response to the event. As reported by the International Association of Campus Law Enforcement Administrators (2008: 74–75), the review panel recommended the following:

1. Universities should conduct a threat assessment and then choose a level of security appropriate for the campus
2. The head of the campus police should be a member of the threat review team that reviews student conduct and actions that may be a threat to the campus community
3. Campus police must train for active shooter incidents and with neighboring police departments
4. The use of the incident command system should be used for events of this nature
5. Regional disaster drills should be conducted to take into account high number of casualties
6. Students, faculty, and staff should be trained in emergency response

In February 2008, a graduate student killed five students and wounded sixteen at Northern Illinois University. He then killed himself as police began responding to the crime scene. School officials were able to send messages to the campus community on the situation, which resulted in people locking themselves in offices and classrooms. Events of these kinds have led to further emergency plans to deal with "active shooter" incidents, with particular attention to inter-agency mutual assistance from adjacent police and emergency service departments. The training program for armed first response personnel today is based on immediate termination of the gunman rather than containing the scene and waiting for special weapons and tactics units. Many schools have adopted notification systems whereby faculty, staff, and students are notified of an emergency situation. These computerized systems include the use of public address systems, public electronic notice boards, emergency siren, e-mail, and texting of messages to cell phones. If there is a weather-related threat or a developing emergency situation, a notice can be sent to stay indoors, take cover, or remain away from campus. These notification systems for office computers and cell phones are only available to members of the campus community who are employed and registered for classes. Some colleges and universities offer these same services to parents of students.

Another major issue involves potential terrorist activities. Because campuses are virtually open to nonstudents, have a wide range of research and social activities, and have a large population of young adults, there is concern that campuses could be targets of violence. Additionally, antiterrorism planners have a concern that certain campus groups or students could covertly support terrorist groups or activities. Foreign students are monitored and federal rules and immigration regulations have caused these students to be registered and accounted for.

SCHOOL SECURITY

In January 2004, the City of New York announced that it was assigning 150 police officers to augment school security personnel at that city's most violence-prone schools. Weeks before, the national media showed pictures of police officers in Charleston, South Carolina, with guns drawn conducting a drug raid at a major high school. Note that no drugs were found and the principal was subsequently dismissed as a result of community outrage. These dramatic incidents underscore the trend whereby many states and school districts in the past five years have adopted various levels of safe school policies and practices. Overall, this is the product of a number of widely publicized shooting incidents that occurred between 1996 and 2001 in Littleton, Colorado; Jonesboro, Arkansas; Edinboro, Pennsylvania; and other locations. In these cases either one or two students brought firearms to school and began shooting and killing classmates and staff.

Across the country, the immediate reaction by many school districts after these shootings was to create zero tolerance policies for weapons possession and other types of criminal behavior and to increase security presence including installing metal detectors. Note that before this time, many urban schools had already instituted perimeter security points and hired unarmed school safety patrol personnel to deal with daily neighborhood and gang- and drug-related violence. There also has been a dramatic interest in CCTV systems. For example, one Louisiana school in 2003 attracted national attention by installing cameras and an audio system in every classroom. This now has become commonplace at many institutions.

National data show that for the most part, schools are relatively safe and that most juvenile homicides occur off school property (Crews and Montgomery, 2000). Because schools are essentially open environments, school and law enforcement planners have begun to consider the overall school environment safety in addition to adding perimeter and internal security equipment and measures. Measuring the extent of school violence and crime is difficult. Most states have enacted legislation that requires state education authorities to create data collection and reporting mechanisms on school violence. The Bureau of Justice Statistics and the National Center for Education Statistics have conducted surveys of crime occurring at schools as well as incidents that could occur to and at school. The majority of victimizations involve theft of property (Bureau of Justice Statistics, 2004). School programs to address violence include interpersonal violence reduction for students and crisis intervention skills for teachers and staff.

A joint project between the U.S. Secret Service and the Department of Education (2002) resulted in the creation of a school threat assessment program. The program begins with an internal review of school safety and how well teachers and staff interact with students. The project report notes that in major school shooting incidents, the attacks were planned, and many students had been warned by the suspects that an event was planned and to stay clear of certain areas or simply stay home. Schools are urged to have a threat assessment group to review intelligence information and take action about potential threats or students with emotional problems who may need help.

The National Association of School Resource Officers has estimated that 8,000 security personnel are assigned to schools on a full- or part-time basis. Some school resource officer programs use off-duty police officers in uniform for security or to augment nonsworn security personnel. Duties for these resource officers include monitoring main entrances and hot spots in buildings. Their long-term assignment is to work with students and staff on personal safety issues. These officers have to gain the respect of and have rapport with students and staff to get a feel for potential violence and overall personnel safety issues. They must also have a working relationship with area police departments to respond to felonies. These officers also have to respond to bullying events and the wide range of property and personal crimes.

Reviewing school security ten years after the Columbine murders, Spadanuta (2009) reports that school security planners agree that a comprehensive plan is needed instead of "one method/solution fits all approach." Metal detector and CCTV systems are often installed in response to a security problem but they need to have trained human monitors to deal with security intrusions. For emergency planning the following are important for a comprehensive program:

1. Access control is perhaps the vital area as many institutions have dozens of ways to get into the main buildings, such as from athletic fields and parking lots. Access control also includes sign-in policies for visitors and establishing main offices in the front of the building near major entryways.
2. Working with students and keeping abreast of what is going on remains an important issue. A threat assessment program of potential student conduct problems and their conduct is also important.
3. There is also the need to have emergency plans that are not only written but also reviewed periodically and rehearsed. Rehearsal could include a tabletop exercise with senior staff and faculty, an extended tabletop exercise with emergency responders, and an extended drill that includes response and recovery steps that would be taken if the school faces a major disaster.
4. A lockdown drill, whereby an alarm is sounded and classroom doors are secured, should be conducted on an annual basis.

What happens to schoolchildren off campus is a major issue. In October 2009 an honors student was killed during a gang fight after school. His death has prompted a national discussion on gang violence and visits to Chicago by the U.S. Attorney General and education officials. Incidents of this nature demonstrate that the "client area" for school security frequently goes off campus to surrounding streets.

HOSPITAL AND HEALTH CARE SECURITY

In addition to colleges and universities, hospitals and medical centers operate as small cities. As discussed by Colling (2001), a medical center offers a certain range of health services within a regional area. A medical center not only provides health services but also conducts a wide range of teaching and medical research and postcare services. A long-term-care facility deals with persons requiring extended care such as the elderly or postoperative patients. Short-term facilities include outpatient, postoperative, and rehabilitative units. A health care facility can be a public or profit or not-for-profit private facility.

Like university and college campuses, hospitals and health care facilities are open and accessible to the public. This sense of openness is not quite evident until one realizes the wide range of activities that occurs on any given day and at any given hour. The most visible activity occurs in the emergency room, which is open to all and provides a wide range of treatments from gunshot wounds to headaches. Some major hospital ERs have been the site of shootouts between rival gangs or persons seeking to "finish the job" after a street episode. Other parts of the hospital include psychiatric units for persons who are a danger to themselves and to others, as well as areas where prisoners from area correctional facilities are treated. Some hospitals have a site for helicopter landings for emergency transports from accident or disaster sites. Many medical centers are teaching facilities or are sponsored by institutions of higher education. These centers have a number of security concerns related to biotechnology research and animal research. Based on data gathered over the years, the most pressing concern for hospitals and health care facilities is the safety of staff, who are often the victims of robbery, larceny, and criminal mischief both in the health facility or in the adjoining parking lots. Medical staff dealing with psychiatric patients are especially vulnerable to physical attacks. Deterrence security at the front door is important for centers with active ERs to intercept gang-related individuals and groups. Emergency rooms are the main source of violence at most facilities. Their staff needs special training to deal with assaults from combative patients (Anchus, Boucher, and Hubbell, 1995).

Hospitals represent an important part of a regional emergency management plan to deal with large numbers of casualties. In the event of a serious incident, hospitals may have to deal with hundreds of patients. They have developed what is called *mass prevention/prophylaxis plans* that call for treatment outside the patient care system. They must be prepared to provide care for victims contaminated by a chemical agent and biological weapons before they enter hospital premises. Because biological weapons are not immediately felt or identified, hospital security service agents must be aware of a sudden rise in unexplained deaths or patient admissions for what appears to be respiratory illnesses.

A hospital's physical plant is always under review and must be able to operate if there is a sudden power loss or the likelihood of a natural disaster. This was immediately experienced by many hospitals in the northeast in August 2003 when the northeastern U.S. power grid failed and many institutions had to switch to emergency power during in-progress operations and other patient procedures. The effect of such events often overwhelms hospital staff. For security service personnel, emergency plans include bringing in outside assistance such as the army national guard during a major event to provide perimeter and internal security.

LABORATORY SECURITY

International terrorism, the anthrax letter cases of October 2001, and the potential for chemical and biological weapons have placed renewed emphasis on laboratory security. This need has also been caused by attacks on laboratories by activist groups who decry the use of animals for experimental purposes.

Since 1999, the U.S. Department of Health and Human Services has issued specific instructions regarding the security at laboratories that deal with pathogens and toxins, involving plants and animals. The Department of Health and Human Services classifies laboratories according to the amount of pathogens or toxins that are present (Richmond and Neby-O'Dell, 2002). The typical high school or college laboratory is classified as biosafety level 1 because microorganisms causing disease generally are not present. At the other end of the spectrum is a biosafety level 3 or 4 for laboratories that have agents that cause serious and potentially lethal infection and provide a high risk of exposure and infection to laboratory personnel, the community, and the environment (U.S. Department of Agriculture, 2002). Security for laboratory research is important for all private sector research facilities and those that exist in universities and hospitals. In all cases, the director of the facility must oversee all security operations and attest that his or her laboratory security procedures meet federal specifications including perimeter access and physical security systems, inventory and specimen control, risk assessment, background checks of researchers for personnel suitability, and breach of security incident reviews.

AIRLINE TRANSPORTATION

Airport and airline security was most visibly impacted by the events of 9/11. Before 2001, airport security was generally provided by private sector vendors hired by airplane companies and airports. These private security personnel were assisted by uniformed law enforcement contracted with a major jurisdiction or airport authority police specifically assigned to the air facility. Before November 2001, a number of major reports had criticized airport security for lax procedures, employees with little or no training, inadequate background checks on security screeners, and poor pay and benefits that contributed to high personnel turnover.

Today most passenger and cargo security is under the control of the Transportation Security Administration (TSA). It was originally created by Congress in November 2001 by the Aviation and Transportation Security Act and assigned to the jurisdiction of the Department of Transportation. It was then transferred to the Department of Homeland Security in November 2002. One of TSA's first actions was to establish new procedures to screen passengers and check carry-on baggage. It hired more than 60,000 security screeners under federal jurisdiction, replacing all contract security screeners. TSA also implemented strict testing procedures to identify contraband items passing through security. Although some mistakes do occur and are gleefully reported by the media, identification of contraband has increased as evidenced by the thousands of items that have been taken from passengers.

TSA also assumed responsibility for the federal air marshal program. Originally created to deter airplane hijackings that occurred frequently in the 1970s, the federal air marshal service had been reduced to just a few personnel before 2001. Since November 2001, more than 5,000 marshals have been hired (mostly by transfer from other federal agencies) and placed on regularly scheduled domestic flights. Checked passenger baggage screening for explosives is currently being carried out by personnel and canine units. The greatest challenges facing airport security operations involve air cargo, general aviation, airport perimeter, access security, and air traffic control. At this time, air cargo, which accounts for about 12.5 million tons on passenger and cargo planes, is currently not screened for explosive and other hazardous materials. Efforts are under way to deploy an inspection program by the TSA. A "known shipper" program has been adopted that requires manifests to be logged with various federal agencies only by shippers with legitimate business histories; however, monitoring with electronic equipment is needed. Airport security, both within facilities and in adjacent neighborhoods, is always in need of continued assessment. Background checks and mandated identification cards are being considered for all employees including airline personnel, vendors, retail workers, and airport maintenance staff. There is also the fear of shoulder-fired rocket attacks by terrorists from areas near runways. FAA air control facilities, which manage aircraft landings and takeoffs, need perimeter and computer/infrastructure safety.

General aviation describes all noncommercial and private pilots, privately owned aircraft, and various support personnel. At this time, the Department of Homeland Security has proposed changes to screen pilots, flight plans, or aircraft at more than 19,000 noncommercial air terminals. For aircraft over 12,500 pounds, proposals include a check on all passengers against terrorist watch lists and background checks for pilots and crew. These efforts are not fully being supported by the general aviation industry (Daniels, 2009: 1, 15).

The TSA is currently researching the creation of a passenger database that would screen individuals by profiling. The former program, called the Computer Assisted Passenger Prescreening System (CAPPS II), reviews personal information (e.g., name, address, and date of birth) and matches it against national databases for suspected terrorists. The project has raised many personal privacy concerns that are discussed in Chapter 10. It did not solve the issue of "false positives" whereby persons with reservations have designations of "do not fly" or "select" for further inspection. The entire program was based on name query. In August 2009 a new program called Secure Flight was instituted. Persons using domestic or international flights are now required to give their date of birth and gender. This information, as well as the travel itinerary, is then given to TSA computers for review. Eventually persons flying to the United States will also have to have their information screened (Straw, 2009: 28–29).

However, verification is based on a driver's license, which can be easily forged. This is an important concern since 9/11 as most of the terrorists who hijacked the planes had some form of forged identity including drivers licenses (Federal Register, 2009). In 2005, a program called REAL-ID was introduced, which required states to implement new procedures for the issuance of a drivers license if it were to be used for federal identification for official purposes such as air travel. These included inclusion of security features for each license and stricter authentication standards of license applicants. A number of states have refused to comply with this program citing reasons of cost, and the program has been revamped under the heading of PASS-ID.

MALLS AND RETAIL AREAS

The shopping mall has replaced "Main Street" for most retail activities. Malls are made to be attractive locations that provide ample parking; protection from rain, snow, cold, and heat; and public areas for a wide range of community and social activities. Conceptually, the enclosed mall grew from the shopping center idea of the late 1950s with the goal of clustering a number of stores together to provide parking for cars. The largest location is always under contention, but our nominee is the Mall of America outside of Minneapolis, Minnesota, which has a wide range of retail shops, a theme park, and other attractions. Similar ventures with carousels, water attractions, and so on are found all over the United States.

As discussed in Chapter 2, shopping malls are private property with public access. Enforcement of vehicle and traffic laws as well as city and town ordinances is often an issue. Often there are memoranda of understanding between a city and mall owners regarding these issues. Very often, security service personnel have to deal with issues involving the First Amendment right of assembly. For example, in Albany, New York, in 2003, a son and his father were arrested by town police for protesting the invasion of Iraq by wearing antiwar T-shirts that had been purchased from a store at the Crossgates Shopping Center. The complaints against the pair were brought by mall security. Not surprisingly, people protested the arrests, which received extensive media coverage.

Behind their glitz and glitter, there is a dark side to mall operations. They are attractive locations for gang activity, youth violence, stalking, child abduction, and robbery, especially in the parking area and remote locations in addition to a wide range of retail-related crimes. Food courts experience fights and drug transactions. As a result of some serious incidents, some malls have enacted regulations on loitering and teenagers being accompanied by a person either over eighteen or twenty-one years of age after certain hours. Accordingly, security service planning for shopping malls begins with the layering concept that starts with patrols and CCTV surveillance in parking lots and in main thoroughfares. Traffic patterns and parking patrols must be planned especially for access from main traffic arteries and drop-off points that are always congested. Enforcement of police powers is an issue, and many malls do not have these powers. Malls often have arrangements with local police departments who place satellite offices or precincts at the malls.

This discussion of shopping mall security must also include retail security, which is a balancing act between open access and security and protection of employees and goods. Retail security encompasses a wide range of enterprises that include retail giants such as Walmart and Price Right to small mom and pop stores. The term *shrinkage* is used by owners to describe the loss of retail goods after their delivery to the store. The National Retail Federation estimated that in 2007 retail stores lost 41.6 billion dollars in shrinkage (Grannis, 2007). The usual suspects for shrinkage are employees and customers which increased because of the economic recession. Generally, employee theft embraces a wide range of activities that include stealing cash, "fudging" inventory, or giving unauthorized discounts to friends and associates. Customer theft includes a host of behaviors such as shoplifting. In addition, retail stores are subject to offenses ranging from robbery to credit card fraud.

A wide range of measures is employed to reduce retail losses. The first involves environmental designs including location of merchandise, creation of open spaces, procedures for dressing room entry/exit, and staff training. Equipment includes CCTV and one-way glass to monitor key areas. Electronic article security tags are a mainstay for major "theft target" items such as electronic goods and designer apparel. An ever-important factor is to conduct background checks of potential employees during the hiring process. To keep track of stock, companies are now installing radio frequency identification (RFID) on products or in shipping pallets. Used every day by millions of drivers going through toll booths, the RFID reader contains a chip with an antenna that is scanned by a reader to verify its location. Used during World War II to scan for friendly planes returning from raid missions, RFID was developed in the 1990s by a group of retailers working in concert with scientists at MIT (Booth-Thomas, 2003). It can also be used to monitor the whereabouts of vehicles and people, which has some privacy groups worried. RFID has become a billion-dollar industry in its application to cargo transportation, military equipment deployment, patient and prisoner monitoring, and retail inventory control. For purchase applications, the customer goes to the checkout counter and simply waves a device to begin the purchase.

Major chains use loss prevention specialists whose job it is to intercept person attempting to steal merchandise. Sophisticated systems use a bank of CCTV cameras that are monitored at high-risk locations such as jewelry, electronic goods, personal use items, and anything of interest from a popular culture perspective.

Aside from employees, retail stores are targeted by shoplifters who range from men and women who occasionally lift merchandise to professional thieves working alone or in concert with others or by themselves. There is no one profile of a shoplifter. Persons charged by one of our students working for a major chain in one semester included high school and college students, housewives, an ex-police administrator, and people employed and unemployed. Professional shoplifters often acquire "persons of legend" status. One professional shoplifter would place items between her calf muscles under a large dress or raincoat and leave the store premises. She developed this trick by practicing with telephone books while ironing and doing household chores.

Recently, major stores have been hit by organized gangs that go from store to store. Working solo, or in pairs, these thieves survey targets for security devices and then hit in systematic fashion with a number of ruses (e.g., one talks to the sales clerks while the others steal merchandize from shelves and racks). What happens to all these items? As reported in a case study by Talamo et.al., 2007, these goods are sold to professional fences who pay about one-third to one-fourth of the price of the item depending on the region. They are also sold with legitimate goods on the Internet. To combat these gangs, the retail industry has formed the Enforcement Retail Partnership Network, which is a secure Web site that reports on organized gang activity for its members. On the law enforcement side, the Organized Retail Theft Task Force was created by FBI to provide a partnership with the industry to identify and control organized gangs.

The retail industry formed the Law Enforcement Research Council, which is a partnership to review data on statistical models for shrinkage, shoplifter profiles, testing electronic systems, studying dishonest employee dynamics, and presenting training programs (Titus, 2007). As with any other endeavor, loss prevention has to be geared to the type of retailer; sporting goods, furniture and pharmacies have different concerns and potential targets for thieves. Although much discussion on loss prevention is directed toward major chains, single proprietor stores are especially vulnerable. Riddell (2007) reports that theft of goods or money often results in dire economic impact and eventually store closure. He recommends that small store owners take a course in retail fraud and protection processes as they plan to enter a business.

RECREATION SECURITY

One of the greatest growth industries in the U.S. economy is in the recreation area. For this discussion, *recreation* includes a wide range of activities such as sporting events, concerts, fun and theme parks, and cultural events. The best examples are Disney theme parks in Orlando and Los Angeles, which draw millions of visitors each day. The Disney idea is for visitors to have a fun-filled vacation at one general location with no inconveniences or hassles. Security at both sites is ever present with patrol personnel and cameras that remain out of sight and out of mind for patrons. All theme parks, ranging from Disney to small venues, must have emergency response plans for severe weather, equipment malfunction, and the various catastrophic events that could affect a city.

For recreation events, such as sporting activities or major community cultural events, planning takes time in order to consider a multitude of risks including severe weather, rioting, illegal drinking, unruly behavior, medical emergencies, and the possibility of a terrorist event. For example, Division I athletic events at major universities, which may draw more than 100,000 spectators, participants, and staff, require considerable event planning and operational interaction between state, local, and campus law enforcement. Since 9/11, there is also concern about flyover zones by aircraft, bomb threats, and the potential for weapons of mass destruction.

The main threat at recreation events still remains the misuse of alcoholic beverages. For large gatherings, achieving an incident-free event requires scores of security and staff assistants at front gates inspecting bags and other carry-in items for alcohol. At some events, attendees are required to walk through metal detectors that screen for guns and knives. Security providers need special training to deal with isolated fights in crowded areas and to protect the goalpost from a crowd charge after big games. Some schools have collapsible posts that come down quickly in the event of a fan rush to prevent damage to them and injury to fans.

Sporting events, particularly between rival teams no matter the level of play, can bring out the worst of fan and player behavior. After-game fights and riots between rival factions during and after a major game at colleges and universities, high schools, and professional venues have become frequent. Often the athletic event becomes an excuse for age-old rivalries between community factions. Police, security, and school officials are often caught off guard when disruptions occur that require wide area police response and the use of force. Returning to our discussion of school violence, it is important to have an open communication with students and a record of sports incidents to be able to plan the security for an event. To avoid violence, games have been played without spectators and teams have been dropped from a schedule.

Post-championship riots are also a concern at major universities and cities after the Super Bowl, the World Series, and the NBA championship game. These events often require a major deployment of patrol personnel and equipment. They also require unusual crime prevention steps such as removing street trash containers and any other item that could be thrown, limiting or prohibiting vehicular traffic into the potential problem area, and having small quick-response teams ready to douse street fires and break up combative fans. The most difficult events to secure are basketball games because fans are so close to the players and referees. A person would have to be quite mad to go onto a football field or hockey rink to attack a player with full gear.

For professional venues such as the National Football League, general procedures include frisking people for weapons and alcohol, high use of CCTV cameras to both scan the crowd for suspicious or rowdy behavior and recording incidents, and using high number of security personnel that can be deployed to surround an unruly group and usher them out of the venue.

Concert security has a number of specific requirements. In the past decade a number of concertgoers have been killed by crowd stampedes and fires. In 2003, at West Warwick, Rhode Island, music fans were killed or injured after a band's pyrotechnics ignited the stage and quickly spread throughout the building. Many communities have revised fire regulations and building codes for crowd capacity and exits. In Chicago, Illinois, a stampede occurred after a security officer used pepper spray in a crowded area to break up a fight at a popular dance club. As a result, concerts require safety and security personnel for crowd management, traffic control, and, at times, protection for performers.

Related to recreation security is hotel security. Depending on the rate of crime in a particular area, the major hotel chains, which operate internationally, have well-planned security operations that rely on CCTV in public areas, particularly check-in areas and parking lots. In countries that have a high rate of terrorist activity, international hotels represent a good target because of their accessibility to the public. This has been exemplified by bombing attacks against hotels in Indonesia and an armed attack in Mumbai, India, in 2008 that killed about 173 people and wounded 308.

Individual room security is an important aspect. Room key operations include door security swipe cards or individually coded access locks. Even with these new systems, hotels use the traditional floor patrol and the doorman, who provides a good set of eyes for street surveillance while helping guests alight from taxis and cars.

GAMING SECURITY

Casino gambling continues to be a growth industry. The Department of Labor reports the need for increased security personnel for both internal and perimeter security and antifraud operations (2009). Casino security requires great attention to detail for crowd control, identifying and monitoring suspected cheats and known criminals, and monitoring casino employees at gaming tables. The cash counting room, portrayed in movies as the location for robberies and inside heists, is a high-risk area. Security personnel at a typical casino might include employees who monitor activities, assist customers, and secure areas. Additional personnel are from state wagering units who monitor financial transactions for state tax purposes. There is also a need for personnel with emergency medical certifications as many venues have a high number of elderly visitors who experience health related problems.

The major casino corporations are Harrah's, Bally's, Trump, and Midwest Gaming. The traditional centers of casino gambling remain Las Vegas and Reno, Nevada, and Atlantic City, New Jersey, and gambling casinos have opened along the Mississippi River, particularly in Missouri and Illinois, in the Gulf Coast states, and at sites owned by Native American tribes. As sovereign nations, Native American tribes can own and operate gambling casinos and are not subject to state regulations. Many operations, such as the Turning Stone Casino outside Utica, New York, and Foxwoods and Mohegan Sun in Connecticut, have been a boon to local economies.

An initial review of fraud in gambling operations by Lane (2009) shows that most losses are from employees who come up with schemes to defraud their employer. In any given day, thousands of dollars are moved from secure "cage" locations to gaming areas. Additionally revenues are also created from hotel, food, and beverage operations. This requires an elaborate system of checks and balances on the gaming floor with "casino pits" based on the type of game, the "pit boss" who oversees the particular game, the "floor person" in charge of a specific number and bankroll of games under his or her control, "box people" who control crap games and their attendant bankrolls and chips, and the "dealer" who runs the game. Casinos with slot machines will have a slot manager who sets policy and directs the operation of the machine, slot attendants, and mechanics. Added to this is an elaborate system of visual and electronic surveillance.

PORT SECURITY

Seaports in the United States are part of the critical infrastructure in the American economy and present a high-risk security problem. Goods are both loaded and unloaded from trucks and railcars requiring a high concentration of machinery and personnel. Ships and their cargoes are under a tight schedule and loading and unloading must be completed in a very short time period.

There are many security problems that start from point of manufacturer to destination. Although consumer goods are shipped in containers, there is still theft and shrinkage from maritime employees. There are multiple terrorist targets in a port area. Some cargoes are liquid flammable or environmentally hazardous and they are stored in tanks that abound the port area. Ships present an attractive target, especially those carrying cargoes such as gasoline, liquid nitrogen, munitions, and other substances. There is also the possibility that a container might contain illegal human cargo or even a nuclear device.

Port security is generally controlled by a port authority in conjunction with private transportation companies and state and local police. Major ports, such as New York-New Jersey, Houston, Tacoma, and Long Beach, have the presence of the U.S. Coast Guard and U.S. Customs and Border Patrol for security checks of ships and cargoes. Custom officials not only conduct sample checks of cargoes but also review credentials of crews. In 2002, the Maritime Safety Transportation Act was passed which required ports to have plans for physical security. A number of initiatives have been undertaken that have domestic and global proportion. As outlined by Bullock et.al. (2006), under the 24 Hour Advanced Manifest Rule cargo descriptions must be forwarded to Custom and Border Protection (CBP) before they are loaded onto vessels headed to the United States. CBP personnel also check container cargoes overseas before they are loaded at certain ports. The Customs Trade Partnership against Terrorism (C-TPAT) is a program involving shipping companies who agree to create and abide by strict security standards for cargoes through the supply chain. This includes cargo verification, background checks for personnel and crews, and documentation of customers. Once validated by CBP, the shipping vessel receives immediate clearance to unload its goods.

DHS has undertaken a Port Security Grant program through security assessments of port facilities. Much attention has been given to port area monitoring and coordination centers for security and major emergencies. There is an increased use of CCTV to monitor activities. Additionally attention has to be paid to tank farms and the areas that abound the port. Workers today must be credentialed through the Transportation Workers Identity Card which included background checks. To date, over 1 million workers have been enrolled in this program. (Stelter, 2009)

Related to maritime security is security from pirate attacks on the high seas. The most volatile area is in the Somalia straits, a key entry point for ships traveling to the Middle East. Using small speedboats, pirate gangs attack freighters, tankers, and private yachts and take them over holding the ship and its crew for ransom for millions of dollars. In April 2009 US Navy sharpshooters killed three pirates that had attacked the *Maersk Alabama* and taken its captain prisoner. The captain was unharmed in the incident. Ironically, the same ship was attacked again on November 18, 2009, but armed guards repulsed the attack. Ships of over 500 gross tons are now required to have a security alert system which can send a covert signal indicating that the vessel is under attack by pirates or terrorists. Since the *Maersk Alabama* incident, ship owners have begun to increase security with specially guards using lethal and nonlethal weapons because of the increased costs related to ransoms, negotiations, and paying crews being held captive.

TRUCKING

Since the Oklahoma City bombing in April 19,1995, when a truck filled with ammonium nitrate fertilizer and nitro methane exploded taking the side off the Murrah Federal Center and killing 168 persons and injuring 680, greater attention has been paid to truck cargoes and the identification of truck drivers. At any given time, thousands of trucks traverse U.S. interstate and local highways containing a wide range of hazardous materials. Haz-mat incidents account for most of the incidents where people have to be evacuated. Thus cargo identification is an important element for first responders at a highway accident scene.

The U.S. Department of Transportation has taken a number of steps to address safety and security related to ground transport. The Highway Information Sharing and Analysis Center in Alexandria, Virginia, maintains general traffic patterns related to terrorist threats, and driver security awareness information, such as what to do if your tractor and cargo are hijacked.

MASS TRANSIT

Mass transit is a term for commuter trains, subways, buses, and light railways and buses that carry people to work and social events. It is estimated that approximately 4.7 percent of the American workforce use trains and subways for commuting to work. Most systems are located in major American cities particularly in the northeast United States. Mass transit trains and facilities are a prime target for terrorists as shown by bombings in Barcelona in 2004 and London in 2005. In these two incidents 247 people were killed and about 2,500 injured. On November 27, 2009, Chechen rebels blew up an express train outside of Moscow killing 39. Many workers also use bus transportation, which can also be a terrorist target as exemplified by suicide bombers against buses in Israel.

In the United States, security at facilities involves addressing the needs of thousands of rail stations, bus terminals, and subway stations. Securing these facilities, as well as trackage, storage and maintenance facilities, and tunnels, is a daunting task for operating transportation authorities and private companies and their security services. Efforts by the Department of Transportation and Homeland Security include increased training of workers, security assessments of facilities, increasing the use of explosive detection sensors, and the spot identification of inter-city passengers. There is increased use of CCTV systems and canine and security service patrols at major terminals. Persons using Amtrak trains must show identification and their limits in going to station platforms. It must be noted that the most serious train wrecks involving deaths and injury have been caused by train engineer inattention and error, such as texting messages on a cell phone.

RAILROADS

The total number of track miles in the United States is estimated at 140,000 (Association of American Railroads, 2009). This number increases with the miles for terminals and freight yards and other connections. The reality is that rail traffic tends to travel through heavily populated areas in the United States. Historically, rail yards have been favorite targets for thieves and homeless persons seeking free transportation on trains. Today many cargoes are in trailer containers or by bulk. Bulk items include a wide variety of hazardous materials including oil, anhydrous ammonia, propane, and sometimes nuclear waste products. Most rail accidents are caused by cars "jumping the tracks" because of faulty track maintenance or collision with motor vehicles at crossings. There is also the factor of human error, such as engineers failing to see signals for a variety of reasons including, as noted above, text messaging or talking on cell phones. As with trucks, rail accidents involving hazardous materials result in the evacuation of residents and destruction of property. The Association of American Railroads and the Department of Transportation have entered into a number of cooperative agreements to assess security risks for right-of ways, bridges, and tunnels. High usage fright lines pose a particular threat for high-density residential areas. Thus railroad security services and local first emergency responders need to have response plans to deal with train wrecks and evacuation of people.

Summary

This chapter reviewed a wide range of security issues faced by specific types of industries. The discussion shows that regardless of the industry, security is dependent on organizational policies, technology, and a dedicated security services workforce. Security practices are ever changing because of changes in the global economy, economic recession, and attack tactics by terrorist groups and organized and individual criminals.

Review Questions/Activities

1. Obtain a copy of the Clery report for your campus. What are the main reporting areas required by Clery? What crime statistics and procedures are included in the report that you obtained?
2. Based on the information in this chapter, prepare a short review of security service operations at a hospital, school, or shopping mall in your area. Interview the head of operation regarding personnel training and any special problems the unit has.
3. Identify developments in aviation security reported in the newspaper and general aviation publications.

What changes have taken place based on the general issues described in this chapter?

4. How do hospitals and health centers present unique issues for security services personnel?
5. From a search of area media, review an incident of school violence. What was the cause of the incident?

What was the response of school officials and area law enforcement to the event?

6. Why is it important that casinos have a viable security services program?

WebSearches

1. Access www.securityoncampus.org and, after reviewing the resources available at that site, access guidelines on preventing campus violence. After studying the recommendations in the guideline, compare the safety measures in place on your campus with the ones recommended in the guideline. Also check if any schools have been fined by the U.S. Department of Education for failure to comply with the Clery Act.
2. Access www.securitymanagement.com and, after reviewing the resources available at that site, click on the shortcut to Physical Security and then the link to an article that deals with physical security at nuclear or laboratory facilities. Summarize the security issues presented in that article.

3. The Department of Homeland and its various sub-agencies deal with mass transit, transportation, and port security issues on a continuous basis. Updates on the programs or regulations under consideration can be found at www.dhs.gov and then typing in a query in the search box.
4. The National Association of School Resource Officers maintains an active Web site at www. nasro.mobi/cms. Reviews of incidents and training programs are readily available at this site.
5. Check the Web site for the National Retail Federation at www.nrf.com. Review the latest reports on retail shrinkage rates and the efforts by the industry to control losses.

References

Anchus, John S., Debby Boucher, and Kelly Hubbell. 1994/96. "An Emergency Department Security Plan." *Journal of Healthcare Protection Management* (Winter): 61–72.

Association of American Railroads. "Economy." Posted at http://www.aar.org/Economy/Economy.aspx. Accessed December 1, 2009.

Booth-Thomas. 2003. "The See It All Chip." *Time*, 22 September, A8.

Bullock, Jane A., George D. Haddow, Damon Coppola, Erdem Ergin, Lissa Westerman, and Sarp Yeletaysi 2006. *Introduction to Homeland Security* 2ed ed. Amsterdam, Netherlands: Elsevier Butterworth-Heinemann.

Bureau of Justice Statistics. 2004a. "Indicators of School Crime and Safety—2003." Posed at http://www.ojp.usdoj.gov/bjs/absract. Accessed January 28, 2004.

Bureau of Justice Statistics. 2004b. "Crime Characteristics." Posted at http://www.ojp.usdoj.gov/bjs/cvict. Accessed January 7, 2004.

Colling, Russell L. 2001. *Hospital and Healthcare Security.* Boston: Butterworth-Heinemann.

Crews, Gordon, and Reid Montgomery. 2000. *Chasing Shadows: Confronting Juvenile Violence in America.* Upper Saddle River, N.J.: Prentice-Hall.

Daniels, Rhianna. May 2009. "Flying under the Radar? Cessna Incident Showcases Industry's, TSA's Debate on Private Plan Security." *Security Director News*, Vol. 6, No. 5. pp. 1, 15.

Federal Register. January 29, 2009. "Minimum Standards for Driver's Licenses and Identification Cards Acceptable by Federal Agencies for Official Purposes: Final Rule." Web posted at http://edocket.access.gpo./gov/2008/08-140.htm. Accessed November 3, 2009.

Hogan, Melissa. 2003. "A Public Policy Review of Hate Crimes." Utica College of Syracuse University.

International Association of Campus Law Enforcement Administrators. 1993. *Handling Cultural Diversity on Campus.* West Hartford, Conn.: International Association of Campus Law Enforcement Administrators.

International Association of Campus Law Enforcement Administrators. 2008. *IACLEA: The First 50 Years.* West Hartford, CT: International Association of Campus Law Enforcement Administrators.

Lane, Curtis 2010. A Study of Occupational Fraud within the Gaming Industry. Unpublished manuscript, Utica College. National Advisory Committee on Criminal Justice Standards and Goals. 1976. *Private Security: Report of the Task Force on Private Security.* Washington, D.C.: U.S. Department of Justice, Law Enforcement Assistance Administration (LEAA).

Grannis, Kathy. June 11, 2007. "Retail Losses Hit $41.6 Billion Last Year, According to National Retail Security Survey." Posted at http://www.nrf.com/modules.php?name=News&op=viewlive&sp_id=318. Accessed October 29, 2009.

Riddell, Christopher. 2007. *Employee Dishonesty Who Can You Trust: Impact on Small Businesses.* Utica College Library, Utica, New York.

Richmond, Jonathan Y., and Shanna L. Neby-O'Dell. 2002. Paper presented at "Laboratory Security and Emergency Response Guidance for Laboratories Working with Select Agents." Posted at www.cdc.gov/mmwr. Retrieved August 7, 2003.

Security on Campus, Inc. 2004. "Clery Act Legislative History-Related Congressional Legislation Incorporated into the Clery Act." Posted at www.securityoncampus.org/congress/cleryhistory, html. Accessed June 7, 2004.

Spadanuta, Laura. 2009. Schools Learn Security Lessons. *Security Management,* August, pp. 55–67.

Stelter, Leischen, April 2009. "TWIC hits one million enrolled." Security Director News, Vol. 6, No. 4, pp. 1,12

Straw, Joseph. October 2009. Passenger Screening Progress? Security Management. Posted at www.securitymanagement.com/article/passenger-screening-progress-006224. Accessed November 4, 2009.

Talamo, John, Paul Kay, Kevin McAlister, and Joe Hajdu. March–April 2007. *Executing the ORC Strategy.* Loss Prevention, Vol. 6, No. 2, pp. 50–61.

Titus, William. March–April 2007. *Challenging Assumptions—Putting LP Under the Microscope.* Loss Prevention, Vol. 6, No 2, pp. 22–32.

U.S. Department of Agriculture. 2002. "USDA Security Policies and Procedures for Biosafety Level-3 Facilities." Posted at www. NERRTC/Campus.org.

U.S. General Accounting Office (November 20, 2003). Testimony Before the Committee on Government Report, House of Representatives: Aviation Security: Efforts to Measure Effectiveness and Strengthen Security Program. Washington, D.C.: GAO

U.S. Secret Service and the U.S. Department of Education. 2002. *Threat Assessment in Schools: A Guide to Managing Threatening Situations and to Creating Safe School Climates.* Washington, D.C.: U.S. Department of Education.

8
■ ■ ■
Investigation of Criminal Security Incidents

KEY TERMS
chain of custody, cyber crime, data mining, device surveillance, due diligence, eavesdropping, fraud, hearsay rule, honeypot, incident response, probable cause, profiling, protective sweep, stop and frisk, wiretap

Ordinarily, investigations are reactive. A properly conducted investigation can be transformed, however, into a successful proactive procedure by obtaining information that can help prevent future crimes or incidents. The successful investigation of a crime or security incident can be preventive in nature by (1) gathering sufficient evidence that results in a criminal prosecution and conviction, civil action, or disciplinary proceeding, thereby deterring future conduct by others and (2) exposing threats and vulnerabilities in security policies and identifying countermeasures that can be employed to mitigate those vulnerabilities. Because investigations can be both reactive and proactive, they are essential to effective security management.

INVESTIGATION

An investigation is the systematic collection of data to enable one to determine what, when, where, and why an incident or event occurred and who was involved. There are many types of investigations, and they are classified according to their purpose or type of incident. The purpose of a *criminal* investigation is to apprehend the perpetrator and collect evidence of the crime for prosecution in the criminal justice system. In criminal cases, security investigators must gather and preserve evidence so that it can be introduced in a court proceeding. Criminal investigations ordinarily are conducted by federal, state, and local law enforcement officers; authorized military personnel (e.g., the Air Force Office of Special Investigations); and security service units with law enforcement powers. As noted in Chapter 2, legal constraints, particularly the Fourth and Fifth Amendments to the U.S. Constitution, apply to investigations conducted by law enforcement and other government personnel that do not apply to investigative personnel in the private sector.

Often information acquired during the investigation of a security incident indicates that the conduct was criminal in nature. At that point, investigators must preserve the evidence and proceed on the assumption that it is a criminal investigation. This need to preserve evidence applies to non–law enforcement federal agencies, such as the Securities Exchange Commission and Federal Trade Commission, as well as private sector businesses and private investigators hired by companies or individuals to locate missing persons, conduct background checks or due diligence investigations to verify critical information for prospective business transactions, and marital infidelity cases.

An all-too-frequent example of investigation of a security incident leading to a criminal investigation is a network administrator's discovery that an employee is downloading an excessive number of image files in violation of corporate policy. Further investigation reveals that the image files contain child pornography. At this point, the corporate network administrator must undertake the required evidentiary precautions. Another example of an investigation that could turn criminal in nature relates to the theft of trade secrets. As discussed in Chapter 6, the theft of proprietary information can result in serious financial loss to a company. For example, the theft and public disclosure of Windows 7 source code would significantly impact Microsoft's business plan. The theft of that source code and its utilization in a competitor's operating system product would cause a similar loss. The theft of such a trade secret is the crime of economic espionage in violation of the Economic Espionage Act of 1996 (18 U.S.C. § 1832), and if it is committed to benefit a foreign government or instrumentality, it is a violation of a different section of the same act (18 U.S.C. § 1831). Upon detection of the theft, corporate investigators commence an investigation with the mind-set that any evidence collected must be handled and preserved so it can be introduced either in a criminal or civil proceeding.

Investigations Related to Security

Investigations of security incidents or events are conducted for a number of other purposes: a civil proceeding for damages for the loss sustained by a security attack, an internal disciplinary proceeding, a post-event internal review of security and response procedures, or compliance with federal and state statutes or regulatory requirements. The victim of a security incident can commence a civil action against the perpetrator for damage inflicted during the attack. The civil action may be commenced even though a criminal action is brought by the government against the perpetrator. The same need exists to collect and preserve evidence for admission in the civil proceeding as exists for criminal proceedings.

Many security attacks, events, or incidents do not result in either criminal or civil proceedings. The event may be no more than an employee's violation of company policy such as the improper use of a networked computer to access the Internet or an employee's entry to the company's facility without scanning an identification badge but by "piggybacking" on another employee's lawful entry. The event such as an employee's inadvertent wandering into a restricted area may violate security but not warrant more than mild disciplinary action. From a management perspective, investigations of such events do not require the same commitment of personnel, equipment, or process as investigations related to legal action.

Security investigations also may be undertaken to comply with regulatory requirements. Financial institutions, health care providers, and insurers are required to maintain the security of customer information and to employ compliance officers or auditors to ensure that security policies are followed. Those audit or compliance activities inherently involve security investigations. In this instance, the investigation may or may not be performed in response to a security incident.

Security investigations may also be categorized according to the type of incident, and, depending on the size of the entity, may involve different security departments or units within the agency or business. The incident may be related to physical security, information/computer/network security, or fraud affecting financial assets or property. The source of the incident or attack may be internal or external. These different types of incident require unique investigatory techniques.

Many domestic corporations and business entities have facilities around the world. Even those businesses that do not have physical facilities outside the country engage in e-commerce or e-business with customers and other businesses located around the world. Those businesses are subject to cyber attacks and breaches of security by employees physically working in foreign countries or by outsiders who reside in foreign countries. A response to such an attack or incident requires either a presence in those countries or the cooperation of private sector or law enforcement personnel in the foreign country. We discuss these issues in Chapter 13 of this book.

STATISTICS ON CRIME AND SECURITY INCIDENTS

Crime data are collected and reported in many ways. The most widely known data collection report is provided by the FBI's Uniform Crime Reports (UCR) program, which publishes annual reports. The data consist of reports filed by state and local law enforcement agencies. Not all agencies participate in the UCR program. Further, the UCR classification of crimes only considers some economic crimes or labels them as larcenies without providing explanation. The UCR will be replaced eventually by the National Incident-Based Reporting System (NIBRS), which may yield more specific crime information. In addition to the UCR, most administrators rely on surveys conducted by professional organizations or private businesses.

Currently, most security surveys relate to information, computer, or network security. Perhaps the most widely read and cited of those surveys is the annual Computer Crime and Security Survey conducted by the Computer Security Institute. The 2008 survey reveals that, of those responding to the question, 47 percent indicated that they had experienced between one to five cyber attacks and that 51 percent of attacks were believed to have been committed by outsiders (Computer Security Institute, 2008). The survey reports that the percentage of respondents who experienced unauthorized access to systems decreased from 37 percent in 2002 to 29 percent in 2008. Insider abuse of network access remains one of the most frequent incidences, at 44%. The 2008 survey, like the twelve annual surveys before it, establishes employees as significant sources of computer crime and security incidents.

Similar results have been established in non–computer-related surveys. The 2009 Global Economic Crime Survey conducted by Price Waterhouse Coopers involved a global study of the exposure of businesses to economic crimes such as asset misappropriation, financial misrepresentation, corruption and bribery, money laundering, cyber crime, industrial espionage, and product piracy. The worldwide respondents indicated experiencing those crimes as follows:

Asset misappropriation	67%
Accounting fraud	38%
Bribery and corruption	27%
IP infringement	15%
Money laundering	12%
Industrial espionage	3%

In that survey, *asset misappropriation* referred to theft by company insiders.

The 2008 National Retail Security Survey by Hollinger (2009) indicates that 43.7 percent, or about $15.9 billion, of inventory shrinkage was caused by employee theft and that 38.7 percent was caused by outsiders, either by shoplifting or vendor fraud. Inventory shrinkage by employee theft and shoplifting increased from the previous year. The survey statistics suggest that information and noninformation security incidents and business-related crimes are committed by insiders and outsiders in approximately equal numbers. Additionally, the surveys indicate that, although violent crime is declining, the number of employee fraud- and information-related crime and security incidents is rising.

INVESTIGATION PROCESS

Security incidents are "events that interrupt normal operating procedure and precipitate some level of crisis" (Mandia and Prosise, 2001: 16). The process of responding to and investigating a security incident, whether by public or private sector groups, is a multistage process that should encompass tasks that take place before the incident occurs and analysis that occurs after the investigation is complete. The essential "response stages" are:

- Preincident preparation
- Incident detection
- Response preparation
- Investigation
- Evidence preparation
- Lessons learned

Preincident Preparation

Although it is difficult to conceptualize a "response" occurring before the incident, one must view incident response as a process, not a physical event. Thus viewed, the first and perhaps most critical stage of incident response is preincident preparation. This first stage includes several activities, many of which are management or policy related. First, the organization must identify the need for and role of incident response as part of its information security policy across the business enterprise. Although we have discussed some of the features related to the development of policy in Chapter 3 on planning and in Chapter 6 on securing information assets, the following concepts apply specifically to investigations:

TARGET   The organization must identify the potential source of attacks, its vulnerability to them, and the different assets that are vulnerable to such attacks. The organization can then identify the different targets that could be the subject of an investigation. For example, a fatal attack by a disgruntled former employee on current employees involves a murder investigation. This investigation deals with a body and requires investigators to answer the following questions: Why the person died, how the attack occurred, and who or what killed the person? Fraud investigations deal with financial documents and records and require investigators to determine how much economic loss was suffered, how and why the fraud was committed, and who committed it. The organization must have trained investigators ready to respond to a variety of targets.

RESOURCE   Upper management of the organization must determine how much time, money, and personnel to budget for security investigations, and security department managers must determine how to allocate the budgeted funds to each investigation. The process for each administrative level can be quite different. Upper management must relate the performance of security investigations to the organization's critical mission and the risks associated with it. For example, upper management could determine, based on records of incidents over prior years and existing security vulnerabilities, that the risk of a violent attack on an employee on the organization's grounds is extremely low and therefore allocate very little budget to personnel who have investigative expertise or to equipment that would be used in response to such an incident. The administrator, on the other hand, must allocate resources on a case-by-case basis. For example, the administrator must respond quickly and without much regard for budget to the mass murder of employees, and, if appropriate resources are not available within the organization, must engage external agencies and personnel to assist in that investigation.

COLLABORATION WITH OUTSIDE RESOURCES   Most organizations, whether public or private, are not large enough to have all of the different types of expertise or resources necessary for all security incidents to which it may need to respond within a given period of time. Thus, administrators must determine whether outside technical experts, consultants, or other security service personnel with equipment or expertise are needed for particular investigations. Many small organizations, for example, may decide to outsource the entire security operation or certain portions of it, for example, computer and network security, on a routine basis.

The investigation of many security incidents also requires collaboration between security services in the private sector and public law enforcement. Many fraud investigations start within a company, but the evidence uncovered goes to a prosecutor. A good working relationship between the corporate fraud department and local and federal law enforcement is essential.

Charles Bock headed the Corporate Fraud Department at Chase Manhattan Bank, now J.P. Morgan Chase & Co., for many years. Charlie took pride, and rightfully so, in the strong working relationship his department personnel had with federal, state, and local law enforcement. He referred to this relationship as "the Chase way." Such partnerships between private sector security departments and law enforcement have increased significantly in recent years. Some of those partnerships have been supported by legislation or used as models.

For example, the New York City office of the U.S. Secret Service, under the leadership of Agent Robert Weaver, formed the New York Electronic Crime Task Force (NYECTF), a partnership of law enforcement, public and private sector organizations, and academic institutions. NYECTF and other regional ECTFs meet on a quarterly basis for information-sharing and networking purposes. The success of this model is reflected in the daily public–private collaboration on specific investigations. The USA PATRIOT Act provides for the development of additional regional electronic crime task forces modeled after the NYECTF. Another partnership model is the FBI's Infraguard program.

STRATEGY   Each organization must develop an investigative strategy that best fits the investigative responsibilities of its security department. We discuss this concept in further detail later in this chapter.

Because investigations may involve different targets (e.g., physical, financial, and digital), each of which requires a different investigative process or strategy, it may be necessary to establish teams of investigators prepared to respond to a specific target. For example, the U.S. Computer Emergency Readiness Team (US-CERT), which is now under the Department of Homeland Security National Cyber Security Division, is responsible for analyzing and coordinating a response to security incidents within civilian agencies of the federal government.

The Department of Defense maintains a Computer Emergency Response Team (DOD-CERT) to coordinate the response to security incidents involving the military, and the National Infrastructure Protection Center (NIPC), which is now under the Federal Bureau of Investigation, is responsible for an incident response to attacks on critical infrastructures. The government-funded Computer Emergency Response Team Coordination Center (CERT-CC) at Carnegie-Mellon University serves as a resource and coordination center for information on various forms of computer and network attacks, responses, and recoveries. Many public agencies and private businesses maintain their own computer emergency response team (CERT) or computer incident response team (CIRT) to handle computer and network security incidents.

After the overall responsibilities for security investigations have been determined, security personnel must implement that policy by hiring appropriate personnel, allocating appropriate facilities, and acquiring equipment. Additionally, the security service unit must determine its policies and procedures for conducting investigations. In the case of most security incidents, very little time exists to consider how the department will respond to an incident. The general parameters that are applicable to all incident responses should be established, documented, and subjected to rigorous internal training.

Incident Detection

Organizations must have in place policies and procedures to detect security incidents. Detection may occur in different ways. A physical assault may be detected in real time (as it is occurring) by personal observation of co-workers or by closed-circuit TV (CCTV) when an employee remains at the facility after hours. The theft of physical property, such as a laptop computer, may be discovered in real time by an observant patrol officer or CCTV. However, the detection of most criminal incidents occurs hours, days, weeks, and sometimes years after the event.

Fraudulent acts typically are not detected in real time. The discovery of a fraud is more often the result of information relayed by an informant or the examination of financial documents and records by an internal auditor or forensic accountant. However, with appropriate technology, some frauds can be detected as they are occurring. For example, credit card companies utilize fraud-scoring technology to determine whether a potential card transaction is fraudulent. The technology uses a three- to five-second pause time between the swipe of the card at the merchant's point-of-sale terminal and the determination to authorize the transaction.

Computer and network security incidents may be detected in real time if the organization has appropriate firewall, antivirus, and intrusion detection technology and is actively monitoring network use on a twenty-four-hour-a-day, seven-days-a-week basis. However, as we repeatedly tell our students, there is no such thing as perfect security. Despite the best technology and expert personnel available, security incidents nevertheless happen without detection in real time. In those instances, detection may not occur until examination of the audit trail left on a particular computer or network server by trained security personnel or computer forensic investigators.

In many cases, the personnel or company engaged to detect an incident does not have the responsibility to investigate it. A procedure must be in place to inform security personnel that an incident has occurred. That procedure should include a standard checklist of information that will be essential to the incident responder: What incident occurred, when it occurred, who witnessed it, where it occurred, and so on.

Response Preparation

Upon notification of an incident, a single investigator responds, or in a major case, a response team must be formed and activated. The investigator or response team must conduct a preliminary examination of the scene or incident and develop a strategy for its investigation. That strategy typically requires the determination of an orderly step-by-step process and the one of several different approaches or courses of action to implement. The determination involves the following processes:

1. *Witness interviews* involve talking to witnesses and canvassing the area for persons who may have seen the event.

2. *Interrogations of employees and suspects* must follow certain rules depending on the type of investigation and organization as well as the prevailing union contract or work rules. With respect to government employees or investigations by government personnel, the Fifth and Sixth Amendments, Miranda rule, and exclusionary rule are important. Defendants in a criminal case have Fifth and Sixth Amendment protections against testifying against themselves in a hearing, courtroom, or interrogation setting. The Miranda rule, which was established by the U.S. Supreme Court in 1966 all revised significantly in 2010, requires government investigators to cease the questioning of suspects in custodial settings. The suspect exercises either the right to remain silent or to speak with an attorney. In some states, Miranda extends to cases in which police question a suspect who is represented by counsel in another unrelated criminal case.

   The exclusionary rule is also important in this context because with some exceptions, it forbids the admission in a criminal proceeding, of evidence found to have been illegally obtained. In many organizations, specific work rules and labor contracts may protect the rights of employees during the course of an internal investigation.

3. *The incident scene* is "owned" by investigative personnel called to that scene for the purpose of collecting and securing evidence. When evidence exists outside the scene, government personnel, including personnel who are not sworn law enforcement officers, must comply with the requirements of the Fourth Amendment. Unless government security personnel are authorized by agency policy or work rules to search without a warrant, they must contact a law enforcement officer to obtain a search warrant to conduct a search.

4. *Examination or testing of machinery, products, or personal items* is a common practice in security investigations to utilize the services of trained analysts to examine the crime scene and evidence obtained at it or elsewhere. For example, mechanical engineers are frequently employed to reconstruct what occurred during motor vehicle accidents suspected of involving criminal activity. Forensic scientists are called to crime scenes to take evidence samples and analyze them in the forensic laboratory. Forensic experts and analysts examine computer hard drives and other electronic devices for evidence of criminal activity.

5. *Video or physical surveillance* may be used in fraud cases to catch the person in the act. "Sting" operations (e.g., in which law enforcement personnel establish their own "swap shop" to catch the criminal who is attempting to fence stolen goods) are utilized. Small camera devices installed in clocks, pictures in ceilings, and so on are used to photograph the transaction. Computer security personnel also can create their version of a sting operation called a *honeypot*, which is designed to attract the person intending to victimize a Web site.

6. *Eavesdropping devices* may be necessary in major cases to record conversations between a person and a target or between co-conspirators. A special warrant is required when the parties to the conversation have no idea that it is being recorded. In other cases, a person may be wired with a recording device to obtain damaging testimony from a suspect. In this instance, a warrant is not required because one or more of the parties knows that the conversation is being recorded.

7. *Conducting undercover operations* is somewhat related to eavesdropping. Although undercover operations usually are conducted by law enforcement personnel for organized and youth gang crimes, they also are utilized for intelligence gathering in both the public (e.g., Central Intelligence Agency) and private sectors. This investigative technique is

particularly useful in private organizations for internal fraud investigations designed to identify instances of employee dishonesty, sexual harassment, and corporate espionage. Such investigation procedures do not run afoul of the law except in unusual cases of entrapment (the act of inducing a person to commit a crime) or breach of an employee's contractual rights.

Certain forms of undercover, or covert, operations can be troublesome, however. Private organizations and governments employ undercover operatives to gather intelligence on competitors. Certain foreign governments engage in this process because the government owns or controls the business operation.

There is a point at which competitive intelligence activities, which are legal, become economic espionage, which is illegal (*see* 18 U.S.C. § § 1831, 1832). That point is when gathering competitive intelligence is performed covertly. There is no criminal problem (we'll leave the ethical issue aside for the moment), for example, when one grocery store sends one of its employees to a competitor store armed with a miniature bar code reader for the purpose of scanning prices of items on the shelves. There is, however, a problem when the employee of Store A is directed to apply for an office position at Store B to learn its pricing and advertising plan for the next two months. That information is proprietary in nature and, by federal law and the law of most states, a trade secret. The covert theft of that information is a crime; the individual and Store A are the perpetrators.

8. *Profiling* is the "process of inferring the personality characteristics of individuals responsible for committing criminal acts" (Turvey, 2002: 1). It is a psychological assessment of characteristics based on information collected at crime scenes that is used to develop the profile, "the set of defined characteristics that are likely to be shared by criminals who commit a particular type of crime" (Shinder and Tittel, 2002: 98). The investigative method of profiling has developed a bad reputation recently because of the improper use of racial characteristics as a profile for vehicle and traffic stops and subsequent searches for narcotics. Profiling, however, can be an effective and powerful investigative technique in certain types of investigations (e.g., serial homicides, cyber crimes, and fraud). The FBI utilized inductive profiling methodology to develop its computer crime adversarial matrix, which categorizes computer crimes by four general characteristics: organizational, operational, behavioral, and resource (Icove, Seger, and VonStorch, 1995: 68–69). Some common characteristics of cyber criminals are:

   • At least a minimal amount of technical savvy
   • Disregard for the law, or a feeling of being above the law
   • Active fantasy life
   • Risk taking and sense of control
   • Strong motivation (Shinder and Tittel, 2002)

   Similar profile characteristics have been established for a disparate variety of crimes such as rape, burglary, and fraud. The use of a profile or the assistance of a profiler is useful when the amount of evidence of the crime under investigation is scant or when the evidence, though voluminous, does not point to a specific suspect.

9. *Data mining* is an information extraction process seeking to identify hidden facts in databases. Because law enforcement and certain private industry groups are engaged in the process of information sharing, the ability to mine the data that may exist in different databases and in different forms will become critical to investigations, especially those related to economic crime, cyber crime, and terrorist-tracking investigations. For example, financial institutions are required to file suspicious activity reports with the Financial Crime

Enforcement Network (FinCEN), part of the Treasury Department. The ability to extract data from reports that make connections to terrorist activity, money laundering, and other crimes is essential for both proactive and reactive purposes.

10. *Seizure and audit of records and digital evidence* from a suspect or third party or requiring a third party to produce the evidence for investigative purposes may be necessary in addition to a search for evidence. Once seized or produced, the evidence can be examined by forensic accountants, scientists, and computer examiners in the laboratory. Such records or evidence may be obtained by a search warrant or subpoena issued by a court, grand jury, prosecutor, or administrative agency (e.g., Internal Revenue Service, and Securities and Exchange Commission). In a grand jury proceeding, a person may be required to bring in files specified under the authority of a grand jury subpoena. A subpoena need not be issued by a court. A prosecutor can issue a subpoena which directs the person served to produce evidence at a time and place designated in the subpoena. Failure to appear or produce the items requested often results in a contempt proceeding and imprisonment.

Investigation

We have discussed the investigative processes that are common to public and private organizations in the preceding pages. At this point, we discuss unique fraud and computer crime investigations conducted by private and public organizations. We would be remiss, however, if we did not discuss one form of investigation that is critical to every public and private organization—the background investigation.

BACKGROUND INVESTIGATIONS   Background investigations are proactive in nature; they are designed to prevent a security incident and fraud on the public or private sector organization. In many organizations—military and sworn law enforcement, for example—background investigations are required. They also are required for certain transactions and in certain industries. For example, the employees of private businesses who will be performing work in classified areas under government contract must undergo background investigations and obtain security clearances. Financial institutions must implement customer identification programs and perform enhanced *due diligence,* which are the fancy terms in the USA PATRIOT Act referring to background investigation, whenever a customer opens a new account or in the event of a suspicious activity. Background investigations also are required for permits to carry a pistol and for licensing as a private investigator and for insurance purposes in certain occupations. For example, because they must be bonded by insurers, bank employees, such as tellers and cashiers, must submit to background investigations before they are employed.

Background investigations can be preliminary in nature (e.g., checking to see if an individual's fingerprint indicates a criminal history) or complex (e.g., a lengthy process that includes interviews with all known associates, including all teachers since the first grade and all previous employers and co-workers). The authors frequently are interviewed regarding the character and habits of current and former students seeking internships or employment. A background investigation may also include polygraph, drug, and psychological testing.

Background investigations also should be conducted whenever an organization decides to outsource certain operations, especially security operations, to another company or individual. Because the outsourced company has access to proprietary information, it should be screened as thoroughly as the company's own employees are screened.

Criminal Investigations by Law Enforcement

FOURTH AMENDMENT IMPLICATIONS   The Fourth Amendment to the Constitution prohibits unreasonable searches and seizures by federal government personnel. However, by virtue of the Fourteenth Amendment, the privacy protections of the Fourth Amendment have been extended to searches and seizures conducted by state and local government personnel and security services personnel exercising law enforcement powers. The Fourth Amendment does not apply to private sector investigators unless they are acting as agents of the government. Because an unreasonable search and seizure can result in the exclusion of evidence from admission at trial, as well as charges of criminal liability by the personnel who conducted it and civil proceedings for damages against the personnel and employer, an overview of Fourth Amendment law and its application to the investigative process is important to security administrators.

As previously stated, the Fourth Amendment prohibits only *unreasonable* seizures. It provides:

The right of the people to be secure in their persons, houses, papers, and effects, against unreasonable searches and seizures, shall not be violated, and no Warrants shall issue, but upon probable cause, supported by Oath or affirmation, and particularly describing the place to be searched, and the persons or things to be seized.

An unreasonable search is one conducted without a warrant issued by a neutral magistrate or judge upon showing probable cause. *Probable cause* in this context means that facts and circumstances "are sufficient to warrant a person of reasonable caution to believe that seizable objects are located at the place to be searched" (Whitebread and Slobogin, 2000: 150). As noted in Chapter 2, the authority to apply to the court for a warrant is conferred only on personnel with law enforcement powers. Government personnel lacking law enforcement status do not have the authority to apply for a warrant, but, as will be noted, may nevertheless be able to conduct a warrantless search.

Law enforcement officials may obtain special investigatory powers in connection with search warrants such as a "sneak-and-peek" warrant. For example, this warrant is used when it can be shown that the execution of a regular search warrant would endanger the life or safety of an officer or other individual or result in flight from prosecution, witness or evidence tampering, or otherwise seriously jeopardize an investigation. In this instance, officers can enter and search premises without notifying the owner or possessor of the property and provide notice of the entry at a later time (18 U.S.C. § 3103a). According to the same source, although officers can surreptitiously search, they cannot seize anything unless there is a "reasonable necessity." In instances when it would be dangerous for officers to announce their presence before entering the premises, the court may authorize a "no-knock" entry (18 U.S.C. § 3109), the type of search portrayed on TV when officers knock down the entry door.

Several investigatory methods do not rise to the level of a search or do not require probable cause as the basis for the intrusion:

- **Stop and frisk** This is the brief detention of a person in a public place and pat down of the person's outer clothing for weapons. It may be conducted when a law enforcement officer has *reasonable suspicion* that criminal activity may be afoot and that the individual is armed and may present a danger to the officer or others (*Terry v. Ohio*, 1968). Reasonable suspicion is less than probable cause; it is based on "specific and articulable facts" that would lead an officer to infer that criminal activity is afoot (*Terry v. Ohio*).
- **Protective sweep** This is a quick look ("cursory inspection") through the premises where an arrest is being made in cases when the officer has reasonable suspicion that other persons who could cause harm to law enforcement personnel may be present.

- **Business inspections** Certain industries are subject to inspection by government officials. Examples include workplace inspections for safety purposes conducted pursuant to the Occupational Safety and Health Act (OSHA) and inspections of liquor establishments, auto junkyards, sanitary wastes (landfills), restaurants, and meat packing facilities. Such inspections may be conducted by government personnel who are not necessarily law enforcement officers. Warrants are not required, and the inspector does not require probable cause to conduct the inspection. However, the inspections must be authorized by legislation, limited in scope to their purposes, and conducted during normal business hours. In many instances, the legislative regulation must limit the number of inspections within a specific time period.

Government security personnel can conduct a search without a warrant in the following exceptions recognized by the courts:

- **Consent** Any person who has ownership or possessory control over the premises and who is of suitable age and discretion consents to the investigation. A guest residing overnight in an apartment may have sufficient possessory control to consent to its search.
- **Plain view** Items observed in plain view by an officer who is where she has a lawful right to be can be searched.
- **Incident to lawful arrest** Items that are on or within the reasonable range of access of the person arrested can be searched and/or seized.
- **Hot pursuit** This enables law enforcement officials to chase a person, who they have probable cause to believe has committed or is committing a crime, and to follow that person into premises where some exigency exists such as the potential use of a weapon or the destruction of evidence.
- **Exigent circumstances** Law enforcement officials need not obtain a warrant when it is suspected that evidence may be destroyed or altered if they do not seize it.
- **Automobile exception** Because of the mobility of vehicles, boats, and so on, police without a warrant may search a vehicle or boat that has been stopped lawfully if there is probable cause to believe that it contains evidence of a crime.
- **Inventory** When property has been impounded, it may be searched without a warrant to prepare an inventory of items within it. The inventory search must be conducted as part of the law enforcement agency's routine inventory procedure, not as a pretext for the discovery of evidence.
- **Border searches** Government security personnel authorized to conduct border searches need not obtain a warrant before proceeding with a search.
- **Airports** The screening of airline passengers, their luggage, and air cargo has become the responsibility of the Transportation Security Administration (TSA), which is under the Department of Homeland Security. The TSA also is responsible for the security of the transportation of hazardous materials and other forms of public transportation.

WARRANTLESS WORKPLACE SEARCHES BY GOVERNMENT SECURITY PERSONNEL   The Fourth Amendment to the U.S. Constitution prohibits the warrantless search of a work area for which the employee has a reasonable expectation of privacy. Private sector employees have a reasonable expectation of privacy in their workplace area unless they share work space with fellow employees or members of the public frequently access the work area.

Public sector employees have a much more limited expectation of privacy. The principal issue is whether, based on actual office practices and procedures, it is reasonable for the employee to expect that no other person would enter the work area (*O'Connor v. Ortega*, 1987; see, CCIPS, 2009).

The search by government security personnel of public and private workplaces presents specific problems. As a general rule, law enforcement officials may search a private sector workplace if they have the consent of the employer or a co-worker who has common use of that space (CCIPS, 2009). For example, if two employees work different shifts but share the same desk, the co-worker can consent to its search. The same would be true if five accountants had access to the same filing cabinets in a particular area. Any one of the five could consent to their search. The issue is whether an employee has a reasonable expectation of privacy with respect to the place to be searched.

The search of a public employee's workplace presents some different issues. Because the Fourth Amendment applies to all government personnel, a search by a government agency's security personnel must comply with that amendment. Thus, the employer (e.g., the employee's supervisor) cannot consent to the search because the employer is the party conducting the search. The critical issue in such cases is whether the public employee has a reasonable expectation of privacy in the assigned workplace. The general rule is that public employees enjoy a reasonable expectation of privacy if they expect that others (e.g., co-employees and members of the public) will not enter their space (*O'Connor v. Ortega*, 1987).

From a managerial perspective, an employee's expectation of privacy can be prescribed by official agency policies that authorize the employer's access to the workplace or that expressly limit employee privacy. Furthermore, assuming that a warrantless search by security personnel at a government agency would not violate the employee's privacy, the search must be conducted for a work-related purpose, and it must be justified at its inception and limited in scope (*O'Connor v. Ortega*). This means that security personnel must possess some reasonable basis to believe that the workplace contains evidence of work-related misconduct and that the scope of the search is related to the nature of the misconduct.

PRIVATE WORKPLACE SEARCH BY EMPLOYER'S SECURITY PERSONNEL   The search of a private workplace by the employer does not violate the Fourth Amendment unless the employer is acting as an agent of the government for purposes of conducting that search. Thus, such searches are permissible unless the employer is restricted by contract or agreement with the employee.

CYBER CRIME INVESTIGATIONS   Cyber crimes may be divided into two types: crimes that can be committed only by a computer or computer system on another computer or computer system and traditional crimes such as securities or credit card fraud committed through the use of a computer. Cyber crimes in the first category include the unauthorized hacking into the computer or network of another for the purpose of altering, removing, or destroying data or damaging the operation of the computer or system by installing a virus, worm, Trojan horse, logic bomb, or some other form of malware (i.e., malicious computer code or software), as well as attacking on Web sites by modifying their appearance or conducting a distributed denial of service attack to interfere with public access to a Web site or to render it inaccessible. This category also includes acts of cyber terrorism (i.e., cyber attacks against military sites or parts of the country's infrastructure, such as power grid, utilities, transportation, and finance).

Cyber crimes also include many traditional crimes committed for numerous years in the physical world that also can be committed (and frequently more successfully) by the use of a computer. That category of cyber crime includes credit card fraud, trafficking in child pornography, securities fraud, identity theft, copyright infringement, economic espionage, insurance fraud, health care fraud, bank fraud, and money laundering.

Cyber crime investigations are unique because of the digital medium that is used for such crimes and the fact that investigators, especially law enforcement personnel, are not necessarily experienced in the use of the technology. The gap is closing, however, with the implementation of cyber crime training programs by law enforcement agencies and professional organizations such as the High Tech Crime Investigators Association and the Computer Security Institute.

Because cyber crime investigations involve matters or places in which individuals have an expectation of privacy, Congress has enacted laws designed to protect the privacy of communications and transactions in cyberspace. The most important of those protections are summarized in the following sections.

WIRETAP   A wiretap involves the interception of a live communication. Federal law prohibits the interception of wire and electronic communications by law enforcement, government personnel who are not law enforcement, or private individuals and organizations unless a party to the communication consents to the wiretap or a court order authorizes it. Because of the highly private nature of phone conversations, Congress prohibits wiretapping unless the applicant can establish (1) probable cause to believe that the interception will reveal evidence of a federal felony or state felony offense that is defined in the wiretap law, (2) normal investigative procedures have been attempted but failed or such procedures are unlikely to succeed or are too dangerous, (3) probable cause indicates the communication facility is being used in the commission of a crime, and (4) the surveillance will be conducted in a manner that minimizes the interception of communications that do not produce evidence of a crime (18 U.S.C. § 2518).

The statute prohibits the interception of both wire (e.g., telephone) and electronic (e.g., instant messaging and e-mail) communications unless a party to the communication has consented to the interception. Consent can take many forms. For example, when a banner appears on the screen of each employee's computer on the corporate network to the effect that communications will be monitored, use of the networked computer for future communications implies that consent has been given for the monitoring. Because the monitoring could involve viewing e-mail communications while in progress, the monitoring constitutes an interception of that communication.

Courts have for several years distinguished between the interception of the *contents* of communications, which is prohibited without a wiretap order, and the gathering of information related to live communications (e.g., the pen register, which records the outgoing phone numbers or IP addresses called by a monitored computer) (18 U.S.C. § 3127 [3]), and the trap and trace device, which records the address of incoming phone numbers or IP addresses to the suspect computer (18 U.S.C. § 3127 [4]). A trap and trace device would be utilized in the case of Internet mail communications because the mail "headers" contain both "to" and "from" information. In the case of a pen register and a trap and trace device, the law enforcement applicant must show that information that will be relevant to an ongoing investigation being conducted by that agency is likely to be obtained (18 U.S.C. § 3122 [b]).

Because the expectation of privacy is much lower for addresses as opposed to contents, the evidentiary showing necessary for an order authorizing a pen register or trap and trace is much lower than that required for a wiretap order. Additionally, amendments to the federal criminal code set forth in the USA PATRIOT Act now enable law enforcement personnel to obtain pen register and trap and trace warrants that are nationwide in scope (i.e., can be applied to any phone owned by a suspect rather than being limited to a specific phone number and that can follow a suspect from state to state).

The FBI claims to have the ability to "sniff" (capture and observe) live electronic communications using a software program initially named Carnivore, now called DCS-1000. According to the FBI, DCS-1000 has the ability to filter incoming and outgoing electronic data traffic, identify those communications covered by the court order, and ignore those that are irrelevant to the investigation (Britz, 2004). Additionally, DCS-1000 can be utilized either to act as a trap and trace device capturing only header information or to capture the contents of e-mail or network traffic, depending on the extent of court authorization (McNamara, 2003). We are most familiar with wiretaps on telephone conversations. The same principles apply, however, to electronic communications such as e-mail and instant messaging. Law enforcement cannot intercept the content of those communications using DCS-1000 or other similar technology without a wiretap order authorizing the interception.

SEARCH OF "STORED" COMMUNICATIONS The Electronic Communication Privacy Act (ECPA) also protects the privacy of wire and electronic communications that are in temporary storage. Electronic storage is the temporary and intermediate storage of an electronic communication incidental to its transmission (18 U.S.C. § 2510 [17]). For example, if someone sends an e-mail addressed to your Yahoo! e-mail account and you have not accessed your Yahoo! account to collect that e-mail, the communication is considered to be in temporary storage on the Yahoo! e-mail servers.

Two types of entities maintain temporary storage of electronic communications under the ECPA: an electronic communication service, which is any service to the public of wire or electronic communications including telephone carriers and Internet service providers such as AOL, MSN, Earthlink, and so on, and a remote computing service, which includes any business that provides data storage or processing services to the public by means of an electronic communications system.

Whether law enforcement is entitled to obtain information relating to a communication in electronic storage depends on whether the government seeks "basic subscriber information" (18 U.S.C. § 2510 [17]), customer transactional information, or contents.

One of the more expansive powers granted to law enforcement under the USA PATRIOT Act is the redefinition of what constitutes basic subscriber information. Before the Act, law enforcement was able to subpoena basic subscriber information from an Internet service provider (e.g., subscriber's name, address, local and long distance telephone toll billing records, telephone number, and length of service provided to the subscriber).

The PATRIOT Act added two critical types of information to the definition of basic subscriber information: the means and source of payment, including any credit card or bank account number, and any temporarily assigned network address. Those additions were designed to ensure that law enforcement officials could trace the origin of e-mail and instant messaging communications to locations such as cybercafés and other public areas such as public libraries and could more accurately determine the real identity of the suspect by obtaining credit card and bank account information. The common means of paying the monthly subscription fee to an Internet service provider is by charging it to a credit card or making an online debit to a bank account.

The ECPA applies only to electronic communications that are held in temporary storage by services available to the public. Thus, if the intended recipient of a communication has downloaded an e-mail to his computer on the corporate network, that communication is no longer in electronic storage, and the restrictions of the ECPA do not apply. Also, a corporate network administrator can monitor e-mail traffic flowing through network servers if such monitoring is necessary to protect the network (e.g., to detect whether the system is being intruded on for the purpose of installing viruses, worms, and other malware).

PRIVACY PROTECTION ACT   The Privacy Protection Act protects publishers from unreasonable searches and seizures. Because the creation and maintenance of a Web site is a form of publication, this act protects those sites as well as the traditional newspaper and magazine facilities.

FRAUD INVESTIGATIONS   Numerous crimes involve nonviolent fraudulent activity typically accompanied by some form of writing. Although the name of the fraudulent activity may vary from state to state, economic, or white-collar, crimes include mail, wire, insurance, securities, health care, auction, cellular, and credit card fraud; Ponzi and pyramid schemes; and occupational and employee frauds such as embezzlement, false statement frauds, bank fraud, and money laundering.

Although the apprehension of fraud perpetrators may require the deployment of armed investigations, the actual investigation does not. The investigation of many of these crimes involves many hours of financial document examination and analysis by specially trained investigators, many of whom are forensic accountants or fraud auditors. Also, these investigators need to be trained in the use of technology specifically designed to aid in fraud investigations such as link analysis programs (Analyst Notebook) and in auditing and data analysis software programs such as ACL and IDEA.

A common characteristic of cyber crime and fraud investigations is that both are usually detected by private organizations, which conduct the initial investigation. It is now common to find fraud investigation units and cyber crime investigation units in financial institutions and in many large businesses.

Evidence Preparation

An objective of any investigation is to gather information that will enable the investigator to determine how, when, where, and why an incident occurred and by whom it was perpetrated. The information gathered must be acquired legally and may be used for a variety of purposes. It may be determined at the conclusion of the investigation that the incident was an inadvertent breach of security policy. In such case, the information acquired during that investigation will be used internally to train employees to avoid such breaches but in all likelihood will not be used in a legal proceeding. However, security personnel did not know, when the investigation started, that legal proceedings would not be involved. The best practice is to treat every piece of information as though it will be evidence that can be used in court. If that practice is not followed, the failure to obtain and preserve evidence properly may result in unsuccessful legal proceedings, in which case the employer will be restricted to internal uses of the information.

We cannot possibly consider in this book all of the evidentiary rules that should be considered during the course of an investigation. It is important, however, to provide an overview regarding the rules that apply to security investigations. The primary evidentiary rule is the hearsay rule. *Hearsay* is any statement, oral or written, made outside of the courtroom that is offered as evidence by someone other than the person who made the statement. For example, a police officer responds to a vehicular accident, asks both drivers and the passengers what happened, and records the statements of the drivers and passengers in the accident report. A year later, the officer is called to testify regarding the investigation of the accident and while on the witness stand is asked what one of the passengers told her. The officer cannot testify to the passenger's statement because it was made outside the courtroom and one of the parties wants the statement admitted for its truth. Also, that portion of the accident report cannot be admitted as evidence because the recorded portion of the witness's statement is hearsay.

There are numerous exceptions to the hearsay rule. One of the more common ones is the business records rule, which allows the admission of hearsay statements recorded in a business record if the record was made in the ordinary course of business of the individual who recorded it, it was the duty of the person recording the statement to make such a record, and the record was made contemporaneously with the statement. Thus, a statement made by a person injured in an accident to a nurse in the hospital emergency room that is written into the hospital record may be admitted into evidence if the statement was relevant to the diagnosis and treatment to be provided by the nurse. Other exceptions to the hearsay rule that may apply to security investigations are:

- **Admissions and confessions.** The accused's statements acknowledging participation in the event at issue.
- **Dying declarations.** The victim's statements, made under the apprehension that he is about to die, concerning the event that caused the death.
- **Excited utterances.** The victim's statements typically made at or shortly after the event and without sufficient opportunity to conjure up the statement.
- **Prior inconsistent statements.** Statements made prior to the court proceedings that are inconsistent with the witness's testimony in court.
- **Prior consistent statements.** Statements made prior to the court proceedings that are consistent with the witness's testimony that are offered because this testimony is challenged as a recent fabrication.

Another evidentiary rule that is critical to investigations is the *chain of custody* rule. Whenever physical items are introduced as evidence in a legal proceeding, it must be shown that the evidence was in the continuous possession of the organization or its agents and that the item has not been tampered with since its acquisition. For example, items collected at the crime scene should be "bagged and tagged" with identifying marks and signatures, and records must be maintained with the date, times, and initials or signature of every individual (e.g., forensic technicians and detectives) who had access to the item before its admission in court. Adherence to this rule should be observed whether the custodian of the evidence is a law enforcement agency or the security department of a business.

Security service personnel often are required to testify in court regarding the investigation of an incident. As part of the investigative process, they must be trained in their role as witnesses and be aware of courtroom procedures. Very often cases are won or lost on the jury's perception of the witness's truthfulness, which in turn depends on the attitude and body language of the witness.

Finally, every stage of the investigation should be carefully documented. It often is necessary several years after the event to testify regarding details of the investigation or to make a presentation at a security training seminar concerning it. Careful documentation will enable security personnel to bring the investigation to a successful conclusion.

Lessons Learned

Regardless of whether the investigation leads to a successful prosecution or legal action for damages, it is essential to utilize information gathered during the investigation to reexamine security vulnerabilities, exposure to attacks, and the value of existing countermeasures designed to prevent or mitigate such attacks. This final stage is proactive in nature because it enables the organization to learn from its failure or mistake, to continually analyze its security policies and procedures, and to upgrade or make changes to prevent or mitigate the next crime or incident.

Summary

The investigation of crimes and security incidents serves an important function in proactive security administration. The successful completion of an investigation enables the administrator to identify the source and method of the attack as well as the internal vulnerability of the organization's security plan and procedures. Many concepts must be incorporated into the administration of a security investigation, including the preparation for the investigation in terms of budget and personnel and postinvestigation analysis. The success of an investigation depends on critical aspects of planning and collaboration between the public and private sectors.

Review Questions/Activities

1. Although investigations usually are considered to be reactive, describe two investigation methods that could be proactive and provide an example of each method.
2. Access the 2010 Report To the Nations at *www.acfe. com*. After reviewing the report, prepare a profile of the typical occupational fraudster. What did you consider in preparing the profile?
3. You are the director of the security services department in a medium-size retail business. What policy recommendations would you propose to upper management concerning the use of the company's networked computers to enable your department to conduct thorough background investigations?
4. A special agent of the FBI just appeared in the security department of your firm and informed you that an employee was suspected of downloading large volumes of child pornography onto the computer that he uses at work. The FBI agent has asked you to secure the computer, remove and bag the hard drive from the computer, and call the agent so that she can retrieve the evidence. As the director of security, what steps would you take to obtain the hard drive?
5. A Secret Service agent in the local field office has asked you as the director of security for your company to become a member of the regional Electronic Crime Task Force in your area. What benefits are there to such membership? Are there any drawbacks?
6. Discuss the meaning of electronic storage of communications. Why does the law treat the live transmission of electronic communications differently from electronic storage?

WebSearches

1. The Web site *www.htcia.com* is the site for the High Technology Crime Investigators Association. Review it, looking specifically for training and education provided by the association.
2. The U.S. Department of Justice, Computer Crimes and Intellectual Property Section, maintains a Web site containing a treasure of documents, articles, and other resources pertaining to computer crime, intellectual property crimes, and economic espionage. The site is at *www.cybercrime.gov*. Access it and locate the current manual for the search and seizure of electronic evidence. After locating the manual, review the material on the Electronic Communications Privacy Act and prepare a short paper describing the various types of electronic communications covered by the Act.
3. Access the Web site of International Association of Financial Crimes Investigators at *www.iafci.org*. Review the information publicly accessible on it, and prepare a brief report discussing the association's mission and objectives.
4. Access the Web site of the Association of Certified Fraud Examiners at *www.acfe.com*. Review the information available at this site, and prepare a brief report discussing the types of investigations conducted by fraud examiners.
5. Access the Web site of the National Association of Legal Investigators at *www.nalionline.org*. After reviewing the contents and resources in this site, briefly describe the principal functions a legal investigator should perform to qualify for full membership in the association.

References

Britz, Marjie. 2004. *Computer Forensics and Cyber Crime: An Introduction.* Upper Saddle River, N.J.: Prentice Hall.

Computer Crime and Intellectual Property Section (CCIPS), Department of Justice. 2009. "Searching and Seizing Computers and Obtaining Electronic Evidence in Criminal Investigations." Accessed May 10, 2010, at www.cybercrime.gov/ssmanual/ssmanual2009.pdf.

Computer Security Institute (CSI). 2008. "Thirteenth Annual Computer Crime and Security Survey." Accessed October 12, 2009, at *www.gocsi.com.*

Hollinger, Richard. 2009. *2008 National Retail Security Survey.* Accessed on May 11, 2010 at soccrim.clas.ufl.edu/criminology/srp/finalreport_2008.pdf.

Icove, David, Karl Seger, and William VonStorch. 1995. *Computer Crime: A Crimefighter's Handbook.* Sebastopol, Calif.: O'Reilly & Associates.

Mandia, Kevin, and Chris Prosise. 2001. *Incident Response: Investigating Computer Crime.* Berkeley, Calif.: Osborne/McGraw-Hill.

McNamara, Joel. 2003. *Secrets of Computer Espionage: Tactics and Countermeasures.* Indianapolis, Ind.: Wiley Publishing.

O'Connor v. Ortega, 480 U.S. 709, 107 S.Ct. 1492, 94 L.Ed.2d 714. 1987.

Price Waterhouse Coopers. 2009. "Global Economic Crime Survey." Accessed March 19, 201- at www.pwc.com/en_GX/gx/economic-crime-survey/pdf/global-economic-crime-survey-2009.pdf.

Shinder, Debra L., and Ed Tittel. 2002. *Scene of the Cybercrime: Computer Forensics Handbook,* Rockland, Mass.: Syngress Publishing.

Terry v. Ohio, 392 U.S. 1, 88 S.Ct. 1868, 20 L.Ed.2d 889. 1968.

Turvey, Brent E. 2002. *Criminal Profiling,* 2nd ed. San Diego: Academic Press.

Whitebread, Charles H., and Christopher Slobogin. 2000. *Criminal Procedure: An Analysis of Cases and Concepts,* 4th ed. New York: Foundation Press.

9

■ ■ ■

Emergency Management and Homeland Security

KEY TERMS

anthrax, C-BNE, CBP, Center for Disease Control, CIKR, command center, emergency management, emergency planning, FEMA, haz-mat, homeland security, ICE, incident command, mitigation, natural vs. man-made, nerve agents, NIMS, potential threat element, tabletop exercise, WMD.

INTRODUCTION

Events in this past decade have shown how vulnerable our economic, political, and social infrastructure is in withstanding terrorist attacks and man-made and natural disasters. In the late 1990s, the authors dealt with a regional ice storm that knocked down trees, blocked roads, and destroyed the electrical grid system. Thus there was no heat, mail, manufacturing, agricultural, and social activities, and transportation in the region for about two weeks. Residents had to endure temperatures that hovered about zero during this time.

Within the past decade many other areas in the United States have experienced the same due to tornados, floods, earthquakes, and forest fires. The terrorist attacks of 9/11 not only impacted the airline and financial systems; there was also a major psychological impact based on the large loss of life and the destruction of major landmarks. The damages caused by hurricanes Katrina and Rita in 2005 continue to have an impact on communities along the Alabama, Louisiana and Mississippi coastlines, and the City of New Orleans, not only because of the devastation caused by the storm and flooding but also the lingering issue of the inability of state and federal governments to rapidly respond to the crisis. Thus, homeland security and emergency management have become major missions for security services on the local, state, and federal level. In this chapter we review the nature of homeland security and the overall operational structure of emergency management. Attention is given to the U.S. Department of Homeland Security, which is the lead agency that plans for and responds to these events.

OVERVIEW

Homeland security is the general term given for all domestic and international activities to protect people and property in the United States from terrorism.

The Department of Homeland Security was formed in response to the 9/11 terrorist attacks and is responsible for the following:

- Preventing terrorist attacks in the United States
- Reducing the nation's vulnerability to terrorism
- Minimizing damage and assisting in the recovery of attacks that occur
- Ensuring that the overall economic security of the United States is not diminished by efforts, activities, and programs aimed at securing the homeland.
- Monitoring connections between illegal drug trafficking and terrorism. (Homeland Security Act of 2002)

As presented in the *History of the Department* (2009), homeland security activities before 2001 were spread across over forty federal agencies. In February 2001, the U.S. Commission on Homeland Security (called the Hart Rudman Commission) had recommended merging these efforts into a National Homeland Security Agency. Soon after the attacks of September 11, President Bush announced the formation of the Office of Homeland Security and appointed former Governor Thomas Ridge as secretary. Executive Order 13228 was issued which established the Office of Homeland Security as part of the Executive Office and charged to create a national strategy for counterterrorism against attacks. The order also created the Homeland Security Council to prepare national policies for homeland security for the president. Additionally, a Homeland Security Advisory Council was established to bring together representatives from the public and private sectors to provide advice on homeland security matters. Organizational and legislative efforts to create a department continued for the remainder of 2001 and well into 2002. The federal budget for 2003 proposed some $37.7 billion for homeland security efforts including border security, bioterrorism prevention, first responder equipment and training, and technology.

On June 6, 2002, President Bush formally announced the creation of a cabinet-level Office of Homeland Security. This required the merger of twenty-two agencies and over 180,000 employees. As discussed by White and Collins (2006), the Homeland Security Act merged various agencies and their missions into five organized directorates according to the following plan:

Border and Transportation Security

Agencies in this group include the U.S. Customs Service, the Immigration and Naturalization Service, Federal Protective Service, Transportation Security Administration, the Federal Law Enforcement Training Center, Animal and Plant Health Inspection Service, and Office of Domestic Preparedness. Together, these agencies had a common mission to protect the nation's borders and dealing with persons who attempt to enter or remain in the United States illegally. The agencies in this group also deal with international trade and agriculture issues.

Soon afterward, a number of organizational revisions were further put into place. The Bureau of Border Security became the Bureau of Immigration and Custom Enforcement, often called ICE, taking parts of the Immigration and Naturalization Service, the Customs Service, and Federal Protective Service. ICE is responsible for enforcing immigration and customs laws. The Office of Detention and Removal for ICE often receives much media attention as it is responsible for removal and deportation of illegal aliens. ICE officers conduct periodic raids on business employing illegal aliens or receive apprehended prisoners from the CBP. Pending immigration law proceedings, these persons are then secured at a number of ICE detention facilities in Arizona, California, Texas, and western New York. Criminal defendants are secured at federal detention facilities.

The National Security Division for ICE is responsible for the investigation of cases related to the illegal importation of weapons of mass destruction and munitions. The Financial Investigations Unit investigates cases dealing with money laundering, cash smuggling, and counterfeit goods trafficking. The Smuggling/Public Safety Division investigates organizations involved with human trafficking. Its subunits include the Federal Air Marshal Service, which provides security on commercial flights, and the Federal Protective Service, which provides security for approximately 9,000 federal facilities.

The U.S. Customs Service was renamed the Customs and Border Protection (CBP) incorporating inspection tasks from Customs, Immigration, the Border Patrol, and Department of Agriculture. At this time CBP has about 41,000 personnel that are assigned to border protection along U.S. land areas and major points of entry. In addition to deployment of personnel, the agency uses a number of data banks that review travelers arriving to the United States which include the Advance Passenger Information System and the United States Visitor and Immigrant Status Indication Technology (USVisit), and the Student and Exchange Visitor Information System (SEVIS). For air and sea cargoes bound for the United States there are several computer systems that provide advance information on cargoes coming to the United States including the Automated Commercial Environment System and the Automated Export System. The agency also has an intelligence function that analyzes threats and information on suspicious person and cargoes. Border patrol operations remain a major mission of the agency. In addition to normal patrol techniques, technology is applied including the use of cameras and sensing systems, remote video, and unmanned aerial vehicles.

The Transportation Security Administration, which was formally a part of the Department of Transportation, became responsible for security at all airports which included passenger and baggage screening. As discussed earlier in this book, all security operations which were held in private contract agencies became federalized with TSA employees. The general issues related to airline and general cargo security are discussed in Chapter 7.

Emergency Preparedness and Response

The focus of this grouping of agencies is for preparation and response to terrorist attacks. The most notable agency in this directorate remains the Federal Emergency Management Agency (FEMA) which is discussed further in this chapter. Other agencies in this grouping include the Strategic National Stockpile and the National Disaster Medical System, Nuclear Incident Response Team, Domestic Emergency Support Teams, and the National Domestic Preparedness Office. The Transportation Security Agency was also added to this grouping.

Science and Technology Directorate

This area was first named the Chemical, Biological, Radiological, and Nuclear (CBRN) Countermeasures. The goal of this grouping was to develop technologies to both prevent and respond to terrorist attacks. These include CBRN Countermeasures, Environment Measurement Laboratory, National Biological Weapons Defense Analysis Center, and the Plum Island Animal Disease Center. The Cyber Security Research and Development Center was established in March 2004 to address cyber security research and developments.

Information Analysis and Infrastructure Protection Directorate

This grouping was tasked with intelligence gathering and analysis of information related to potential terrorist attacks against the United States and protecting the nation's infrastructure including cyber security. Agencies under this umbrella are the Federal Computer Incident Response Center, National Communications System, National Infrastructure Protection Center, and the Energy Security and Assurance Program. This group works closely with the Central Intelligence Agency, the FBI, the National Security Administration, and other intelligence groups. As will be discussed, this directorate was tasked with developing a national infrastructure protection plan to protect the nation's critical assets.

The management of this new endeavor would be coordinated by a fifth directorate headed by the Under Secretary of Management. This grouping was responsible for budgeting, operations, public information, and human resources. A legislative proposal for this new agency was prepared in July and sent to both houses for review. The House of Representatives passed the measure in July 26, 2002, and the Senate version passed on November 19, 2002. On November 25, the bill was signed into law and March 1, 2003, was set for the new department to become operational. The final measure signed into law brought into the Department of Homeland Security the United States Coast Guard and the Secret Service.

In July 2005, the Department underwent an organizational review process which eliminated the directorates for Border and Transportation Security, Informational Analysis and Infrastructure Protection, and Emergency Response and Preparedness. The current organizational makeup is presented in Figure 9-1.

The heads of FEMA, CBP, TSA, ICE, and other entities today directly report to the secretary. Two new areas headed by an undersecretary were established in the areas of Policy and Preparedness. Policy was charged with reviewing overall operational policies for the department while Preparedness combined the chief medical officers, fire administration, and cyber and telecommunications. Between 2005 and 2009 there were further organizational changes. Due to the criticism of the federal government's response to Hurricanes Katrina and Rita the Undersecretary of Federal Emergency Management became the administrator of FEMA and principal advisor to the President and the Homeland Security Council.

Discussions on the Department of Homeland Security invariably bring forth the position and role of the Secret Service and the Coast Guard. Although part of the Department, the two agencies are considered as independent entities as they have a number of other duties linked to their historical missions. What follows is an overview of these two agencies as related to security services and emergency management.

The United States Secret Service

First formed in 1864, the Secret Service was created to deal with the flood of counterfeit money brought on by the Civil War. After the assassination of President McKinley in Buffalo, New York, in 1901, its duties were expanded to provide executive protection for elected presidents, their immediate families, and foreign dignitaries visiting the United States. This also includes investigating threats and securing major events if the president or a foreign dignitary is in attendance.

The Secret Service is also responsible for protecting the White House, the home of the Vice President and residences of foreign dignitaries. Perimeter security of foreign embassies is carried out by the uniformed branch of the department. These protection activities require the use of intelligence analysis and threat review. Today its mission has further expanded in dealing with

U.S. DEPARTMENT OF HOMELAND SECURITY

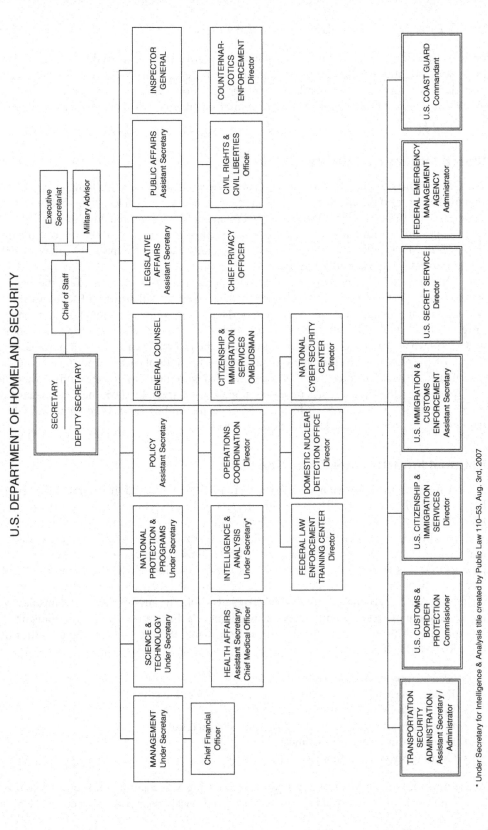

* Under Secretary for Intelligence & Analysis title created by Public Law 110–53, Aug. 3rd, 2007

FIGURE 9-1 Current organizational chart for Department of Homeland Security. *Source:* Department of Homeland Security (2008).

business fraud, especially those cases brought on by Internet commerce, credit card use, and theft of personal identity (United States Secret Service Strategic Plan, 2009). The Service has also provided training and recommendations related to school safety. The overall relationship to Homeland Security is obvious with regard to international terrorism and protecting the president against attacks.

United States Coast Guard

The Coast Guard is both a military and civilian service organization with a long history. In 1795 Congress authorized the creation of a Revenue Marine with its principle assignment to intercept smugglers. In 1915 it was combined with the Lifesaving Service and renamed the United States Coast Guard. In wartime it operates as a department of the Navy in protecting coastal areas. In peacetime it has both a military and civilian missions that involve maritime safety, environmental protection, and law enforcement.

Operating a fleet of helicopters, patrol boats, buoy tenders, and ice breakers, the agency is responsible for protecting U.S. coastal waters that abound the Atlantic and Pacific oceans, the Great Lakes, and inland ports on major rivers. There are seventeen regional districts that are divided into Atlantic and Pacific Ocean operations. Its role has expanded to drug interdiction in what is known as the "Transit Zone" which includes the Eastern Pacific, the Gulf of Mexico, and Caribbean. In 2008, it intercepted approximately 33,000 pounds of cocaine and 20,000 pounds of marijuana (U.S. Coast Guard, 2009). It is also charged with intercepting illegal immigrants that attempt to enter the United States in vessels along coastal areas. In 2005, the Coast Guard was widely praised for its rescue efforts by boat and helicopter to thousands of residents stranded in their homes by flooding caused by Hurricane Katrina.

National Infrastructure Protection Plan

As outlined in the Homeland Security Act and later defined in Homeland Security Presidential Directive 7, the Department was charged to develop a National Infrastructure Protection Plan. The purpose was to review actions to deter threats, mitigate vulnerabilities, and to minimize consequences associated with terrorist attacks or other man-made or national disasters. The focus of the plan is on Critical Infrastructure and Key Resources (CIKR) that involve security, health, and economic activities. CIKR, as defined by the plan and commonly used in the field, are physical and virtual systems and assets that are vital to the nations security, economy, public health or safety, and the environment. The incapacity or the destruction of these systems and assets would have a dire impact on federal, state, or local jurisdictions (National Infrastructure Protection Plan, 2009: 109). Planning activities here include the following:

- Security protocols and target hardening
- Building resiliency and redundancy for critical operations
- Initiating active or passive countermeasures
- Preparing and conducting related training and exercises
- Implementing cyber security measures
- Creating business continuity planning

At this time the Office of Critical Infrastructure is working with state and local agencies to review critical infrastructures that could be major targets and review their risk management plans and programs. Agencies involved in the Department of Homeland Security must address a wide area of concerns as shown by the following examples:

- Transportation Security Administration—postal, shipping
- Transportation Security Administration and Coast Guard—transportation systems
- Immigration and Customs Enforcement/Federal Protective Service—government facilities

Other federal government offices outside of the Department of Homeland Security must deal with homeland security issues. These include the following:

- Department of Agriculture—agriculture and food production
- Department of Defense—defenses industries
- Department of Energy—energy creation and supply
- Department of Health and Human Services—health care and public health
- Department of Treasury—money and banking
- Environmental Protection Agency—water

Many key assets, such as communications, energy, financial services, and transportation, are privately owned. In other cases, certain operations, such as water districts, roadways, and airports, are owned by the government and operate under government license. Terrorist organizations understand the impact of CIKR on a region and, as discussed in the beginning of this chapter, attacks would have important impact on the nation's economic, political, and social systems.

In his review of homeland security initiatives, Chertoff (2009) discussed how DHS partnered with the chemical industry to undertake increased security measures for high-risk facilities. Based on the Chemical Facility Anti-Terrorism Standards (CFATS), Congress directed DHS to conduct a risk assessment of facilities in terms of threat, vulnerability, or the likelihood that an attack on a facility would be successful, and the consequence if an attack should occur. The department created risk-based performance standards applicable for each facility. After an assessment, facilities were assigned a rating of risk from high (Tier 1) to low (Tier 4) based on the chemical being produced and the serious consequences should an attack occur "The National Infrastructure Plan also includes an all-hazards approach in that human and natural disasters that can also have a devastating effect on critical infrastructure. All-hazards is a grouping classification that includes all environmental and man-made conditions that have the potential of causing physical injury, death, and damage to or loss of equipment, infrastructure services, or property. These conditions could also cause a functional degradation to social, economic, or environmental conditions" (National Infrastructure Protection Plan, 2009: 109). For example, in fall 2005, national gasoline prices rose dramatically after the shutdown of oil refining plants in the Gulf of Mexico region due to hurricanes Katrina and Rita.

HOMELAND AND CYBER SECURITY

The economy today depends on or operates on an interconnected series of global network of information forged by the Internet. Cyber security is a growing field that is tasked with preventing damage or preventing the unauthorized use or exploitation of electronic information and communications. Cyber security is also involved with restoring electronic information and communications systems in the event of a terrorist attack. The goal here is to ensure confidentiality, integrity, and availability of information (National Infrastructure Protection Plan, 2009: 109).

One expert termed the Internet and related computer systems as the "soft underbelly" of the United States that has introduced a level of vulnerability that is unprecedented (Baldor, 2009). Thus, the United States is subjected to a wide range of cyber attacks that threaten to shut down operating systems or gain access to secure information and tamper with systems. Examples abound. The Pentagon computer systems are probed 360 million times a day and one power company acknowledges that its networks see up to 70,000 scans a day (Baldor, 2009). Cyber security planners must deal with scenarios whereby a computer system fails or is sabotaged resulting in planes not being able to land, floodgates being opened, or trains switching to wrong tracks. In 2004, the department issued the National Strategy to Secure Cyberspace Plan. This plan has five general components: a national cyberspace plan, a national security threat and vulnerability reduction program, awareness and training, securing government cyberspace, and creating national and international cyber security cooperation. A key factor of the plan is to respond to cyber attacks, reduce vulnerabilities, and minimize damage and recovery time from such attacks (p. 73). As outlined by Chertoff (2009: 97) cyber attacks launched from IP addresses in Russia virtually shut down or impacted government and civilian Web sites during the Georgia–Russia conflict in summer 2008.

The directorates of Information Analysis and Infrastructure Protection (IAIP) and Science and Technology are charged with dealing with cyber security matters. Science and Technology develops research and development in this area. In the IAIP area, the National Cyber Security Division sponsors the U.S. Computer Emergency Response Team (U.S. CERT) which coordinates defenses against cyber attacks in the country. U.S. CERT also analyzes and reduces cyber threat and vulnerabilities with federal agencies, industry, and the research community (U.S. CERT, 2009).

CURRENT ISSUES RELATED TO THE DEPARTMENT OF HOMELAND SECURITY

The Department of Homeland Security has a vast number of critics who point to a number of operational and organizational problems. These include the following issues and concerns:

- The agency is too large to manage because of the vast array of agencies with varying missions related to homeland security. Critics have called for the Coast Guard and the U.S. Secret Service to be separated from the Department based on their historical missions.
- Funding is allocated without regards to a risk assessment of where attacks might occur. Critics point out that states with low risk, especially in the Midwest, receive higher funding than those with greater risk and target appeal, such as New York, New Jersey, California, and Washington, D.C.
- Money is spent on projects that have nothing to do with homeland security such as funding for athletic equipment, vehicles, and some training programs.
- There is little assessment of myriad of programs in terms of how well they are doing or if they are truly needed.

There are some observers who point out that priority should be given to natural and man-made disasters instead of terrorist attacks. Some call this the post-Katrina syndrome, but the agency is still dealing with the aftermath of responding poorly to the hurricanes that affected New Orleans and the Gulf Coast areas in 2005.

FEDERAL EMERGENCY MANAGEMENT

Emergency management is the management of emergency situations that have the potential to have a long-term negative impact on the economic, social, and political life of a community. Emergency management is also concerned with identifying risks to communities and potential responses to these risks. Historically, emergency management was a local or state function that dealt with disasters. There was very little federal government involvement with the exception of limited financial aid and the provision of federal troops to secure disaster-affected areas. In the years following World War II, emergency management became associated with civil defense in providing warnings and postattack procedures for the potential of a nuclear attack from the former Soviet Union.

As with other areas of public administration after World War II, the federal government assumed more of a role in disaster management especially with large-scale events such as hurricanes, earthquakes, and floods. By 1970 there were over five agencies dealing with emergency management such as the Department of Commerce (weather warnings), Nuclear Regulatory Agency (nuclear events), and General Services Administration, Department of Housing and Urban Development (housing and flood insurance). After a series of major hurricanes in the late 1960s, and a call for reform by legislative representatives affected by these disasters, the Federal Emergency Management Agency was created in 1970 to consolidate disaster preparedness and response.

The early days of FEMA were not spectacular. As discussed by Bullock et.al. (2007), the agency did not have a clear sense of mission, operated under poor leadership, and employees and functions were geographically and operationally dispersed. The agency received scathing criticism for its response to a series of hurricanes that affected Florida and North Carolina, and an earthquake that caused massive property damages in the Bay area of California. By the 1990s, the agency was credited in successfully dealing with disasters and having a clearly defined mission under the administration of James Witt, who was appointed as agency head under President Clinton from 1993 to 2001. Witt was credited with opening communications with Congress, emergency managers, and the media, and professionalizing the agency with trained personnel, upgraded equipment, and predicting a clear sense of mission. The agency also began to place an emphasis on risk assessment and mitigation for disaster preparedness. As discussed by Bullock et.al. (2007), responding to terrorist attacks became part of its mission as the agency provided a coordinated response to the Oklahoma City Bombing of April 26, 1995. Witt became part of President Clinton's cabinet which underscored the importance of emergency management.

With the election of President Bush, Witt was replaced by Joe Allenbaugh. The agency responded to the attacks on World Trade Center in 2001 with search and rescue teams, housing assistance, unemployment relief, counseling, debris removal, and emergency services overtime.

FEMA, as well as other federal and state agencies, was again criticized for the response to hurricanes Katrina and Rita which devastated the Louisiana and Mississippi coastlines and caused severe flooding in the City of New Orleans. Over 1,300 people died in these disasters. Major complaints included the lack of an operable evacuation plan for the city of New Orleans and a confused response by FEMA personnel. As fully discussed in *The Great Deluge* by Douglas Brinkley, the agency was overwhelmed by severity of the disaster, and the storm and the succeeding floodwaters virtually made areas in the city and elsewhere uninhabitable. There was no electricity, roadways, and communications and governmental control. Brinkley (2006) recounts in great detail a series of mishaps such as food and emergency supplies being held up because of lack of organization and logistics planning. To be clear, much of the blame was also directed to state and local officials for their lack of planning and inaction in planning for and responding to the disaster. Over the ensuing weeks and months after the hurricanes hit, aid and relief finally

FIGURE 9-2   A tabletop exercise is conducted for a group of first responders using the layout of a small city. The presenter gives the responders various situations, and each must deploy personnel and equipment to the specific situation.   *Source: Photo courtesy of the authors.*

arrived to those areas affected by the disaster. Although the most commercial and tourist areas today have been rebuilt, there are certain areas in New Orleans (Figure 9-2), such as the Ninth Ward, and throughout Louisiana and Alabama that will never be restored because of the devastation caused by these storms.

NATIONAL RESPONSE FRAMEWORK

The major federal plan for responding to disaster is found in Federal Response Plan which was originally issued in 1992 and later updated in 1999. FEMA was designated as the chief coordinating agency. In all, there are thirty-two federal departments and several nongovernmental agencies (e.g. American Red Cross) that are active participants in the plan. In response to criticism of FEMA after Hurricane Katrina, the plan was retitled the National Response Plan. Today it has once again been revised as the National Response Framework. The purpose of the plan is to mobilize all facets of the federal government to address major emergencies including natural and man-made disasters and terrorist attacks. This plan consists of the following areas:

1. Policies and scope of operations on how the federal government and its agencies and assets will assist state governments. In general, the governor of an affected state can make a formal request to the president seeking federal assistance when a disaster overwhelms state resources. The request is evaluated by FEMA and a recommendation is sent to the

president. The president makes the final decision on whether to declare an area or an event eligible for disaster aid. In some cases, the president can designate an event as a disaster eligible for federal aid

2. Emergency support functions with regard to the response by first responders and the delineation of agencies responsible for major problem areas such as transportation, communications, public works, firefighting, information and planning, mass care, medical and health services, disaster relief resources, and energy

3. Recovery functions related to operations that help disaster victims and affected local governments return to normal

4. Support functions that assist with communications, logistics, and health and safety

5. Incident annexes related to mission and concept of operations for specific events

Responsibility for emergency planning and response to major emergencies are local responsibilities. As stated in the document, "The responsibility for responding to incidents, both natural and man-made, begins at the local level with individual and public officials in the county, city, or town affected by the incident." Further, "A mayor, or city manager, or county mangers, as a jurisdiction's chief executive officer, is responsible for ensuring the public safety and welfare of the people of that jurisdiction" (National Response Framework, 2008: 15). In practice, the day-to-day planning of emergency management rests with law enforcement, fire, and public health officials. In like manner, the role of state government is to supplement and facilitate local efforts before, during, and after incidents (p. 21). Thus many states have created departments of homeland security or state emergency management in order to coordinate responses that go well beyond local and county boundaries. Partnerships with agencies, the business community, and other nongovernmental organizations are deemed as essential, especially those deemed as CIKR. Businesses are thus encouraged to work with state and local government in developing emergency management plans and response. Thus private security services and their equipment are viewed as an asset for emergency response.

The National Incident Management System

On February 28, 2003, in Homeland Security Presidential Directive Number 5, President Bush ordered that the U.S. government have a single response plan for major emergencies and terrorist attacks. The order designated the Secretary of Homeland Security as the principle official to coordinate this response in conjunction with state and local officials. The order also called for the attorney general to investigate criminal incidents and for the military to render assistance if called upon by the president. The Secretary was designated to create a National Incident Management System (NIMS), which is based on the following principles:

- Use of the Incident Command System (ICS)
- The need for interoperable communications between agencies during events
- The need for preparedness for events, which includes forecasting, training, and standardization of qualifications and certifications
- The importance of communications and information management to provide a common operating picture for the public and media
- Resource management of critical personnel, equipment, and supplies to emergency areas
- Ongoing management and maintenance of the plan occurs through the National Integration Center and support from various sources such as the Science and Technology Directorate of the Department of Homeland Security

FOCUS ON HOMELAND SECURITY AND HIGHER EDUCATION

As discussed in this chapter, the events of 9/11 and other natural disasters have raised wide interest in homeland security and emergency management. One of the by-products has been the creation of academic programs that offer courses and degrees in these two topics. Over two hundred academic institutions now offer certificate, associate, and baccalaureate programs in homeland security. These institutions also offer the Master of Science graduate degrees. The programs come under the titles of Homeland Security, Emergency Management, Disaster Management, Emergency Preparedness, and Public Security Management. Other colleges and universities offer specific courses and elective concentrations in these same areas.

Course offerings for both graduate and undergraduate programs include a number of titles and content—those most common are Introduction to Homeland Security, Terrorism, Critical Infrastructure, Risk Analysis, Research and Policy Analysis, Planning, Critical Infrastructure Protection, Intelligence, and Cyber security.

Relatedly, as an academic discipline, homeland security has begun to develop a body of knowledge. Journals that have been established include the *Journal of Homeland Security* (www.homelandsecurity.org/journal/), the *Journal of Homeland Security and Emergency Management* (www.bepress.com/hsem/), and *Homeland Security Affairs* (www.hsaj.org).

EMERGENCY PLANNING

Emergency management involves governments and businesses to have a business or operation contingency plan if a serious emergency were to occur. Emergency planning consists of the following activities: hazard identification, mitigation, recovery, and emergency operations.

Hazard Identification

In emergency planning, agencies and organizations have to take a candid review of what natural and man-made situations could become emergencies. Natural hazards include weather-related events (e.g., tornado, lightning fire, hurricane, violent storm, and heavy rain), earthquakes, and other ground movements such as mudslides caused by heavy rains in an area. Man-made situations include a wide array of events that include terrorist attacks, long-term utility outages, a plane or train crash, violent crime and civil disturbances, fires and explosions, planned events where large crowds will gather, explosions or gas releases caused by hazardous materials, and chemicals and nuclear plant events. Related to our discussion on information security in Chapter 6 are cyber attacks and failures. What planners try to do is predict worst-case scenarios and prepare business continuity plans for restoring operations.

The most obvious situations are natural because over time, residents and planners have, from experience, an idea of what major disasters might occur. Coastal areas are subject to hurricanes, and the Midwest United States is called "Tornado Alley" because of such storm activity from April to August. California and other areas in the western United States are prone to wildfires during the summer. All areas in the United States are subject to violent storms and lightning. With natural disasters, planners address the great unknown. For example, one community in upstate Vermont was not too pleased to learn that it was located on a major earthquake fault that could have the same devastating effect as an earthquake in California. For both man-made and natural disasters, planners predict the possibility that such an event could occur and the impact that it could have on the community or the organizations.

Another concept with assessment is inventorying. Planners and other emergency response providers examine a community or area and ask business owners to inventory hazardous materials stored on their property. In some areas, local laws require this inventory.

Mitigation

As discussed by Buck (2002), mitigation actions involve making lasting reductions to exposure and losses from hazardous events. *Mitigation* is often applied to physical and building planning in high-risk areas such as floodplains, coastal regions, and earthquake-prone areas. For example, in coastal regions that are exposed to hurricanes and fierce storms, mitigation efforts might include passing zoning codes for building construction and methods that businesses and individuals can employ to reduce life and property losses if an event were to occur. Mitigation can also include initiating plans and procedures to reduce the likelihood of man-made emergencies. For example, an organization wishing to reduce workplace violence might initiate an incident review committee, prohibit weapons on company grounds, and conduct visual and electronic inspections of its property.

Recovery

This activity involves addressing recovery from both physical and psychological standpoints. *Recovery* is generally understood to mean the overall actions an organization will take to make itself "whole" or to return to its previous operating condition. Recovery efforts involve a series of activities over a long period of time and include financial and other resource assistance from a number of sources including federal and state governments. For major disasters, FEMA lends important assistance in recovery activities. After a disaster has occurred, the agency brings in experts and support personnel to lend financial assistance to homeowners, organizations, and localities.

The psychological recovery from a disaster often receives little attention but is important. Survivors of natural or man-made disasters may need counseling and the time to recover from the mental effects of an event. Both victims and first responders may experience nightmares and difficulty in adjusting to the world after the event.

Emergency Operations

The core of emergency management planning is an emergency operation plan. As cited by Federal Emergency, the purpose of an emergency operations plan is to accomplish the following:

- Assign responsibility to organizations and individuals for carrying out specific action at projected times and places during an emergency.
- Define the lines of authority and organizational relationships in terms of actions.
- Identify personnel, equipment, facilities, and resources that are available to either an organization or a jurisdiction.
- Identify initial steps to begin response and recovery activities.

PLAN FORMAT A written plan consists of the following sections:

1. **Introduction and purpose.** This section introduces the concept of emergency management and includes a statement by the chief executive officer for support and guidance.

2. **Team members.** For communities and organizations, this section lists the team members by agency or office and the contributions they can make in a disaster situation. It lists position titles rather than exact names because personnel can change. For public agencies, the most obvious members or "sections" in the command center with their general duties are as follows:

Office of the chief executive designates chain of command and who is in charge.

Fire department renders first response for fire and explosions, which includes fire suppression and containment and victim recovery.

Security service department conducts initial response to many situations. Security services are involved in securing an area and controlling traffic and crowds, and conducting criminal investigations. Emergency response or special weapons and tactics teams are also used in shooting situations.

Emergency medical services (EMS) include all first aid and hospital services in a community or organizational unit. It often includes mental health, environmental health, mortuary, and identification services. EMS personnel render first aid to victims and transportation to area hospitals. Emergency room personnel in the hospital continue emergency care and facilitate follow-up treatment. Many hospitals operate under a medical response system plan that focuses on bringing in additional personnel and resources and suspending normal operations to deal with mass casualties.

Hazardous materials personnel known as "haz-mat" provide information and response for various chemical and radiological events. They often have special equipment for detecting chemicals, poisons, gases, and radiation. It is not uncommon for hazardous material personnel to be a specialized unit under the fire department command structure. Critical for haz-mat operations are container labeling and identifying chemicals and the threat they pose for humans and the environment. These guidelines, which also include policies for controlling chemical fires and spills for firefighters and security service personnel, are published in the *Emergency Response Guidebook* published by the U.S. Department of Transportation (2000).

Public information officer (PIO) prepares public announcements and conducts press briefings and news conferences under authority of the chief executive. The PIO also assists emergency responders by directing media representatives to a site that can be used for press briefings during an emergency situation.

Legal counsel renders opinions regarding legal and public policy impact of actions and directives taken by the emergency team.

Planning office is responsible for information regarding mitigation and recovery plans, maps, and demographic data.

Human services provide financial assistance and other resources to victims in terms of basic life needs such as food and shelter. It also may be called on to provide psychological assistance to victims and emergency providers.

Education Educational facilities may be used for evacuation and other resource purposes.

Public works include water, sewage, utility, road and bridge conditions, and maintenance, all of which are essential especially for evacuation and business recovery purposes.

Communications including radio, telephone, Internet, and satellite communications systems are critical for all emergency operations. Communications for emergency management also includes arranging interfaces between various agencies that may not have common communications channels.

In private sector organizational plans, the chief executive or representative gathers people from various offices who would deal with an emergency. These include emergency services, media relations, human resources, physical plant, and institutional safety. For all types of emergency plans, other individuals or personnel may be brought in, depending on the nature of the event. In one case study, persons who could speak French were kept on a language list and activated when a bus carrying French Canadian tourists crashed in a remote area.

ACTIVATION AND COMMAND CENTER

Just when an emergency plan goes into effect depends on the nature of the emergency event or the warning time that planners are given for a public gathering or a weather-related event. Each plan must have a mobilization protocol that activates the emergency team under the authority of the chief executive. Private organizations have a chain of command that calls for mobilization and activation. Chains of command identify a line of authority, which places a person in charge if the chief executive officer is not available.

The first steps in an emergency event involve critical incident management (CIM). This requires first-responding officers and supervisors to take a series of steps to contain the crisis. As presented by Faggiano and Gillespie (2004) the steps include the following:

1. Accessing the situation in terms of immediate threats to victims and responding officers
2. Establishing communications with responding units by clearing radio channels for operations
3. Identifying the area called the *hot zone* or *kill zone* that contains immediate hazards for responding emergency personnel
4. Establishing a staging area and a command center for future actions
5. Identifying and requesting additional resources

The goal during this first response phase is to identity the extent of the problem and to prevent further injuries. For example, a fire at farm supply store would require a series of actions that might include evacuation, traffic control, and identification of hazardous materials and potential threats to the natural environment. Following the immediate crisis stage, emergency responders would then create a temporary command center from which to take further actions to deal with the crisis. A command center can be established anywhere, such as in a strip mall, school house, and convenience store parking lot, depending on the circumstances of the event. The location must provide response supervisors a place to meet and take future actions at a safe distance from the scene. Similarly, a staging area near the event would be established where emergency responders can be deployed and await orders. This area also allows incident supervisors to prevent emergency vehicle traffic congestion and confusion in and around the event scene.

For long-term emergency planning purposes, most organizations and governmental units have created stationary command centers where representatives of the emergency team can meet to coordinate operations that move beyond the immediate crisis stage. Theoretically, state and county command centers are often located in secure public buildings with up-to-date communications and computer links to federal agencies and county command area centers. These centers also must have telephones, computer capabilities, food, and restrooms for long-term situations. In our travels around the country, we have found that many counties and municipalities do not have defined command sites and the command center may be nothing more than an office in the police department or sheriff's office. There is also a need for a secondary backup center should the main area be destroyed. Recall that on September 11, 2001, the New York City emergency command center was located in Building 7 of the World Trade Center and had to be evacuated.

To assist in this mobilization, most plans have defined various categories of emergencies. For this discussion, an *emergency* is an event that negatively impacts the daily operations of an organization or a community by shutting down services, commerce, and social activities. Emergency events can originate in a location immediate to or far from the site but still have a serious operational and psychological impact on the surrounding area, state, or nation. For example, many states initiated emergency management procedures in the wake of the 9/11 attacks even though they occurred in New York, Washington, D.C., and Pennsylvania. At that time, there was fear that a second wave of attacks might occur.

Not all emergencies require activation of regional or national emergency management plans, however. Most communities and organizations are quite adept at dealing with crisis on a daily basis. When the crisis reaches proportions that threaten to kill large numbers of civilians, destroy huge areas, or shut down all business and social operations, emergency management plans go into effect.

For emergency planning, events are often categorized into three levels:

LEVEL I   Events of this category are limited in terms of threat and victimization to an area or organization. Although they require serious attention by either law enforcement or emergency service personnel or both, they present no overall danger to the entire community or organization. Members of the emergency response team may be notified of the event but mobilization is not required.

Examples

Death or violent crimes involving few individuals per incident

Fire of limited duration and scope

Typical weather situation such as snow

Utility failure of a limited duration

LEVEL II   A Level II event requires mobilization of the emergency response team because the event has the potential for or is disrupting overall operations for an extended period of time. External emergency assistance will be required. There is limited access to affected areas.

Examples

Fire or bomb threat/detonation affecting a large area

Serious weather situation affecting a specific area

Major crime victimization affecting an area or continuing over a period of time

Chemical/radiation event that results in limited evacuation

National or state emergency event

Major crash of computer services

LEVEL III   An event of this category involves the actual or potential widespread loss of life and property. There is need to evacuate entire community areas. Organizations shut down all operations and evacuate. Access to the community is limited to designated staff and emergency services.

Examples

Major weather disaster

Airplane crash

Area that needs a medical quarantine

Terrorist event involving a weapon of mass destruction (e.g., chemical, biological, nuclear, incendiary, and explosive)

Emergency Operations Annexes

The annexes of a plan contain general guidelines for handling emergency events and coordinating emergency-related operations. Emergency plan annexes describe general actions to be taken by each agency but do not go into detail on those actions. It is understood that agencies represented have the requisite knowledge and skills to deal with the situation. Emergency plans have to be tested to see whether they actually work before a real event takes place. This is undertaken using tabletop exercises, scenarios, and actual drills discussed later in this chapter.

In areas with a potential for a serious weather event, the annex outlines the steps that all agencies will take to deal with the weather and the services provided by a range of agencies for evacuation or mass care after such an event. The annex of a plan outlines the chief operations person for the emergency type and how each service unit or team member contributes to addressing it. The annex also contains information related to logistics, moving people and equipment, available resources, closing businesses and schools, suspending nonemergency services, and evacuating people to a safe location. Evacuation plans are the cornerstone for many plans that address weather-related events such as a hurricane or tornado. These plans are the most difficult to execute because people do not want to leave their homes, pets, and belongings.

The following is a list of emergency operations annexes (Buck, 2002: 87):

- Evacuation
- Shelter
- Mass care
- Health and medical services
- Law enforcement response
- Fire
- Search and rescue
- Radiological defense
- Engineering services
- Agriculture services
- Transportation
- Auxiliary resources
- Terrorism and weapons of mass destruction

INCIDENT COMMAND SYSTEM

The objective of emergency planners is to deal with natural and man-made situations. Because of the size of the United States and the decentralized nature of its government, it is important that first-responder agencies and jurisdictions be able to be "on the same page" in dealing with situations. Nationally, disaster planners and responders use an incident command or the incident command system (ICS). Developed in the 1970s under the FIRESCOPE program after a series of serious forest fires in the state of California, ICS addresses issues related to authority, command, communications (always a problem), and interagency coordination to deal with the various problems related to a major forest fire. As outlined by the National Interagency Fire Center (1994), ICS became the national standard used by FEMA and the U.S. Coast Guard for dealing with a wide variety of situations including large-scale fires and disasters, search and rescue operations, pest eradication, oil spills, air and ground transportation accidents, major law enforcement incidents, and planned events. It is now the national protocol for all government agencies and states designated by presidential directive to create a national incident management system that sets forth common operations principles, terminology, and training programs that will be used by state, federal, and local emergency agencies in responding to domestic events.

Organization

ICS is built around five major management activities: command, operations, planning, logistics, and finance/administration. The group or person in charge of the overall operation is the incident commander. The command section has a section chief for each area. What follows is a basic outline of each area's roles and functions.

COMMAND   The question that often arises when an emergency threat or event occurs involves who is in charge. There are two concepts under the command model. One is that a single agency incident manager is in charge either by government decree or the ability of one agency such as the police or fire department or the county executive to manage the event. The second model involves multiple agencies coordinated under unified command in which fire, police, and haz-mat units speak as a single voice.

The command section has support personnel who represent the following areas: information and media relations, safety, liaison services, and recorder to organizations outside the ICS structure. The information officer is the chief spokesperson to the media and other groups seeking information related to the incident or event. There may be public information officers from other agencies working with the information officer, but only one person issues press releases and arranges press briefings related to the event. The safety officer advises the incident commander on issues related to the safety of response personnel. The liaison officer becomes the chief point of contact for outside agencies. Finally, the recorder makes a chronology of the event from the perspective of the command center in terms of when orders were issued and when various pieces of information were obtained. A deputy incident commander assists the incident commander during the event.

Operations

Operations members in the field rescue people, provide assistance, and strive to contain a situation. For a major hazardous materials situation involving a fire, an explosion, and the release of harmful fumes, operations and their general tasks include the following:

Fire departments and haz-mat units contain and extinguish fires, rescue victims, and prepare site disposal procedures for equipment cleanup.

Police conduct crime scene investigations, control the inner and outer perimeter and traffic, and evacuate area residents near the scene.

EMS services stabilize patients and transport them to hospitals.

Social services arrange food and shelter for evacuees.

This seemingly simple arrangement also includes a section for each area that might be further broken down into working subgroups to address problems. For example, a firefighter and a police officer may be teamed to review the need to extinguish a fire but try to keep some semblance of order for the protection of the crime scene.

LOGISTICS   The logistics group moves people and resources (e.g., communications, medical needs, facilities, and food,) to provide support for the operations area.

The key concepts related to logistics involve the incident command post, staging area, incident base, and—for long-range events—potential campus, helibases, supply areas, and even airports.

Planning

The planning group anticipates activities related to information and documentation related to the emergency situation. It may include technical specialists who can provide assistance to safety and operations personnel. For a hazardous materials event, the group would also strive to predict the harm to living things by chemicals and the best methods known for cleanup and disposal.

Administration and Finance

Administration and finance may be the most overlooked aspect related to emergency management. After the first responders arrive, someone has to determine where financial assistance will come from. This area keeps a record for future compensation efforts. FEMA provides financial assistance and compensation to localities for major disasters, but it requires documentation and information. In general, insurance companies require documentation regarding physical injuries of people, losses of equipment, and damage to buildings. The administration and finance section thus records information for potential insurance claims and lawsuits.

As a concept, ICS can be used for major event planning purposes such as gatherings involving large crowds or warrant raids or drug raids.

WEAPONS OF MASS DESTRUCTION

An important topic in emergency management planning deals with weapons of mass destruction (WMD) either launched by a terrorist group or caused by human error. A WMD is an item that when weaponized can be used to threaten or kill large numbers of people and bring about a negative lasting effect on the economic, political, and social lives of a community. Planners today use the acronym C-BNE for chemical, biological, nuclear, and explosives. C-BNE weapons (except nuclear ones) have been used by armies and navies in various applications for centuries; their use by terrorists or rogue countries within the context of modern-day life raises a chilling specter especially when vehicles and aircraft are weaponized for terrorist purposes. Remember that it was a commercial aircraft commanded by al-Qaeda operatives that crashed into the World Trade Center and Pentagon, resulting in widespread destruction and loss of life.

WMD and Terrorism

The possible use by a terrorist group of any WMD against a population is important for emergency and security planning. For our purposes, *terrorism* consists of actual or threatened criminal acts by a person or group in the furtherance of a political or social cause. The Federal Bureau of Investigation defines *terrorism* as the unlawful use of force against person or property to intimidate or coerce a government, the civilian population, or segment thereof, in the furtherance of political or social objectives (FBI, 1999). Terrorists' targets are nonmilitary, often chosen to obtain maximum media coverage. In her book on terrorism, Cindy Combs suggests that planners need not confine themselves to a perfect definition. Terrorist acts have violence, an audience, innocent victims, and the creation of fear for political motives and goals (Combs, 2002: 7–8). Included in the broad definition of terrorists is a wide variety of national and international groups that may be supported by a regime to destabilize a region or another country. At this time, the U.S. Department of State has labeled approximately thirty-three groups as terrorist. As outlined by Richmond (2002), thirteen are based in the Middle East including high-profile organizations such as Hamas, Hezbollah, and the Popular Front for the Liberation of Palestine. The State Department also keeps a list of terrorist incidents by region. Before 9/11, Colombia and other parts of Latin America had the largest number of bombings and shooting incidents that fall under this broad definition.

Types of Weapons of Mass Destruction

BIOLOGICAL WEAPONS   Biological agents are living organisms that either cause disease to incapacitate or kill human beings, plants, and/or animals (Buck(b), 2002: 173). The exposure comes from aerosols, liquid droplets, or dry powders. They are absorbed by the respiratory system or skin or are ingested. Unlike other weapons, they may not have an immediate impact but incubate for a period of time before they are discovered. Because of global economic operations and transportation, a group of persons exposed to a biological agent may be dispersed around the world and may inflict the disease on others. The Center for Disease Control in Atlanta, Georgia, and other health care task forces watch for sudden increases in emergency room admissions or fatalities involving respiratory illnesses at health care facilities. One problem with biological weapons is to realize that an attack has occurred and then to locate the source site or exposure event so that treatment and quarantine procedures can begin. The three classifications of biological weapons are viruses, bacteria, and toxins.

The most noted bacterial weapon of concern currently is anthrax. After September 11, 2001, twenty-two anthrax attacks resulted in five deaths. The U.S. mail was used to disperse the agent in envelopes after it was created in an unknown laboratory. The targets included the Senate Office Building in Washington, D.C., various publishing and media outlets, and mail transfer stations. The fatalities were persons who were either intended or accidental targets or handlers in mail facilities. The victims first experienced fever with skin irritation from inhaling or being exposed to the virus.

The anthrax attacks resulted in thousands of false or mistaken anthrax reports. There was also a limited understanding of anthrax and a lack of protocols to address every report on the local and state level. Within weeks, a state and national protocol that included the following emerged:

1. Identification procedures for suspicious packages and emergency notification if a substance is found
2. Deployment of a haz-mat team to obtain the item and remove it in a safe manner for testing
3. Identification and immediate decontamination of those persons who might be contaminated from the substance

Rather than go through massive evacuations and decontamination procedures, many localities created small chemical and biological response teams to test suspected materials being reported.

Another agent of significance is smallpox, which is highly contagious. After being inhaled, the virus spreads into the body and causes muscle rigidity, chills, and vomiting. Scabs form that leave deep pigmented scars on victims. The only nations that are known to have smallpox for use as WMD are the United States and Russia, but there is fear that rogue countries or terrorist groups may obtain small samples of the virus. Smallpox can be controlled by an inoculation, but many first responders are reluctant to be vaccinated because of rare but potentially lethal side effects.

NUCLEAR WEAPONS   Use of a nuclear weapon would have a devastating effect based on its blast power and the spread of poisonous gamma radiation. The immediate blast would result in hundreds of thousands of deaths if a device were detonated in a populous area. The "hot zone" would be uninhabitable for some time. Other affected areas impacted by radiological contamination would be identified only after victims develop radiation sickness symptoms (nausea, vomiting, fatigue, loss of appetite, and respiratory illness). A lethal dose of radiation, which is measured at more than 400–500 roentgen equivalents in man (rem) will cause death. Today only seven countries have the technology to develop and deliver nuclear devices. Although the Cold War between the United Sates and the former Soviet Union has ended, it is estimated that thousands of warheads are still in service by both countries. The general policy of the United States and its allies is to stop other nations from obtaining or developing nuclear capacities. Certain rouge countries such as Iran and Iraq have been identified as attempting to create nuclear weapons programs. The fear that Iraq might have such weapons was one of the reasons that the United States opted to invade it in 2003. Diplomatic difficulties have occurred between North Korea and the United States because the former has developed nuclear capacity.

It is difficult to build a nuclear or fission bomb without massive resources and scientific expertise, but there is the potential to create a "dirty" bomb, which is a conventional explosive device with radiological or chemical materials packed around it. One of the efforts of the U.S. Energy Department's Nuclear Incident Response Team is to conduct searches for such materials and to provide state and local police with radiation detection devices. There are also fears that radiological materials may have been stolen from former Soviet military arsenals for trade on the international black market. Another fear is the explosion of a conventional bomb near a nuclear power plant or weapons storage area. This fear is one reason that security remains high for nuclear weapons storage and nuclear commercial sites located near population areas.

INCENDIARY WEAPONS   The ignition of many flammable liquids causes widespread fires and consumption of oxygen. It is estimated that incendiary devices, such as handheld gasoline bombs, rockets, and planted devices, account for some 25 percent of all bombing incidents in the United States. What these incidents have in common is an ignition source and combustible material. For example, the gasoline in a truck or airplane can cause a large number of deaths and serious damage if it is ignited by an explosive or incendiary device. The problem is that many flammable liquids in tanks represent thousands of potential bombs being transported by truck or train throughout the country. Increased attention is now being paid to access to tank farms and to perform background checks on drivers.

CHEMICAL WEAPONS   Chemical weapons include a wide range of poisonous gases, liquids, and solids that have toxic effects on people, animals, and plants. They are classified as nerve, blister, blood, and choking agents, and irritants. The impact on the victim depends on the agent, the duration of the exposure, and the strength of the agent in an area. For emergency response purposes, *persistent agents* remain in a target area in lethal concentrations for more than twelve hours. While many classified agents are easy to make, they require large quantities and an appropriate delivery system to be lethal. The impact of chemical weapons depends on weather and wind conditions.

The last widespread use of chemical weapons occurred during World War I when artillery shells dispersed chlorine and mustard gases. These weapons caused so much physical and psychological damage to both Allied and German soldiers that most nations signed international treaties against their future use. The most recent use of a chemical weapon was the use of sarin by a terrorist cult group in Tokyo, Japan, in 1995. The suspects released the chemical on various subway trains during rush hour causing more than 5,000 injuries and twelve deaths. Emergency services were simply overwhelmed by the rush of patients, and many health care providers became ill from the chemical on patients' footwear.

A chemical event could also be caused by accident at a chemical-producing or storage facility. For example, a farm supply store fire can become a chemical event because of the large quantities of fertilizer and other products on its premises.

The following is an overview of the most common chemical weapons (Emergency Response, 2002).

Nerve Agents   Types include tabun, sarin, soman, and V agent. Their common characteristic is high toxicity resulting in death in minutes if large exposures are involved. They attack the nervous system and cause convulsions and uncontrolled muscle or glandular reactions.

Blister Agents (Vesicants)   Types are mustard, distilled mustard, and lewisite. They cause skin blistering or damage to the eyes and respiratory system similar to contact with bleach or lye. The persistence rate for mustard ranges from one day to several months, depending on the type and weather conditions.

Blood Agents   Hydrogen cyanide, used for various industrial purposes, is most commonly used. The agent can be absorbed, inhaled, or ingested. Exposure causes rapid respiratory arrest and death as the agent blocks oxygen from entering to cells.

Choking Agents   Chlorine and phosgene are common choking agents. These readily available industrial chemicals can cause chest tightness and airway irritation (choking) if exposure levels are high.

Irritants   Tear gas, mace, and pepper spray used for crowd control and self-defense are dispersed by aerosol containers. A high concentration can cause serious injury or death to someone with a respiratory problem.

EXPLOSIVES   By definition, explosives are materials that when ignited result in violent decomposition and instantaneous oxidation. There is a sudden release of gas followed by high temperature, shock wave, noise, and light. People are injured and killed by blast pressure, heat (thermal), and fragments (e.g., glass, metal, and debris) produced by the explosion. Buildings are damaged or destroyed. Explosives remain the most commonly used item to destroy people and property. They remain the weapon of choice by terrorists as witnessed by the recent wave of car and suicide bombings in the Middle East and domestic incidents in the United States. Recall that a vehicle bomb was responsible for the first World Trade Center bombing in 1993 and the Alfred P. Murrah federal building bombing in Oklahoma City in 1995. Various kinds of explosive materials are classified as primary, secondary, and tertiary. A primary item, such as lead azide or mercury fulminate, is used as a detonator because it ignites very quickly. It is used for electric and nonelectric detonators. Secondary items, such as TNT, dynamite, C-4, Flex-X, and ANFO, require a detonator for activation. Tertiary explosives include ammonium nitrate, dinitrotoluene, and mononitrotoluene; they require a greater charge and confinement to detonate.

The most common explosive elements are black powder and dynamite used in most construction projects (Barrett, 2002). Military grades, such as C-4, are more powerful but are more difficult to obtain and require advanced training to use.

Although bombings are rare in the United States, their threats to persons and organizations are commonplace. Some agencies have a policy to evacuate at all times when a threat is received, but others review the elements of the threat and then make a decision to inspect the area for suspicious packages, disregard the threat, or evacuate. The final decision is based on a correlation of information provided by the caller and general events going on in the workplace. For example, a threat received by a school during final examinations would be viewed differently than a threat received by a manufacturing firm during a contentious labor strike. Finding a suspicious package or dealing with a serious threat requires technical assistance from bomb experts. If it is suspicious, then leave it alone.

WMD Impact On Emergency Responders

The first action to take when any emergency, particularly a WMD one, occurs is to identify what has happened. Then it must be contained and not allowed to cause more casualties, particularly among emergency first responders or civilians who want to assist at the scene. Terrorists sometimes use secondary devices to inflict casualties on first responders. The use of incident command and the establishment of a command site become very critical during the first minutes of the response. The general response protocol includes the following:

Approach or evacuate upwind of the suspect area.

Wear protective masks including a self-contained breathing apparatus and clothing and cover all exposed skin surfaces.

Minimize exposure in radiological material incidents and maximize distance from the contaminated site (U.S. Department of Justice, 2002: 6–27).

The second action is to determine how to treat persons exposed to the substance. A chemical event requires containing the scene and decontaminating victims in portable showers. A person exposed to serious radiation cannot be saved, and the contaminated area has to be cordoned off to prevent further casualties. Thus, it is important that first responders have a general training in WMD for assessment, notification, control, and containment purposes. A patrol unit coming to an office complex where employees are blistered and gasping for air are most likely dealing with a chemical attack that will require massing additional personnel and equipment under an incident command system format. Site training for the event includes establishing a proper command center and taking natural and environmental factors into consideration.

There is also the need for special equipment. Various classes of emergency response attire are available. The typical gear worn by a firefighter is Type C with a self-contained breathing apparatus worn on the back. Gear worn by haz-mat specialists range from Levels B to A, which are constructed to have zero exposure with the external environment and self-contained breathing equipment. Additional equipment is required to decontaminate victims such as portable showers or fire hoses with fine spray nozzles that can be used to remove gross contaminants from the victims before they receive triage and medical attention. This means removing all clothing and eventually showering with soap or a mixture of water and bleach. Not every fire department or emergency service unit has the resources and training to deal with these kinds of situations. Outside of major metropolitan areas, there remains the need to create regional response teams.

THREAT ANALYSIS

Security service units must review potential threats and target vulnerability in their client area. While there is a tendency to look at groups or sites that appear most obvious, a concentrated review with other organizational units and law enforcement and rescue personnel may yield interesting results.

The first step in threat analysis is to review the existence of potential groups, termed *potential threat elements* (PDE). (Department of Homeland Security/State and Local, 2005) A PDE is any group that advocates violence for political, social, or religious reasons. Identification of a PDE is often difficult because it is based on a number of intelligence factors that must be analyzed and reviewed and among federal, state, and local agencies under the auspices of a federal or joint terrorism task force. Although there is great concern for al-Qaeda and other foreign-based terrorist groups, attention must be focused on domestic groups that include white supremacists, environmentalists, anti-Semites, and antigovernment groups. Often these are local or regional groups. A complete review has to be conducted, however, as to their ideology, potential violent intentions, possible capability, and history. Whether their members are undergoing training or have access to finances and resources to obtain explosives or chemical or biological weapons must also be determined.

The second step in threat analysis is reviewing target vulnerability. A *vulnerability* is a weakness that can be exploited by an adversary to gain access to information. Returning to the discussion of risk in Chapter 4, security service units have to review client vulnerabilities by considering building characteristics, equipment properties, and personal and operational practices. For most organizations, potential targets are site facilities, internal operating systems, and special event situations. The five factors that are important in this part of the review are as follows.

1. **Level of visibility.** This pertains to how well outside groups know the target. A government building may be well known, but the computer operations center within it may have very low visibility because it is tucked away outside of normal pedestrian and vehicle traffic. On the other hand, a highly publicized cultural or sporting event can be viewed as a potential target.
2. **Criticality of target site to jurisdiction.** This pertains to a target that is either highly useful or critical to organization or the client area. Power plants, water reservoirs, and bridges have a profound impact if destroyed. Often the reviewers have to asses the effect of the loss outside the immediate jurisdiction.
3. **PDE access to target.** This refers to access of the perimeter of a target. A target that has unlimited access presents a larger problem than the one that has restricted access with an alarm system and armed personnel.
4. **Potential hazard threats.** From an operations perspective, reviewers have to determine whether the site or facility has concentrations of potentially dangerous materials. A nuclear plant, an oil-pumping facility, and a laboratory conducting high-level biological research will be viewed as a high hazard threat. Another site that must be reviewed is a water treatment facility that has concentrated amounts of chlorine. If released into the environment, the chlorine could affect the population for about a three-mile radius.
5. **Target site population capacity.** More people in an area present a high potential for mass casualties. Analysis also has to include the population in the area immediate to the target site. (Department of Homeland Security/State and Local, 2005)

In considering these factors, reviewers may use a point system to rank each item or present an open-ended threat assessment. This review, however, should be simply undertaken by the security service unit in conjunction with other organizational units such as fire, haz-mat, facilities operations, computer systems, and others.

DRILL AND TRAINING

Once plans have been established and resources identified, there is a need to train personnel. Training must include all members of an organization from nonparticipants to emergency responders. For example, employees at a manufacturing plant need to know the internal warning devices that signal evacuation from work stations and to safe areas to report to. Workers need to know whom to call if a bomb threat is received and what important notes to write about the threat. Many companies have created quick checklists that are used for training and response. For example, many companies issue policies for dealing with crimes in progress. Unwittingly, one of the authors was present in a bank when the cashier was robbed after the suspect gave her a note demanding money. A review of procedures for the bank afterward showed that she followed the institution's procedures which included:

1. Call security or a supervisor as soon as possible
2. Write down a description of the suspect: sex, race, approximate age, height, clothes worn (e.g., jacket, hat, and glasses), and unusual body features
3. Do not attempt to apprehend the person or confront the perpetrator in a threatening manner

After the robber left, the bank was locked down until police arrived. The culprit, meantime, fled into an adjacent parking lot and boarded a city bus and escaped. He was caught the next day after a CCTV video of his attempt was showed over local media. In venues with the potential for civil disturbances, employees are directed to take defensive measures such as staying away from public areas near the facility, looking out windows, and locking offices down should demonstrators enter into the building. In some cases, the business will be shut down and employees directed to stay home for the duration of the disturbance.

Emergency responders normally receive training on first response to situations such as motor vehicle and mechanical accidents, various injuries, and crimes. Treatment of victims and related topics are presented in Chapter 12. They may not have training, however, in responding to catastrophic events with multiple victims or involving a weapon of mass destruction. In these cases, it is important for security service organizations to train from the plan and use actual situations in which personnel might be involved. Training is also important for emergency planners to see whether a plan works or to measure its strengths and weaknesses. Typical training courses can include the following:

Scenario. This is a specific emergency situation that the work group uses to determine how each unit would respond. Results can be used to prepare general emergency plans.

Tabletop exercise. This simulates a situation for which members of the work group role-play to identify responses and solutions as the emergency unfolds. For first-responder training, the replica of a city or area with model buildings, roads, and facilities constructed to H-O train scale is used (see Figure 9-3). Responders must move vehicles, equipment, and personnel as the situation occurs. The presenter of the emergency acts as the dispatcher, giving each responder new or critical information. Responders often have to deal with two or more unfolding situations.

FIGURE 9-3   A FEMA worker inspects damage to neighborhood in New Orleans.
Source: ANAM Collection/Alamy.

LIMITED SIMULATED SITUATION   In this scenario, a building or park is used for first responders to deal with a situation such as the report of anthrax contamination or a gunman holding a
hostage next to a chemical tank. This model is often used for team or unit response evaluation
and review.

ACTUAL DRILL   This involves testing the overall plan or specific response protocols among
country and regional response units. Volunteers pose as victims with stage props such as,
blown-up vehicles. There is one specific site scene, but the entire city or county may be
involved in the overall response. A drill of this nature involves much planning and coordination among the various agencies, and volunteers must be recruited to act as victims (free
lunches often work for this). "Consumable" items such as blankets, stage blood, bandages, cots,
wrecked cars, and the like must be purchased. Most drills of this nature often identify problems
with communication among responding units, incident notification, and creation of correct
incident command responses. Gross decontamination issues always appear because some
"victims" are able to leave the scene and make their way to the area hospital, thus contami-
nating it. Some states have training sites that can present all of these situations. A notable site is
at Texas A&M University in College Station, Texas, which has an entire training facility—called
Disaster City—that includes oil refinery facilities, wrecked trains and planes, destroyed
concrete buildings, bus and car wrecks, and the superstructure of a ship. Since 9/11, other
states have created homeland security training sites. In New York State, a former airport is now
being used for homeland security training and provides facilities for active training scenarios
including hostage taking, emergency vehicle operations, disaster recovery, and firearms
training for first responders.

Summary

Homeland security and emergency planning have become important issues for security service personnel as a result of both natural disasters and the terrorist attacks of 9/11. This chapter discussed the development of the Department of Homeland Security, the role of FEMA, emergency planning topics, categories of emergencies, incident command system, terrorism and response to weapons of mass destruction, and terrorist threat evaluation.

Review Questions/Activities

1. Review the main roles of the following agencies of the Department of Homeland Security and their contributions to security services: CPB, ICE, FEMA, Secret Service, Coast Guard, and TSA.
2. What are the main objectives of emergency planning? Find out if your campus or organization has an emergency response plan. Determine what emergency procedures it has for the staff.
3. Conduct a vulnerability assessment of your home or apartment. What weaknesses do you have?
4. List at least two main threats from C-BNE that would impact a community and emergency service provider.

5. You are a security patrol officer and have been dispatched to a traffic incident involving three vehicles and a gasoline truck. Three people in each vehicle are injured, and gasoline is leaking from the truck. Apply CIM to this situation using all available resources that exist in your community.
6. Review a major emergency that took place in your area or state. From newspaper articles, Web site reviews, and perhaps interviews from first responders, analyze how governmental agencies responded to the situation. To what extent were private sector businesses involved in the incident?

WebSearches

1. Access www.fema.gov, the Web site of the Federal Emergency Management Agency. After reviewing its resources, click on careers in homeland security. What are the types of positions available at this time?
2. Most states have Web sites on emergency management or preparedness. Review the sites for your state and list the resources that are available. Compare this site with that of another state to know the resources available for each state. Discuss the features that are common to each site as well as the differences. Why do the resources of some states differ from those of the others?
3. Access the Web site of the *Journal of Homeland Security and Emergency Management* or *Journal of Homeland Security*. Read one of the journal articles that is archived at that site, and prepare a summary of the issues discussed in that article.

References

Baldor, Lolita (October 5, 2009). "Feds Warn of Dangers Afoot in Cyberspace." Albany Times Union, p. A4.

Barrett, Jerry. 2002. "Bombs and Explosives." Presentation at Utica College.

Brinkley, Douglas. 2006. The Great Deluge. New York: Harper Collins.

Buck, George. 2002. *Preparing for Terrorism: An Emergency Services Guide*. Stamford, Conn. Delmar.

Buck, George. 2002. *Preparing for Biological Terrorism: An Emergency Services Planning Guide*. Albany, NY: Delmar.

Bullock, Jane, George Haddow, Damon Coppola, Erdem Ergin, Lissa Westerman and Sarp Yeletaysi.

2007. *Introduction to Homeland Security.* New York: Butterworth Heinemann.

Chertoff, Michael. 2009. *Homeland Security: Assessing the First Five Years.* Philadelphia, PA: University of Pennsylvania Press.

Combs, Cindy. 2002. *Understanding Terrorism.* Upper Saddle River, N.J.: Prentice-Hall.

Department of Homeland Security. 2008. *Brief Documentary History of the Department of Homeland Security 2001–2008.* Washington: DC: United States Department of Homeland Security. Web posted at www.dhs.gov. Accessed September 2, 2009.

Faggiano, Vincent, and Thomas Gillespie. 2004. *Critical Incident Management.* Tulsa, Okla.: K&M Publishers.

Federal Bureau of Investigation. 1999. "30 Years of Terrorism: A Special Retrospective Edition." Accessed June 20 2004 at www.fbi.gov/publications/terrpr/terror99.pdf.

Homeland Security Act of 2002, (Public Law 107–296), November 25, 2002.

National Interagency Fire Center. 1994. *Incident Command System National Training Curriculum.* Boise, Ida.: National Interagency Fire Center.

Richmond, Nathaniel. 2002. "The Geography of International Terrorism." Presentation at Utica College.

U.S. Coast Guard. 2009. "USCG: Drug Interdiction." Web posted at www.uscg.mil/cg5/cg531/drug_interdiction.asp. Accessed October 12, 2009.

U.S. Computer Emergency Response Team (U.S. CERT). "ND.". Web posted at www.us-cert/aboutus.htm. Accessed November 25, 2009.

United States Department of Homeland Security-State and Local Government Coordination and Preparedness. 2005. Campus Preparedness Assessment (CD). Washington, DC: United States Department of Homeland Security/International Association of Campus Law Enforcement Administrators.

United States Department of Homeland Security. 2008. *National Incident Management Plan.* Washington, DC: United States Department of Homeland Security.

United States Department of Homeland Security. 2008. *National Response Framework.* Washington, DC: United States Department of Homeland Security.

United States Department of Homeland Security. 2009. *National Infrastructure Protection Plan: Partnering to Enhance Protection and Resiliency.* Washington, DC: United States Department of Homeland Security.

U.S. Department of Justice. 2002. *Emergency Response to Terrorism: Law Enforcement Response to Weapons of Mass Destruction Incidents.* Baton Rouge: Louisiana State University.

United States Department of Transportation. 2000. *Emergency Response Guidebook.* Washington, D.C.: United States Department of Transportation.

United States Secret Service Strategic Plan. 2009. Washington: D.C.: United States Department of Homeland Security/United States Secret Service.

White, Richard, and Kevin Collins (eds). 2006. *The United States Department of Homeland Security: An Overview.* Upper Saddle River, NJ: Pearson Custom Publishing.

10

■ ■ ■

Human Resource Management in Security Services

KEY TERMS

affirmative action, background check, collective bargaining, credit check, evaluation, human resource, labor market, job description, quality of life, set aside, sexual harassment, square badge, staffing model, terms and conditions of employment, turnover.

An important factor in security service operations is finding and retaining quality personnel. For most organizations, roughly 90 percent of management activity involves *human resource administration*, which is defined as recruiting, training, and motivating the organization's workforce. Returning to the model of security services in Chapter 3, it is obvious that the right fit has to be made between the duties and expectations of a particular position and the education, training, and skills of an employee. Too often, this match is not made.

BASIC PREMISES

There are several fundamental axioms in human resource management. First, people must be paid for working. In addition to a salary or an hourly rate, "pay" includes a "benefit package" that might include health insurance, vacation days, personal days, and a retirement fund. It is also fundamental that a large number of people will apply for those positions that pay high salaries. Employees may be expected to stay with an organization if there are opportunities for advancement (which equates to higher pay), and if they are treated in a humane fashion.

From the employer perspective, salaries are paid based on requisite education and job-related attributes and skills. In other words, employees who have a higher level of skills often can command higher salaries.

There is also the concept of the *human resource labor market*, a term that attempts to describe the total range of positions compared to the number of qualified people who are either in a particular region or can be recruited to move into the area. The number of qualified people that can be recruited for an area is often determined by *quality of life factors,* a term that describes employment rates; salaries and wages; housing costs; crime and personal safety perceptions; weather conditions; and social, cultural, and recreational opportunities. Against this background, security service administrators have the important task of finding and retraining the right person for the job.

The human resource function also involves keeping accurate records. Computerized software programs allow companies to keep continuous records of employees from their application until their retirement. Employee documentation is necessary for potential disputes and lawsuits that often arise over training, time and attendance, and wages.

JOB ANALYSIS

One of the first things that security service agencies have to determine is what they want employees to do and under what circumstances. These essential functions of the position are important for many legal and technical reasons. What is needed is a job analysis, which is simply a review of tasks required in a particular position and the skills needed to perform them. There is also the need for an assigned risk factor to the position. In another words, the importance of the position to the agency and what will happen if a mistake is made in its performance must be assigned.

In general, security service positions involve high risk for any organization. The employee has the "keys to the kingdom" in terms of access to physical and electronic assets. Personnel in Level III and IV security service organizations are armed and legally entitled to use force, even deadly force. The following is a general job description for a security service agent at a state mental health facility that would be classified as a Level III security services organization:

> You will be trained to become a security service agent with various police powers. You would then be responsible for detecting and preventing crimes and enforcing laws, rules, and regulations for the protection of persons and property and the general maintenance of peace, order, and security. You would develop and maintain positive relations with all segments of the company to obtain cooperation and support in conducting successful security program. Typical activities would include crowd control, foot and mobile patrol, response to situations involving patient disorders, and participation in crime and personal protection programs. This position requires a drivers license and completion of a medical and agility testing because it involves necessary physical fitness in performing a wide range of duties.

From this general list, a description of tasks would be required. A job description includes the working conditions, which include number of hours of employment, shift assignment, and environmental conditions such as inside/outside duty. For example, the described position included this information:

> Normally patrol officers are assigned to regular eight-hour shifts including evenings, nights, weekends, and holidays. You may be assigned to work irregular hours in the event of a major event or emergency. You will be working inside and outside facility buildings and in all kinds of weather conditions.

GENERAL OVERVIEW OF HIRING PRACTICES

As described in preceding chapters, security in the United States is provided by a number of public and private sector agencies, organizations, and enterprises. Our model of security services as described in Chapter 3 becomes a useful tool for identifying the current challenges facing the industry. The most significant challenge is with minimum service model agencies that include contract guard positions that generally pay minimum wage and have few, if any, job benefits. Personnel receive little or no training, and the person is there just to provide a presence in case something should happen. Generally the position is referred to as "rent a cop," "square badge," or other dero gatory term that denotes a security officer without official powers.

Positions in this level have high turnover. *Turnover,* for our purposes, refers to the number of personnel in a specific position for one year. We use one year because it takes that time for a person to be trained and to learn the basic functions of the position. Here we must emphasize "basic functions" because many positions may require two to five years to learn the technical requirements of the positions. Security service organizations can have either positive or negative turnover. *Positive turnover* is described as few people leaving an organization or a job function on an annual basis. It is important to realize that all positions have turnover as people leave for retirement, promotion to a higher rank with another firm, or family responsibilities. Family responsibilities include employment of a spouse at another location, raising children, and taking care of a seriously ill family member. *Negative turnover* would be defined as a high number of people leaving the job position. One hospital, classified as a Level I organization, had a turnover rate that exceeded 100 percent in one year. We believe that negative turnover begins somewhere above 10 percent, which means that the administration is trying to keep 90 percent of the work-face intact while recruiting and training new employees.

This situation with Level I organizations is not going to change unless state governments take proactive steps to increase training and organizations raise their salaries to recruit and retain employees. The federal takeover of airport security positions after 9/11 illustrates this. Most airport security officers were in the minimum categories with low hour wages and no benefits. Many agencies reported more than 100 percent turnover. The takeover of this function by the Transportation Security Administration, which now is part of the Department of Homeland Security, increased wages and benefits. This was financed, in part, with a security tax on airplane tickets.

Hiring procedures in public and private sectors are vastly different. In public sector hiring, especially in those states that have competitive civil service examinations, it takes longer to hire an employee because the person has to take a competitive test and, after the score has been posted, complete a supplementary employment hiring process consisting of a background check, psychological testing, a series of oral interviews, and physical and medical testing. In the private sector, a person may be hired based on his or her education, training, and work experience. For Level III and Level IV agencies, the candidate may be required to pass oral examinations, polygraph and psychological testing, and physical agility exercises.

STAFFING

Persistent issues in staffing are the number of personnel needed to complete assignments and determining the right number of staff to deploy. Security service managers are constantly trying to justify the need for additional personnel to upper management or policy makers. To address this, the International Association of Chiefs of Police created a staffing model that has been adopted in many states (McDougall, 1992) that is quite useful in addressing these personnel issues.

A main concern for security services personnel is the fact that assignments are for twenty-four hours a day, seven days a week. One person cannot normally work three shifts, so one person is limited to one traditional shift assignment of 7 A.M. to 3 P.M., 3 P.M. to 11 P.M., and 11 P.M. to 7 A.M. and so on. In total, a person works only approximately 180 days of the 365-day year based on a forty-hour work week with one week of vacation and five days off for holidays.

To make staffing assignments, the first step is to decide how many "posts" are needed. A *post* can be a patrol area, a critical entrance at a front door, a communication desk, or just about any assignment. Post creation is often difficult for security service organizations that are responsible for patrol over a wide area. Some units simply divide the area into sector zones and determine post assignments based on geography or best guesstimate. Another method is to base shifts according to the number of calls with which patrol units must deal.

For example, one department determined that it answered 3,810 calls for service during a one-year period between the hours of 3 P.M. and 11 P.M. A call for service was any assignment such as assisting a motorist, conducting a crime investigation, and responding to a call for service. The manager then multiplied this figure by .75, which is the average time that is spent on each call.

$$3,810 \times .75 = 2,857.5$$

The manager then multiplied this figure by 3, which is a buffer for routine patrol. This total is then divided by 2,920, the total number of hours needed to fill an eight-hour shift. The quotient from this calculation mathematically showed that three posts were needed for this shift:

$$2,857.5 \times 3 = 8,572.5 \div 2,920 = 2.93, \text{ rounded to } 3$$

The manager then conducted a similar analysis for the other two shifts. Obviously, it is important that data on "calls for service" are collected to conduct this calculation.

Once the number of posts has been determined, it is necessary to staff them with personnel. As discussed earlier, a person is not available to work 365 days of the year based on regular days off and holidays. To determine the number of days that employees actually work, the calculation has to include personal days, sick days, training days, court time, and any other paid time when the employee would not be on post. For example, the manager calculated the following days that her patrol officers were not able for post assignment:

Regular days off	104
Vacation	5
Personnel leave	3
Sick days	5
Holidays	8
Training days	3
Other	1
Total	**129**

She then multiplied this total by 8, which is the number of hours in the shift. This number was then subtracted from 2,920, the number of hours in a staff year 1365 × 82, as follows:

$$129 \times 8 = 1,032 \text{ average hours off}$$

$$2,920 - 1,032 = 1,888 \text{ average hours available}$$

The average number of hours a patrol officer was available, 1,888, was then divided by the total number of hours in a staff year to determine an availability factor.

$$2,920 \div 1,888 = 1.55 \text{ availability factor}$$

Thus, the availability factor of 1.55 was then multiplied by the number of posts for the shift. Thus, for the 3-to-11 shift, the manager needed five patrol officers assigned all year to answer calls for service ($1.55 \times 3 = 4.65$, or 5).

Any mathematical calculation must account for the intrinsic events that occur with each organization. For example, at one department, the shift was responsible for locking down ten buildings each night in addition to other calls. The manager then calculated posts needed by using this number as ten individual calls for service. Determining officer availability must consider personal leave and sick days. In many organizations, personnel can accrue sick days or personal days. In one case review, we found that on paper one officer did not have to work for the entire year because he had accrued an equivalent number of personal days off. Thus, many organizations place an upper limit on the number of days a person can accrue for personal time. Also one immediately has to take into account the flow of action that occurs with each shift. At a nuclear power facility, it was found that the 3-to-11 shift was the busiest for the security services unit because of local traffic problems caused by "day" people leaving work and evening workers arriving between 2 to 4 P.M. at staggered times.

Proper staffing is important for a number of reasons. If the security service unit is understaffed for a long period of time, managers will be dealing with overtime, forced overtime, "blue flu" (calling in sick to get a day off), and high turnover. This was the case at one agency because policy makers did not replace patrol officers who retired or left for other positions. At first the employees enjoyed the overtime but then found that they could not take regular days off, plan for vacations, or use personal time for family events. Eventually, staff would call in sick, thus resulting in forced overtime, which means that a person could not leave her post because a replacement was not available. This, in turn, caused people to leave for other positions and higher costs involved in finding and training new workers.

EMPLOYMENT CONSIDERATIONS

Education

Most security service positions require at least a high school education. This is the national benchmark to ensure that the person can read and write and make basic mathematical computations. In application to security services, this benchmark is used to determine that a person can report orally and write a sequence of events and make notations on report forms. Positions that appear in the upper levels of our planning model, particularly in federal and state agencies, often require a college education that ranges from an associate degree (60 credit hours) to a bachelor's degree (120 to 126 credit hours). Many high-level positions require graduate education or specialty training in computer science, electrical engineering, accounting, or business management.

College education for law enforcement and security personnel and managers began in the 1970s as a result of the President's Commission on Law Enforcement and the Administration of Justice. Policy makers and many public safety executives argued that patrol officers and investigators needed to have higher analytical, ethical, social, and technical skills to deal with a myriad of social problems. Supervisors and administrators needed additional skills related to budgeting, planning, and dealing with the organization's external environment.

Not all law enforcement and security executives have embraced the need for college-educated personnel. Many call for the need for "common sense," not education in dealing with security problems. As discussed by Thibault et.al. (2008), early criminal justice and security administration programs were seen as extensions of the police academy with retired police officers teaching academy-type "handcuffs 101" courses. Some colleges were also found to offer courses of questionable academic value at police stations since applicants were able to obtain federal grants in aid. At this time, approximately 15 percent of all police departments surveyed by the Justice Department require college education. However, many departments use education as a way to obtain promotions (Bureau of Justice Statistics, 2003).

Background Checks

A typical job description for a security service employee states that the person must be of good character. This means that an organization is looking for a person who is not going to commit crimes under the auspices of the agency, sell drugs, misuse agency equipment for personal gain, steal and rob fellow employees or service clients, or steal or sell the company's intellectual data. The organization is also looking for a person who will arrive on time, work well with employees and supervisors, complete tasks in a timely manner, generally use common sense, and do "the right thing" during critical incident situations. Importantly, the person has to be trusted by not only the employer but also the client service population. High-level positions require background checks to ascertain that the person has the necessary education and technical skills required for the position. Very often, original higher education transcripts and training credentials must be presented. To lessen the likelihood of criminal and unethical behavior and to determine whether the person has good job habits and the right skills, security service agencies have instituted a number of procedures to make a reasonable determination of a candidate's qualifications.

The first step is for the candidate to complete the employment application and a background questionnaire such as those in Figure 10-1. Employment applications normally request basic personal information which includes name, address, home phone number(s), recent employment history, employment references, education, and training. Application forms often ask whether the person has been convicted of a crime (a misdemeanor or a felony offense). Note that *conviction* for these purposes does not mean arrest. For security service agencies, the question of arrest is important and can be answered by a review of rap sheets and fingerprint checks.

For security service positions, a candidate employment questionnaire used for the background investigation should include the following:

- Residence for the past twenty years
- Job history since high school
- Five work references with addresses and telephone numbers
- Five social references with addresses and telephone numbers
- Military experience and history
- Credit rating
- Driving record including convictions for moving violations
- Arrests and convictions for crimes
- Self-reported health history

This information serves as the basis for phone and field interviews with references and continuance in the application process. In talking with references, investigators first describe the

Application for Employment

NAME: _____

ADDRESS: _____

_____

_____

LEGAL ADDRESS (if other than above)

_____

1. E-mail address _____
2. Date of birth _____
3. Telephone number _____
4. Do you have a motor vehicle conviction record? _____ yes _____ no
   If yes, please specify:

   _____

   _____

5. Do you have a criminal conviction record: _____ yes _____ no
   If yes, please specify:

   _____

   _____

6. Were you ever involved in a motor vehicle accident that resulted in property damage, personal injury, or death? _____
7. Do you have a valid driver's license? _____ State: _____
8. Do you own a car? _____ Registration number: _____
9. Military service record:

   Organization: _____ Rank: _____

   Date entered: _____ + _____ Date discharged: _____
10. If you are a member of a military reserve, name organization:

    _____

11. Social Security number:

    _____

12. Kind of position applied for:

    _____

13. Would you accept temporary _____ or part-time employment _____?
14. Are you a citizen of the United States? _____
15. Have you ever been barred by any Civil Service Commission from taking examinations or accepting civil service employment? _____

FIGURE 10-1 Typical Security Services Agent Application (Continued)

If yes, explain: _____

_____

_____

16. Are you an employee or an official of any state, territory, county, or municipality?_____

17. Have you ever been discharged (fired) from employment for any reason? _____

If yes, explain: _____

_____

_____

18. Have you ever resigned after being informed that your employer intended to discharge you?

_____ Yes _____ No

19. List your residence addresses for past ten years, including length of time and dates of each:

_____

_____

_____

20. Previous employment: List last three (3) places of employment.

A. Dates of employment (month and year) from _____ to _____

Exact title of your position_____

Salary or earnings (starting) $ _____ per _____

(final) $ _____ per _____

Place of employment _____ City _____ State

Name and address of employer (firm, organization, etc.)

_____

_____

Name and title of immediate supervisor

_____

Reason for leaving: _____

_____

Description of work: _____

_____

B. Dates of employment (month and year) from _____ to _____

Exact title of your position _____

Salary or earnings (starting) $ _____ per _____

(final) $ _____ per _____

Place of employment _____ City _____ State

Name and address of employer (firm, organization, etc.)

_____

_____

Name and title of immediate supervisor

_____

Reason for leaving: _____

_____

Description of work: _____

_____

C. Dates of employment (month and year) from _____ to _____

Exact title of your position _____

Salary or earnings (starting) $ _____ per _____

(final) $ _____ per _____

Place of employment _____ City _____ State

Name and address of employer (firm, organization, etc.)

_____

_____

Name and title of immediate supervisor

_____

Reason for leaving: _____

_____

Description of work: _____

_____

21. Education:

_____

Name Grade School Address Grade Comp.

_____

Name High School Address Grade Comp.

_____

College Address

_____

Years attended Graduated Concentration Degree

_____

College Address

_____

Years attended Graduated Concentration Degree

List any school in addition to the above and the period in attendance. Include correspondence courses, night school, trade schools, and similar education. Include service school in the armed forces or Merchant Marine.

_____

_____

_____

FIGURE 10-1 (Continued)

22. Athletic Activities:

High school: _____

College or university: _____

23. List and describe hobbies: _____

_____

_____

Have you had any experience in commercial photography or advanced work in photography?

_____

Can you swim? _____ Excellent _____ Good _____ Fair

24. Special skills:

a. Kind of license or certificate (e.g.: pilot, teacher, registered nurse, lawyer, radio operator, CPA, etc.) _____

b. State or other licensing authority _____

c. Year of first license or certificate _____

d. Year of latest license or certificate _____

e. Special skills you possess and machines and equipment you can use _____

_____

_____

(for example, short wave radio, computers, key punch, transcribing machine, scientific or professional devices)

f. Typing? _____ Shorthand? _____

g. Special qualifications not covered in application (e.g.: publication, patents, inventions, public speaking experience, membership in professional or scientific association, honors or fellowships received.)

_____

_____

_____

_____

_____

25. Have you previously tested for entrance to the Police Academy? yes _____ no

_____

If yes, approximately when and for what police agency?

_____

_____

NOTE: A FALSE OR DISHONEST ANSWER TO ANY QUESTION IN THIS APPLICATION MAY BE GROUNDS FOR RATING YOU INELIGIBLE OR FOR DISMISSING YOU AFTER APPLICATION EMPLOYMENT APPOINTMENT. ALL STATEMENTS MADE IN THIS APPLICATION ARE SUBJECT TO INVESTIGATION, INCLUDING A CHECK OR YOUR FINGERPRINTS, POLICE RECORDS, AND FORMER EMPLOYERS.

I certify that all of the statements made in this application are true, complete, and correct to the best of my knowledge and belief, and are made in good faith.

Date: _____

Signature of applicant: _____

(Sign in ink)

Authority for Release of Information

I hereby authorize any investigator or duly accredited representative of XYZ Security Department bearing this release, or a copy thereof, within one year of its date, to obtain any information from schools, residential management agents, employers, criminal justice agencies, or individuals relating to my activities. This information may include, but is not limited to, academic, residential, achievement, performance, attendance, personal history, disciplinary, arrest, and conviction records. I hereby direct you to release such information upon request of the bearer. I understand that the information released is for official use by XYZ Security and may be disclosed to such third parties as necessary in the fulfillment of official responsibilities.

I hereby release any individual, including record custodians, from any and all liability for damages of whatever kind or nature which may at any time result to me on account of compliance, or any attempts to comply, with this authorization. Should there be any question as to the validity of this release, you may contact me as indicated below.

SIGNATURE (full name): _____

FULL NAME: _____

OTHER NAMES USED (include maiden name): _____

DATE OF BIRTH: _____

CURRENT ADDRESS: _____

_____

TELEPHONE NUMBER: _____ DATE: _____

FIGURE 10-1 (Continued)

position that the person is applying for and a general review of the tasks to be performed. Then the reference is asked questions such as these:

How long have you known the applicant?

Is the applicant involved in questionable activities?

Would you hire the person for the position?

Do you know the names of other people who could assist us in our review?

Has the candidate been involved in activities that are a threat to the security of the United States?

Do you have any personal information regarding the candidate's drug or alcohol use?

Through fingerprints, the person's name is matched against criminal data banks by fingerprint submission, or name and date of birth submissions. Some candidates run into a problem when the "rap sheet" or fingerprint response shows arrests for offenses that were not reported in the employment background application.

One of the problems with background checks is that they are very time consuming. People in today's society are very mobile. Some agencies send an investigator to each site where a prospective employee worked; others rely on telephone interviews or hire other agencies to complete interviews in distant localities. Because there have been instances in which candidates have sued their former employers for poor work reviews, most agencies require the candidate to sign a waiver of liability stating that she is aware that a background investigation is being completed and that former employers and associates will be contacted.

CRIMINAL HISTORY   Most applicants report violations of the law on applications or in background investigation questionnaires, but there are some who "forget" about past felony and misdemeanor offenses. This information can usually be identified by submitting the candidate's fingerprints to state criminal justice information agencies and the Federal Bureau of Investigation's data bank. Although most public sector law enforcement and security agencies require the submission of fingerprints for job applicants, some states do not require private sector agencies to do so. As a basic tenet, we believe that any person involved in security service operations must submit to a fingerprint check that is verified against state and federal data banks. Additionally, the print submission should be filed on a "search-and-retain" basis, which means that the prints are left in the database for future reference should the person change positions or be arrested for a criminal offense anywhere in the United States.

Candidates with a felony conviction are generally prohibited from employment in security service organizations because they are bad risks, and they may be prohibited by federal law from carrying a weapon. We have seen, however, instances where some states do not bar candidates with nonviolent felony offenses or offenses that occurred while they were sixteen to eighteen years of age. A candidate with a misdemeanor offense or someone who had been charged with a crime and has pled to a lesser charge will be reviewed based on the time, place, and manner of the offense.

CREDIT HISTORY   Some agencies place a great deal of emphasis of credit ratings for they serve as an indicator that the candidate is living within his or her economic means and is responsible in paying debts. Some employers believe that a person with a bad credit rating creates a risk for committing economic and property crimes. There are three major credit reporting agencies used by most card companies, financial institutions, and retailers: Experian, Equifax, and Trans Union. Using national information from banks, credit card companies, home lenders, and so on, these reporting agencies assign numbers or values based on the number of credit cards and loans a person has and her payment history. There are extraordinary reasons that candidates may have a bad credit rating that are not their fault. These include identity theft victimization and economic fallout from a previous marriage.

DRIVING VIOLATIONS   While we have all received a parking ticket or may have received a moving violation summons at some point in our lives, there are those candidates who have received numerous moving violations or parking tickets and their licenses are suspended or revoked based on the number of violations or the failure to appear in traffic court. Repeat offenses and not showing up at court are signs that a person has little discipline and a total disregard for traffic laws. Obviously, a person without a driver's license cannot perform many elements of the security service positions and, except in major metropolitan areas, will have a hard time getting to work.

EMPLOYER REPORTS   There are certain "flags" that immediately appear when a candidate has worked at multiple locations for a short period of time. This usually means that the person has a hard time keeping a position for personal reasons, is unable to get along with supervisors and co-workers, or fails to perform job tasks. It is imperative that the background check include, at a minimum, telephone interviews with past employers on the following:

1. How long did the candidate work for you?
2. Please comment on his or her reliability and attendance.
3. Did he or she perform tasks in a competent manner? Give examples.
4. Were there any problems with ethical behavior on the job? If so, please comment.
5. What areas or performance areas or tasks needed improvement?
6. May I have the names and telephone numbers of two people who worked with the candidate for interview purposes?
7. If you were in my position, would you hire this candidate?

POLYGRAPH EXAMINATIONS   Polygraph examinations are a standard employment practice for many law enforcement agencies. Their application to the security services is based on state laws and the organizational level of the company or agency (usually Level IV). The information provided by the candidate and from the background check is used for a polygraph examination for verification purposes. The polygraph is an electronic machine that measures three items—breathing, blood pressure, and perspiration—when a person is asked specific questions related to the background information. People who are lying will register high on the chart that records these three elements. The key to a successful polygraph examination is a detailed interview about the veracity of information presented to the agency before the actual test.

We know of some individuals who claim that they can beat a polygraph examination. While there are, no doubt, people who have been trained or are simply psychotic, the vast majority of people will register appropriate responses when tested. Because of the cost of the polygraph, many companies are looking at other verification means. These include paper and pencil tests that bring up "red flags" based on answers to the questions.

In addition to the polygraph, voice stress analyzers (VSA) are also used for truth verification in background investigations. Developed in the 1970s, the purpose of the VSA is to detect stress and deception in voice communication. VSA proponents report that this technology is less expensive than polygraph examinations in terms of instrument training and field applications (Pease, 2010). There are several brands that are currently available and in use in the security services field.

DRUG TESTING   Drug testing has been constitutionally upheld since the Supreme Court reviewed a number of cases in 1978. Based on landmark rulings in *National Treasury Employees Union v Von Raab* (109 S. Ct. 1384) and *Skinner v Railway Labor Executives*

Association (109 S.Ct. 1402), courts have ruled that there has to be a relationship between the position and the need for the test in view of safety, ethical, and security reasons. Drug testing may be used in these cases:

Random testing for all employees

Preemployment testing

Testing based on suspicion

Testing for particular positions such as helicopter pilot, drug task force investigator

The most common form of drug screening is the urine test. If a person tests positive, there may be follow-up testing. The reasons for drug testing are clear. Persons who use controlled substances—marijuana, cocaine, uppers and downers, LSD, and chemicals, for example—are violating the law. Also, persons who are misusing prescribed drugs or are using controlled substances are not physically and mentally fit to perform the essential elements of the job and can be a risk to themselves and the client group. Both sets of users may steal agency assets or commit crimes under the authority of their office to feed their habits.

FITNESS REQUIREMENTS AND THE AMERICANS WITH DISABILITIES ACT   Physical agility and fitness requirements have long been viewed as bona fide job-related requirements. Security service employees must be physically able to perform a range of tasks that relate to the position. They must also be in good health, which means being free from diseases or physical aliments that would prevent them from performing assigned tasks or being disqualified from employment. The term of *good health* is rather broad and must be applied to specific requirements for a position. In general, most health standards relate to general agility motion, eyesight, use of hands, breathing, speaking, and reaction to stressful events.

In 1990, President George Bush signed into law the Americans with Disabilities Act (ADA), which expanded regulations related to discriminatory hiring and personnel practices for persons with disabilities. Based on the original legislation and subsequent Supreme Court cases, a *disability* is defined as an impairment that "substantially limits" a major life function. If a person has such a disability, the employer must be able to provide a reasonable accommodation for that person unless it causes undue hardship on the employer. As outlined by Bennett and Hess (1995: 278–283), accommodations for the ADA might include modifying work schedules, training, work stations, assignments, and obtaining special equipment. The first step in dealing with the statute is defining the essential physical functions of the position. Returning to our service model, managers must be able to articulate what tasks personnel must actually perform using our model as follows:

Level I: watching and reporting serious incidents through visual contact or monitoring computers, monitors, and alarms; driving a motor vehicle; filling out reports

Level II: performing emergency first aid and basic restraint of individuals, performing reviews of risk incidents, using a computer keyboard

Level III/IV: responding to critical incidents that may require the use of physical and deadly physical force, driving a motor vehicle in emergency response and pursuit, subduing persons who are resisting authority, running after a person who is the suspect of a crime, responding to a chemical or biological incident and wearing protective clothing as the event requires

Since the passage of the law, case law related to the ADA is very specific related to questions regarding a disability and what is a reasonable accommodation Furthermore, persons who are drug addicts, while they may be disabled, are not eligible for security service positions because they are unable to perform the essential functions of the position and would not pass a background investigation as to character. Thus far, most of the case law involves situations in which current employees are injured and then wish to return to work (Oakstone, 2000).

The other question that is raised by the ADA is the linkage between the position and the actual physical tasks to be performed. Some decades ago, the authors took physical agility tests that attempted to measure the ability to perform tasks that might be required in a security position. These events included running, jumping over walls, dragging a dummy a certain distance, and so on. Job-related physical tests of this type have been replaced by tests for general physical fitness. The most commonly used models in law enforcement are those developed by the Cooper Institute of Dallas, Texas (2010). Over the past decade, the Institute has reviewed validation studies conducted by various state and local law enforcement agencies to validate physical agility for job relatedness. What has resulted is a determination that the following can measure physical fitness.

Fitness Area	Task
Aerobic capacity	1.5 mile Run
Anaerobic power naerobic Power Vertical jump	300 Meter run
Muscular strength	1 RM bench press and/or 1 minute push-up
Muscular endurance	Situps either timed for 1 minute or maximum number

Candidates perform these activities and are scored based on the time and rate of repetitions. Several years ago these tests were gender based with different norms for scoring. As outlined by Cooper (2003), separate standards are now viewed as being against federal antidiscrimination laws; the benchmark for the same job and same standard must be employed. In the next section, we will further discuss federal laws and regulation that have an important impact on hiring.

MAJOR FEDERAL LAWS AND HUMAN RESOURCE ADMINISTRATION

Discrimination

It is against federal law to discriminate against persons in employment considerations which include recruitment, selection, training, evaluations, and promotions. The basis for most labor laws and regulations include a series of presidential executive orders and Title VII of the 1964 Civil Rights Act, which states, in part, that it is illegal to discriminate in employment decisions on the basis of race, color, national origin, sex, and religion. This law and subsequent amendments provide for federal review and regulatory measures for discrimination complaints. It is the benchmark by which most state regulations have been created.

Since the passage of this law, public sector law enforcement hiring has been a target for laws and civil suits related to Title VII. Historically, since the early 1800s, public sector positions, especially those of police officer and firefighter, have been the domain of white males because these positions provided upward mobility for immigrant groups and were used as patronage by politicians. Women and other minorities were rejected at the applicant stage through a variety of formal and informal regulatory and occupational subcultural mechanisms. It was not uncommon for recruiters to tell certain applicants "don't even bother to apply" or to have them rejected unfairly on the basis of physical agility tests and background checks or other reasons.

We would like to say that it is important for employment decisions to be fair. Thus, companies cannot refuse to hire or discharge a person based on race, color, religion, sex, national origin, disability, handicap, or veteran status. Companies cannot discriminate against a person based on these same factors with regard to compensation and the terms and conditions of employment. For this discussion, *terms and conditions of employment* might include scheduling, work assignments, training and promotional opportunities, and retaliating against an employee who made a complaint based on discrimination against the agency. The employer must have physical facilities to accommodate people of both sexes such as lockers and shower areas. Women cannot be discriminated against because they may be of child-bearing age or need to take maternity leaves.

As a business practice, employers have to keep documents and records that document decisions related to hiring, promotions, and work assignments based on acceptable operational standards, qualifications, and seniority requirements. Employees must be notified in writing regarding these employment-related decisions.

Charges involving employment issues can be filed with a number of venues related to alleged discrimination. Persons who have issues related to employment discrimination can make complaints to state regulatory boards or to the federal Equal Employment Opportunity Commission (EEOC) or federal courts. In organizations that have collective bargaining, this complaint ability becomes even more important because there has to be adherence to the collective bargaining agreement regarding pay, benefits, and conditions of employment. *Conditions of employment* is a rather broad concept that might include provision of uniforms, equipment, training, shift assignments, overtime assignments, the type of weapon issued, and staffing levels.

Affirmative Action

A controversial public policy that emerged in the late 1970s was affirmative action. A basic definition of *affirmative action* is the process by which employers take proactive steps to recruit employees from populations underrepresented in the workforce and not discriminate against minority applicants. Despite these efforts, women and minorities were consistently excluded from graduate programs and certain "male" occupations such as police and fire positions across the county. Through a series of Supreme Court cases and federal regulatory orders, many organizations—particularly fire and police—were required to sign consent orders to take affirmative steps to hire and promote minority and women candidates. In many cases, these programs became controversial and were viewed, particularly by white males, as quota programs.

During the last decade, many consent programs have been dismantled based on the increased numerical representation of minority employees and revisions to hiring procedures. Recent Supreme Court cases, such as *Adarand Constructors v Pena* (132 L.Ed.2d 158), however, allow set aside programs only if it can be shown that there was a compelling reason for why an agency initiated the program in terms of hiring minority applicants and so on. At the present time, lawsuits related to promotions in the public sector are often filed by white candidates over charges of reverse discrimination.

Fair Labor Standards Act

The Fair Labor Standards Act (FLSA) which was passed by Congress in 1938 to address working conditions for children and the concept of "work week," requires employers to pay employees one and one-half times the regular wage for work requiring more than forty hours a week. The FLSA was deemed to not apply to public sector agencies because of the operational flexibility needed to staff twenty-four-hour shifts. This exemption ended in 1986 with the decision in *Garcia v San Antonio Metropolitan Transit Authority* when the Supreme Court ruled that FLSA was applicable to state and local law enforcement agencies.

Thus, for security service operations, employees must be paid the time and one-half rate for time worked over forty hours. There are a number of exceptions. For example, the "40-hour" rule does not apply if the employee was paid overtime by agency or collective bargaining agreement after eight hours. Executives, managers, sales personnel working on commission, technical support personnel, and those deemed professional employees (e.g., teachers, lawyers, and physicians) are exempt under this act. Certain seasonal employees at parks and recreational sites are also exempt. Operationally, a manager must be able to classify employees as either exempt or nonexempt in dealing with the FLSA. The key here is including in the job description the extent to which the employee is deemed a manger or a policy maker and using personal judgment to deal with overall agency or company decisions.

Age Discrimination

The Age Discrimination in Employment Act of 1974 (ADEA) prohibits discrimination on the basis of age for employees age 40 and older. Often, certain companies would find ways to lay off employees in this age bracket as an effort to cut costs and hire younger workers. In 1990, this law was amended to also prohibit discrimination with regard to benefits such as wage, medical, disability, and retirement. For security service agencies, age cannot be used as a reason for not hiring or retaining an employee unless it can be shown that the age requirement is related to a bona fide occupational requirement. This affects many security service organizations that have age limits in hiring and mandatory retirement ages in the range of fifty-five to sixty years of age. The reason for these age limits is the relationship between age and the physical rigors of the position.

Sexual Harassment

It seems that in every decade there are some high-profile case studies about sexual harassment. Events related to the topic of sexual harassment during the presidency of William Clinton are still used by trainers to illustrate complicated issues regarding this topic in the workplace. Sexual harassment cases that are settled either before or after a trial with high payments for damages to victims always are reported with large headlines. There are three types of sexual harassment complaints:

1. Making unwanted advances toward an employee, including touching, physical violence, and continued pressure for sexual favors.
2. Making sexual demands in return for promotions, assignments, or job security.
3. Creating a hostile work environment, which includes a wide range of behaviors such as sexually explicit posters and jokes, or harassing an employee by taping sex paraphernalia to bulletin boards, locker room doors, and mailboxes.

The first stage in dealing with sexual harassment is creating a policy and conducting training programs for *all* employees—including supervisors and management—on what sexual harassment is and methods by which employees can make complaints. It is critical that supervisors and managers document and take proactive steps to address complaints when it comes to their attention. The information contained in Figure 10-2 shows a sample policy on sexual harassment.

Purpose:

Utica College affirms the principle that its students, faculty, staff, and guests have a right to work, study, and enjoy the society of the College community without being subjected to sexual harassment or sexual assault, including rape. The academic community depends on the integrity of its members to maintain an environment in which all may function free of intimidation. Sexual harassment subverts the mission and the work of the College, and will not be tolerated in any form or context at Utica College. All members of the College community have a responsibility to ensure that the College is free from all forms of sexual harassment.

Definition:

Sexual harassment constitutes a form of sex discrimination and all forms of sexual harassment are prohibited, including the following: an unwelcome sexual advance, request for sexual favors, or other expressive, visual or physical conduct of a sexual or gender-motivated nature, when:

1. submission to such conduct is made either explicitly or implicitly as term or condition of an individual's employment or status in a Utica College course, program or activity; or
2. submission to or rejection of such conduct by an individual is used as the basis for employment-related, educational, or other decision affecting an individual; or
3. such conduct has the purpose or effect of unreasonably interfering with an individual's work, educational performance or status; or
4. such conduct has the purpose or effect of creating an intimidating, hostile, or offensive environment.

What behaviors may be considered "sexually harassing"?

Most sexual harassment falls into two categories: verbal and physical. Verbal harassment may include:

- Sexual innuendoes and comments about clothing, one's body, or sexual activity
- Suggestive or insulting sounds
- Turning work, class, or individual discussions to sexual topics inappropriately
- Whistling in a suggestive manner
- Humor and jokes about sex or women/men in general
- Sexual propositions, invitations, or other pressure for sex
- Implied or overt threats

Physical harassment may include:

- Patting, pinching, and any other inappropriate touching or feeling
- Brushing against the body
- Attempted or actual kissing or fondling
- Coerced sexual intercourse
- Assault

Other types of sexual harassment may include:

- Leering or ogling
- Making obscene gestures
- Giving unwanted materials or gifts of a personal nature
- Sending unwanted letters, e-mails, or making unwanted telephone calls
- Stalking

What should I do if I believe I have been harassed or assaulted?

Employees and students have recourse through the formal and informal grievance procedures of the College. Any employee or student may present a complaint without fear or reprisal.
Depending on the seriousness of the offense, the employee may wish to:

- notify the alleged harasser that their behavior is offensive and unwelcome
- note date, time, location, and witnesses of the alleged harassment
- meet with the alleged harasser, with a third party, to discuss your feelings toward what is being said or done

1. Individuals with a complaint regarding sexual harassment may have initial contact with the individual's supervisor, department head, division dean, or the Director of Human Resources. Depending on the individuals involved, the Vice President for Academic Affairs, the Vice President for Student Affairs, or the Associate Dean of Students may also be appropriate initiate contact people.
2. Supervisors, complainants, etc. may also wish to consult with Academic Support Services Center staff; if counseling support is desired, counselors are available through the Academic Support Services Center or the Employee Assistant Program.
3. All serious and formal complaints must be taken to the Office of Human Resources, and complaints will be investigated in a prompt and confidential manner to the degree possible.

FIGURE 10-2   Sample Policy on Sexual Harassment

Related to this is harassment. Harassment is unwanted or hostile behavior directed at an employee on the basis of race, color, national origin, religion, age, physical or mental disability, or any other basis protected by applicable law (Bagyi and Boyd, 2009). This can include a range of behaviors as threats, derogatory comments, hostile jokes, hardcopy or electronic drawings or cartoons, and physical contact. Another area that has gained attention is bullying. Bullying refers to unreasonable actions of an individual or group of individuals directed towards an employee, or group of employees, which is intended to intimidate and creates a risk to the health and safety of the employee(s) [Department of Labor and Industries (2008)]. Bullying involves either a repeated pattern of behavior or the "culture" of the work unit or organization—some examples include unwarranted criticism, being treated differently, and being shouted at or humiliated.

Policies on sexual harassment, harassment, and bullying should outline the various behaviors that are prohibited and where employees can make complaints to in order to have the issues resolved. Policies in these areas should also include a statement against retaliation, which often occurs when a person makes a complaint and then is subject to harassment or adverse employment action (e.g., transfer to another unit, moved to a smaller office, and having rank and tasks taken away).

FAMILY MEDICAL LEAVE ACT

The Family Medical Leave Act, that was signed into law in 1993, entitles employees to take unpaid leave up to twelve weeks to take care of newborn or recently adopted children or to care for a seriously ill family member. The law covers unmarried domestic partners who have to take care of children from the relationship. It also allows the employee to take an unpaid leave if he or she has a serious medical condition (Weiss, 1998).

The act resulted from company practices to fire people for having to leave work to take care of children or their own medical conditions or those of others. The law also prohibits employers from modifying health plan coverage related to these illnesses or leaves.

DISCIPLINARY ACTIONS AND REWARD SYSTEMS

In all organizations there is the need to define the rules and expectations for employees. As discussed in Chapter 3, this is formally included in the employee handbook, job description, and what is called *past practice*. The term refers to the unwritten behavior of organizational members based on daily rituals commonly understood by all members of the organization (e.g., "we have always done it this way"). In unionized environments, past practice may suddenly become formalized as a work rule or memorandum of agreement after a dispute between labor and management. In one department, the past practice of having two officers in a patrol car was an unwritten rule for years. After a new director of public safety questioned this practice, the union filed a grievance, and the practice became part of the memorandum of understanding between labor and management.

The behavior of organizational members is governed by a number of laws, regulations, and rules including state and federal criminal codes and state and organizational rules and regulations that define the daily conduct of the organization's members. All security service organizations are concerned with acts of misconduct by their members because it reflects badly on the agency and its ability to perform its mission. Misconduct by for-profit companies, has a negative impact on future contracts or relations with clients. There is also the possibility of civil action against the agency by a client or victim. For example, patrol officers who use street justice against low-level drug dealers may subject their employer to a whole range of civil rights violations and civil suits.

For our discussion, *misconduct* is broadly defined as any violation of law or agency practice. Misconduct is also used with regard to corrupt activities in which a security services officer uses her position for personal gain. This might include stealing property, using classified information for personal reasons, and accepting a payoff to be absent during the commission of a crime. Using a scale of one (minor) to ten (serious), committing a felony offense while on duty would be a ten while failing to get to work on time might be a one or a two. However, a person who is late ten times in one month may move from a lower classification to an eight.

To deal with these issues, agencies must have disciplinary policies that are widely understood by employees. These can include a verbal or written warning, counseling, fine, loss of days off, suspension, and termination. All textbooks speak to progressive and consistent discipline. *Progressive discipline* is dealing with a situation in a timely, just, and progressive manner related to the scale given earlier. The employee who is tardy for work but has never been late before deserves a kind verbal warning in comparison to someone who is late all the time. On the other hand, an untrained officer who attempts to deactivate a bomb device and presents a danger to himself or others may require suspension and termination. Thus, it is important that the organization have a disciplinary system that is operational. The system also should have a formal process whereby clients, visitors, victims, and other employees can make complaints for agency or company action.

EMPLOYEE EVALUATION AND REWARDS

Few textbooks on human resource administration address positive ways to encourage and motivate employees and subordinate managers. It is an issue that requires looking beyond uniforms, training, and salaries. First and foremost, security service managers must be viewed as leaders and be visible by line personnel rather than sitting in the office all day. Fire chiefs and captains know this well, for they are judged by leading the troops in serious situations, not standing in the background. The most basic method to reward employees is through positive oral or, on more important occasions, written acknowledgement. There should be a written performance evaluation of the employee on an annual basis at a minimum to address performance indicators related to completion of tasks; establishment of satisfactory relationships with supervisors, co-workers, and clients; and self-improvement through training or education. Although many evaluation forms and formats are available, employee evaluation can be a very exhausting process. What often happens, however, is that supervisors do not document enough information during the total evaluation time period and instead rely on memory of incidents or events that took place weeks before the evaluation.

The criteria used for employee evaluation include a number of factors. A review of several evaluation formats used for security services personnel shows several common themes as follows:

1. Dependability—ready for duty; reports for work on time and ready for duty; completes assignments in a timely manner.
2. Judgment—ability to solve problems; uses good judgment in dealing with situations.
3. Relationships with Clients/Public/Co-Workers—shows courtesy to clients and the general public and is able to work with co-workers and supervisors.
4. Initiative—interest in work and desire to learn new skills.
5. Job Knowledge—understands the dimensions of assignments; undergoes training to learn new tasks.

For supervisors, the same criteria apply with the additional factors of providing leadership, motivation, and evaluation of employees. Thus, it is important for supervisors to keep records on such items as attendance, personal observation, extraordinary service, letters of praise and complaint, and training attendance and completion. Negative items, such as lateness or poor performance, must be brought to the employee's attention immediately and not fester until the next formal evaluation. In short, employee evaluation must be viewed as a continuous interaction between the supervisor and the subordinate that involves daily feedback, coaching, and encouragement.

With regard to rewards, it is no secret that employees at all levels like to be recognized for a job well done and are likely to stay with the unit if they receive such recognition. Many security service organizations have service awards (e.g., plaques, award ceremonies, monetary bonuses, and service or award ribbons) for uniformed personnel. These should be made for "real" contributions of service to the organization or for heroism at a particular incident. Quite often a thank-you note given to an employee or a unit immediately after a great performance goes a long way. Small thank-you rewards for a job well done might include bonus days off, tickets to a concert or athletic event, and coupons for a meal while on duty.

The extent to which a person can move up an organization to either a specialized or supervisory position depends on the career ladder that exists in the agency. This, in turn, is dependent on agency size, complexity of tasks and mission, and scope of operations. Because of the 24/7 nature of security services, security officers are deployed usually by shift and the need to fill posts or functions. For supervisory purposes, the general rule for "span of control" is that one person can supervise five to six people. The general scope for supervisory duties include planning, organizing, and controlling the activities of the security unit. Supervisors assign and review work assignments, evaluate performance, and deal with issues involving motivation and discipline. They may also become the persons in charge of an emergency situation or investigation.

In public sector organizations, promotions are based on time on the job, work history, completion of special training, and testing. Tests may include a written examination that deals with job-related functions and the ability to make a decision given a set of circumstances. This is further reviewed by an interview with a promotion or managerial panel that would assess the candidate's history and her decision-making ability.

Executive Positions

While the focus of our discussion is on entry level and supervisory positions, some attention must be paid to executive leadership in the security services organization. At one time, most senior positions, particularly in the private sector, were comprised of retirees from federal and state police forces. Today there is a trend where many positions are being filled from within the organization of people who have risen through the ranks.

What are the necessary qualifications for leadership positions in the security services organization? These will vary according to the dictates of the position and the services being provided. In general, candidates must be able to complete the same background, psychological, and related checks as with entry level and supervisory candidates. Furthermore, candidates must have the following attributes:

Excellent interpersonal and written communication skills.

Technical expertise or experience in the field related to the business of the company or agency undertaking the hiring (e.g., health care, higher education, and financial fraud).

Leadership skills for working with a wide range of stakeholders including employees, senior management, and external groups such as law enforcement. All of these undertakings may be done in a global environment.

Formal higher education and certifications in the security services and related fields. For corporate level leaders it is not unusual for incumbents to possess graduate degrees in business, criminal justice, public administration, and computer science along with training certifications in law enforcement and security.

Good health. Executive positions do require much mental and physical stamina in dealing with people and situations. Candidates for organizations with global operations must be able to travel and deal with time zones.

Following the theme of this text, the candidate should have the ability to address problems from both an immediate and long-term planning perspective. This involves having an undertaking of enterprise risk management and strategic planning.

COLLECTIVE BARGAINING

You may recall from Chapter 1 that security service personnel were often used to "break" union organizing in the nineteenth and well into the twentieth centuries. Many security service managers deal with the issue of unionism or collective bargaining. *Collective bargaining* is the process by which employees bargain with an employer for wages, benefits, and conditions of employment. If there is a major disagreement between the employer and the union, the union can withhold its services through a strike or boycott. Since the passage of the National Labor Relations Act of 1935, employees in the private sector are allowed to form unions if a majority of those in a work unit vote for a collective bargaining group. Government workers were allowed to form unions under the Civil Service Reform Act Title VII of 1978 (Schermerhorn, 2002). However, only certain states and federal agencies allow security service employees to form unions, and none have a strike provision. This means that serious disputes over contract negotiations or grievances are settled by a third-party arbitrator or referee.

Collective bargaining is an economic activity, and an ultimate disagreement between the employer and the employees can lead to a strike, which is the withholding of labor by the employees. In the public sector, only certain states allow public employees to form unions because there is a fear that strikes would lead to widespread disruption of vital services such as police/security, health, and fire protection. On the federal level, however, many security service agencies are allowed to unionize. One issue that arose with the passage of the Homeland Security Bill was whether unionized federal workers would be allowed to continue with their union affiliations. The administration of President George W. Bush wanted all employees to work as direct appointees of the president, but various members in the Senate and House of Representatives stalled the security measure until the union issue was resolved. The issue was resolved in that most unionized workers retained their collective bargaining rights.

In collective bargaining, most contracts include a grievance procedure to deal with issues that arise during the contract. A grievance procedure typically deals with employment disputes and discipline of union members by management. In most contracts, there is a stepwise process that deals with differences between the union and the employer. Most contracts call for informal discussions between the union member and the employer to resolve the issue. If this cannot be achieved, the employee may request a formal hearing between the union and the employer. If the hearing does not resolve the dispute, an outside mediator may be brought in to resolve the issue. If the mediator is unsuccessful, there may be a binding arbitration hearing at which the case is heard by a state-appointed arbitrator. In all contracts there is usually a strict time limit in which grievances can be filed by the employee and responded to by the employer.

A standard item that appears in collective bargaining agreements is the management rights clause, which defines those areas over which management exercises exclusive decision-making authority. Such authority includes the right to determine an agency's mission, budget, general employee duties and internal security matters (Department of the Interior, 2004). However, in practice, some bargaining agreements may have management items that have been bargained or are established as a past practice with regards to job assignments. A common area that intrudes into management rights is the use of seniority or time on the job for work and shift assignments. Unions are also free to file civil suit in state and federal courts over major issues. In those states that have comprehensive collective bargaining statutes, there is also an improper practice procedure available when union members allege that the employer is interfering with union activity or failing to negotiate in good faith. On the other hand, employees may sue their union if believe feel that they are not being represented in a fair manner.

In the security service industry, union organizing activity appears to be very active in a wide range of Level I organizations because their employees typically receive low wages and limited benefits. This situation has caught the attention of many national collective bargaining groups—such as the Service Employees International Union (SEIU), which represents more than 1.5 million workers—that seek to raise wages and employment standards. Public sector security service workers are generally union affiliated in the Northeast, Midwest, and West Coast. Traditionally, states in the South and Southwest have prohibited or discouraged public employees from joining unions, but that appears to be slowly changing in such growth states as Florida, Texas, and Arizona. Most public sector unions are related to the employer's political basis—federal, state, and local—because negotiating issues are driven by operational or local political considerations. For example, the American Federation of State, County and Municipal Employees (AFSCME), which is affiliated with the American Federation of Labor (AFL), has local and state chapters for security service and police personnel for collective bargaining purposes. Some federal security service operational and clerical personnel are represented by the American Federation of Government Employees. Note that employees of certain federal law enforcement agencies such as the FBI, Secret Service, and Drug Enforcement Office, are prohibited from joining collective bargaining groups and their wages, benefits, and conditions of employment are regulated by Congress. The Fraternal Order of Police (FOP), which has affiliate social and collective bargaining groups, represents certain security service agencies such as college and universities. Overall the nature of contracts and collective bargaining remains regional and local in nature for most security services organizations.

Collective bargaining for many security service units must be viewed in the larger context of the national and state political arena. Union membership dues may be used to lobby for union-specific programs in state legislatures, and candidates constantly vie for endorsements and campaign contributions from unions. It is not surprising that union political lobbying occurs across the country on a wide variety of topics related to security in this country. For example, the FOP, which represents many police and security unions, has been lobbying for the right for off-duty police officers to carry concealed firearms anywhere in this country as a means of dealing with terrorism. Very often, state statutes and agency policies prohibit carrying firearms outside of the officer's jurisdiction. Another agenda item for the FOP is to oppose revised Department of Labor regulations that would increase the classification of nonexempt workers from earning overtime. It is feared that this would apply to many police supervisors who earn time and one-half and double time for overtime purposes.

The SEIU has been calling for higher wages and training for security officers through federal legislation. In 2009, it has been recognized as the collective bargaining agent for many security officer unions in the northeast United States and has settled contracts in the New York, New Jersey, and Washington, D.C., areas for municipal employees, and private sector organizations contracting with municipal governments such as Allied Barton, Guardsmark, and Securitas. Contract negotiations have resulted in raises and health insurance and related benefits for security officers.

SOCIAL NETWORKING ISSUES

Social networking sites on the Internet, such as Facebook, Twitter, and others, have become favorite platforms for global human interaction. As reported by Mintz (2009), these sites have raised four issues: employer review of these locations for background investigations; review of actions and comments that reflect badly on either the employee or the employer; disclosure of confidential information related to the nature of business; and use of company equipment and time for social networking. Many major companies have begun exploring policy developments that deal with the following:

- The use of company computers and work time
- Company confidentiality policies of proprietary information
- Compliance with policies related to harassment, affirmative action, and discrimination.

Most policies include a disclaimer that the views expressed by an employee do not represent the views of any other person or the company.

Summary

The main administrative activity related to security service administration involves human resource administration. Simply stated, human resource personnel find the best person for a position and administer training or retaining programs, competitive salary and benefits, promotional opportunities, and work challenges so that the company or agency can retain the employee. It is also important that employees be recognized through formal and informal thank-you programs. If these criteria cannot be met, the employee may leave or be dissatisfied.

This discussion of human resource administration for security services provided an introductory review of major human resource issues and laws. These statutes and state regulatory rules are very complex and, if anything, show the need for due diligence in dealing with labor matters. Employers must be able to define, document, and discuss their hiring, disciplinary, and termination decisions.

Additionally, some security service administrators must deal with collective bargaining groups in day-to-day operations.

Review Questions/Activities

1. Why is there high turnover in Level I security service units? Does that appear to be the case with any of the organizations in your area that you have reviewed for earlier chapters?

2. Apply the post and staffing model to an agency after obtaining information regarding its calls for service, days off, and so on.

3. John and Jane Jones are candidates for the position of patrol officer with a major medical center. Both graduated from college with a bachelor's degree and have great work habits and part-time school employment references. Jane is an infrequent user of marijuana. Who would you hire for the position?

4. Define *progressive discipline* and discuss how it can be applied to an employee who in one year did the following:
   • Fell asleep while on duty
   • Discharged a firearm at a deer in a parking lot by accident
   • Dented the rear bumper on a patrol car

   The employee has ten years of exemplary service and several commendations for heroism. She is assigned to patrol security at a nuclear plant facility.

5. Obtain a copy of a collective bargaining agreement for a security service organization. Outline the provisions that deal with wages, benefits, conditions of employment, management rights, and the grievance procedure for contract disputes and discipline.

6. Discuss with a security service manager or supervisor the various ways or methods that the unit or agency rewards employees for outstanding work performance.

7. Decide whether the following situations constitute sexual harassment:

   a. Bill Jones tells a series of dirty jokes to a group of male officers in the squad area one morning. Debbie Long, a new officer, walks in and blushes after hearing some of his stories.

   b. Fred Ray, a supervisor, likes to touch the shoulders of all his employees while he is giving instructions. The female officers walk into the manager's office one day and demand that Fred be removed.

   c. Maxine Reynolds, an officer with twelve years of experience, is attracted to Joe Williams, who has been transferred to her shift. Maxine asks Joe out for a date, but he says no and adds that he is a married man. He then goes to the human resource office and files a complaint against Maxine.

   d. During an emergency first aid training session, Lou Jones, a five-year officer, places the CPR dummies into sexually provocative positions. He takes some masking tape and writes the name of Mary Joan White and sticks it to the dummy. Mary Joan walks into the room, and the students erupt in laughter.

Web Searches

1. Access the Web site for *Security Management* magazine at www.securitymanagement.com. Search the archives for articles pertaining to the management of personnel in security services agencies, select an article, and summarize the issues highlighted in that article.

2. Use your favorite Internet browser to locate published articles on the subject of personnel management in security operations. After reading the articles, prepare a summary of the issues they raised. Note when doing your search how many of the resources you located dealt with discrimination by age, sex, and marital status.

References

Adarand Constructors v Federico Pena, 132 L.Ed. 2d 158. 1995.

Bagyi, John, and Matthew G. Boyd. 2009. *Harassment Prevention.* Security Management, January 2009, pp. 46–55.

Bennett, Wayne, and Karen Hess. 1995. *Management and Supervision in Law Enforcement.* Minneapolis/St. Paul: West Publishing.

Bureau of Justice Statistics. 2003. "Law Enforcement Management and Administrative Statistics—Local Police Departments." Washington, D.C.: U.S. Department of Justice. Accessed January 3, 2003, at www.ojp.usdoj.gov/bjs.

Cooper Institute for Aerobics Research. 2003. Common Questions Regarding Physical fitness Tests, Standards and Programs for Public Safety. Accessed January 10, 2010 at www. http://www.cooperinstitute.org/education/law_enforcement/index.cfms.

Department of Labor and Industries—State of Washington. *Workplace Bullying: What Everyone Needs to Know.* April 2008, Report 87-2-2008.

Mintz Levin. *The Increased Use of Social Networking Websites and the Important of a Social Networking Policy for Your Workforce.* Web accessed at http://www.mintz.com/publications/1962/Employment_ and_Labor_Alert_The_Increased_Use_of_Social_Networking_Websites_and_the_Importance_of_a_Social_Networking_Policy_for_Your_Workforce. Accessed January 20, 2010.

National Treasury Employees Union v Von Raab, 489 U.S. 656, 109 S.Ct. 1384, 103 L.Ed.2d 685. 1989.

Oakstone Publishing. 2000. *Deskbook Encyclopedia of Public Employment Law.* Egan, Minn.: Oakstone.

Pease, William (2010). Background Investigations and the Use of Lie Detection Machines. Uica College, unpublished report.

Schermerhorn, John R. 2002. *Management,* 7th ed. New York: Wiley.

Skinner v Railway Labor Executives Association, 489 U.S. 602, 109 S.Ct. 1402, 103 L.Ed.2d 639. 1989.

Thibault, Edward A., Lawrence Lynch, and R. Bruce McBride. 2008. *Proactive Police Management,* 7th ed. Upper Saddle River, N.J.: Prentice-Hall.

U.S. Department of the Interior. 2004. "Personnel Manager: Employee's Guide to Labor Relations." Accessed June 20, 2004 at www.doi.gov/hrm/pmanager/labfaw.htlm.

Weiss, Donald. 1998. *A Manager's Guide to Safely Hiring, Managing and Firing.* American Management Association: Washington, D.C.

11

■ ■ ■

Security Management: Compliance

KEY TERMS

compliance,   electronic personal health information (EPHI),   Gramm-Leach-Bliley Act (GLBA),   HIPAA,   NIPP,   PCI,   DSS,   Red Flag rules,   Sentencing Guidelines.

Why does the subject of *compliance* find its way into a text on security? What is compliance, and what role does security play in the compliance effort? Tarantino (2007: 21) states that compliance "is a fairly straightforward concept of acting in accordance with established laws, regulations, protocols, standards, and specifications." Bishop and Hydoski (2009: 84) define compliance as "the act of adhering to, and demonstrating adherence to, external laws and regulations as well as corporate policies, procedures, and controls." Biegelman (2008: 2) describes *compliance* this way:

> "Knowing the law and following it is only one side of compliance. Compliance goes much deeper than that, true compliance anyway. Simply following the law so that one doesn't get into trouble is not full compliance. State-of-the-art compliance involves a successful blending of compliance—following rules, regulations and laws—with ethics—developing and sustaining culture based on values, integrity, and accountability, and always doing the right things. True compliance ensures consistency of actions to eliminate, or at least lessen, opportunities for harm from criminal conduct or other compliance failures."

Every type of entity—for-profit businesses, non-profit businesses, and government agencies, must engage in the task of compliance. Most large entities and those businesses engaged in certain industries have a member of the C-suite who serves as the chief compliance officer (CCO). In some instances, the position is mandated by law or regulation. The Sarbanes-Oxley Act (SOX) requires public companies to designate an individual as the CCO, and the Financial Industry Regulatory Authority (FINRA), an independent regulatory authority, requires its member security firms to designate an individual as the CCO. In other cases, it is required by the courts or regulators following a major breach of the law, a compliance failure. Some businesses have voluntarily undertaken compliance as part of their business plan and mission. Public-sector agencies also have adopted compliance policies and designated a top-level executive to serve as the compliance officer. The growth of private- and public-sector compliance programs in the past decade has been significant, and certification programs have been implemented to ensure adherence to standards and best practices. This chapter discusses compliance mandates for security services in certain industries (e.g., financial institutions) and with respect to certain types of assets (e.g., client information) and the need for compliance even when not mandated by a law or regulation. The chapter also describes the role of security services in an organization's compliance efforts.

DATA SECURITY

The security of data, whether it is our personal health information, credit card information concerning an individual's account or transaction, or employee payroll records on the network server of a government agency, has become a major issue in this millennium. Lawmakers are sensitive to the privacy and security of consumer personal information and have enacted several measures designed to ensure the privacy and security of such data. We will focus on five of those measures: the Gramm-Leach-Bliley Act (GLBA, also known as the Financial Services Modernization Act of 1999), which applies to personal financial information in the possession of financial institutions; the Health Insurance Portability and Accountability Act (HIPAA), which applies to personal information held by health care providers, suppliers, and insurers; the Family Educational Rights to Privacy Act (FERPA), which applies to the privacy and security of student records held by academic institutions; the Fair and Accurate Credit Transaction Act of 2003 (FACT Act), which requires the Federal Trade Commission and other industry regulators to establish guidelines for the prevention of identity theft and to require financial institutions and creditors to institute procedures and policies (the "Red Flag" rules) to address their risk of identity theft; and the Fair Credit Reporting Act (FCRA), which protects the personal information and credit history of individuals and businesses held by credit reporting agencies. The chapter also discusses industry security standards applied to certain transactions, notably the Payment Card Industry data security standards (PCI DSS) applicable to those who process or retain personal information in the context of credit, debit, or certain prepaid card transactions.

Financial Institutions

The Gramm-Leach-Bliley Act of 1999 (GLBA) eliminated restrictions on the types of products that various financial institutions could offer. For example, prior to GLBA, banks could not engage in the insurance business, securities firms could not engage in banking, and so on. Under GLBA, financial institutions, such as J.P. Morgan Chase & Co. and Citigroup, can perform all of these services. At the same time, because of an apprehension or concern that client personal financial information would be readily shared with affiliated businesses and product lines and unaffiliated vendors, Congress imposed requirements designed to ensure the privacy and security of customer information.

The GLBA authorized various regulators to develop privacy rules designed to ensure that consumers be given notice of the manner in which their financial institution will handle customer and consumer nonpublic information and enable consumers to inform the financial institution that they do not want information disclosed to certain parties. The institution must provide an annual notice to its customers (those individuals with significant or long-standing relationship with the institution) of its privacy practices, how customer information is collected and shared with affiliated businesses and unaffiliated third parties, and how that information is safeguarded. The institution's consumers (those who have obtained a financial product or service, but who do not qualify as a customer) are entitled to a notice when the institution shares the consumer's financial information with an unaffiliated third party.

The role of security services applies most significantly to the GLBA's safeguard rules mandate. GLBA requires that standards be established relating to administrative, technical, and physical safeguards that are designed to:

1. to insure the security and confidentiality of customer records and information;
2. to protect against any anticipated threats or hazards to the security or integrity of such records; and
3. to protect against unauthorized access to or use of such records or information which could result in substantial harm or inconvenience to any customer. (15 U.S.C. § 6801 [b])

The Federal Trade Commission, which is a principal regulator of GLBA mandates, has established its Safeguards Rule, which requires all financial institutions to:

1. designate the employee or employees to coordinate the safeguards;
2. identify and assess the risks to customer information in each relevant area of the company's operation and evaluate the effectiveness of current safeguards for controlling these risks;
3. design a safeguards program and detail the plans to monitor it;
4. select appropriate service providers and require them by contract to implement the safeguards; and
5. evaluate the program and explain adjustments in light of changes to business arrangements or the results of security tests. (16 C.F.R. § 314.4)

The identification and assessment of risks to customer information must include three areas of operation: "employee training and management; information systems, including network and software design, and information processing, storage, transmission and retrieval; and security management, including the prevention, detection and response to attacks, intrusions or other system failures" (16 C.F.R. § 314.4).

The design of a safeguards program may include consideration of the financial institution's size, nature, and scope of activities and the sensitivity of the consumer information that it possesses (16 C.F.R. § 314.3 [a]). Finally, the Safeguards Rule includes specific requirements for contracts with nonaffiliated third parties. In summary, the ability to offer diverse business products to customers is balanced by strict mandates for the security of nonpublic customer information, security requirements that are technology based.

It is important to recall that the safeguard standards are risk based. Thus, application of the principles and processes discussed in Chapter 4 are critical to a financial institution's compliance with the GLBA safeguard rules.

Financial Institutions and Creditors

Section 114 of the FACT Act requires federal banking agencies, the National Credit Union Administration, and the Federal Trade Commission to establish guidelines for each financial institution and creditor (those who extend credit or who defer payment and bill customers later) to use in connection with transactions and customer accounts for the prevention of identity theft. The Federal Trade Commission (n.d.) promulgated the Red Flags Rule, which sets forth those guidelines and requires financial institutions and creditors to institute an Identity Theft Prevention Program that sets forth the policies and procedures designed to prevent and detect identity theft.

The guidelines provide that each ID theft program should have a four-step process: (1) identify relevant red flags—that is, "a pattern, practice, or specific activity that indicates the possible existence of identity theft" (16 C.F.R. § 681.2 [b][9]); (2) detect red flags; (3) prevent and mitigate ID theft; and (4) periodically update the program to reflect changes in technology and the tactics of identity thieves. Within each step of the process the guidelines provide examples. In step 1, for example, the guidelines suggest that the entity consider risk factors presented by the types of accounts it maintains, the sources of red flags, and categories of common red flags. The guidelines (Appendix A to 16 C.F.R., Part 681) further specify, for example, categories of common red flags, such as alerts from a credit reporting company, suspicious documents, suspicious personal identifying information, suspicious account activity, and notices received from other sources. In the prevention and mitigation of identity theft, the guidelines mention several privacy and security measures such as changing passwords and security codes, monitoring an account for evidence of identity theft, and reopening an account with a different account number. Notably, the guidelines require that a member of senior management be designated to communicate with, and report to, the board of directors. That designee must submit a report at least annually that informs the board and senior management of the entity's compliance with the guidelines and the effectiveness of its program.

Health Care Providers and Insurers

The Health Insurance Portability and Accountability Act (HIPAA) was enacted in 1996. One of its purposes was to reduce health care costs by eliminating paper records and claims and by providing for the electronic transmission of many documents. Because of increased use of and reliance on electronic transmission of personal patient information, the regulatory agency in this case, the Department of Health and Human Services, has imposed standards for the security of that information. The HIPAA security rule, 45 C.F.R. Part 164, is extensive in scope and rigorous in its requirements, and many, if not most, health care providers and insurers have made extensive technology upgrades or acquisitions to comply with them.

The rule's security requirements apply to three categories: administrative, physical, and technical safeguards.

Administrative safeguards include the implementation of information security policies and procedures designed to prevent, detect, contain, and correct security violations; the designation of a single individual responsible for security of the entity's electronic personal health information (EPHI); implementation of policies and procedures that limit access to EPHI to those employees who need it; implementing a security awareness and training program for the entity's entire workforce; implementing policies and procedure for incident response, including incidents that damage systems containing EPHI; performing continuous periodic technical and nontechnical review whether existing policies and procedures meet ongoing security requirements; and ensuring that, if the security process is outsourced to any other organization, such organization has provided assurance that it will satisfactorily safeguard EPHI (45 C.F.R. § 164.308).

Physical safeguards include the implementation of policies and procedures that:

- Limit physical access to information systems and facility locations where they are housed to those individuals requiring such access
- Specify appropriate work station functions, the manner of their performance, and the nature of the physical surroundings of workstations that can access EPHI

- Govern the receipt and removal of hardware and other electronic media that contain EPHI into and out of the entity and from one location to another within the entity
- Govern the implementation of physical controls that limit access to work stations that can access EPHI. (45 C.F.R. § 164.310)

Technical safeguards include the implementation of policies and procedures that:

- Control the access of authorized personnel and software programs to electronic information systems that contain EPHI
- Protect EPHI from improper modification or destruction
- Verify the identity of persons or entities seeking access to EPHI
- Implement audit controls and logs of activity in information systems that involve EPHI
- Implement security measures to prevent unauthorized access to EPHI while being transmitted over a network (45 C.F.R. § 164.312)

Educational Institutions

The Family Educational Rights and Privacy Act (FERPA) requires schools (K-12) and higher educational institutions to maintain the privacy of a student's educational record and imposes penalties upon those academic institutions that fail to protect the privacy of those records. The Act has specific limitations upon disclosure of a student's record by campus safety officers, but carves out exceptions for disclosure to law enforcement and, under certain circumstances, to the parents of students.

Consumer Reporting Agencies

The Fair Credit Reporting Act (FCRA) regulates access to nonpublic personal information held by consumer reporting agencies. The term *consumer reporting agency* is not limited to the three widely known credit bureaus: Equifax, Experian, and Trans Union. All three are consumer reporting agencies, but any organization that aggregates nonpublic personal information of a consumer, such as LexisNexis, or the myriad of security-related investigatory agencies who provide employee prescreening, or background checks are governed by the Act. A failure to comply with the disclosure limitations of the FCRA can subject the violator to civil liability and, in the case of a willful violation, criminal liability. Thus, an improper disclosure of information, or the failure to comply with data security, can result in liability.

GOVERNMENT COMPLIANCE STANDARDS

National Infrastructure Protection Plan (NIPP) Compliance

The 2009 version of the National Infrastructure Protection Plan is a 188-page comprehensive plan for the protection of critical infrastructures and key resources (CIKR) of state and local governments and the private sector. NIPP (2009: 7) observes that CIKR protection can be provided in a number of ways including "improving security protocols, hardening facilities, building resiliency and redundancy, incorporating hazard resistance into facility design, initiating active or passive countermeasures, installing security systems, leveraging 'self-healing' technologies, promoting workforce surety programs, implementing cybersecurity measures, training and exercises, and business continuity planning, among others."

NIPP mandates that federal agencies comply with the plan and take all actions consistent with Homeland Security Presidential Directive 7 (HSPD-7), which essentially requires certain agencies to develop a plan (NIPP) to protect CIKR assets from terrorist attack. NIPP further provides that state, local, tribal, and territorial governments who do not implement CIKR protection plans will not be eligible for federal grants. Thus, although NIPP is a plan, not a list of mandated activities the violation of which could lead to some liability, there are negative consequences that could flow from the failure to comply with NIPP.

Federal Information Security Management Act (FISMA) Compliance

The Federal Information Security Management Act of 2002 requires government agencies, or contractors acting on behalf of government agencies, to develop and implement agency-wide programs for information security of data and systems. FISMA establishes a compliance framework that encompasses seven attributes: (1) an inventory of information systems; (2) categorization of information systems according to risk levels; (3) security controls; (4) risk assessment; (5) a system security plan; (6) certification and accreditation; and (7) continuous monitoring. The National Institute of Standards and Technology (NIST) has established standards and guidelines for the performance of that framework.

Industry Standards

Not all compliance mandates are created by statute or regulation. In many instances, standards are established by a particular industry. The failure to comply with the established standards can result in civil liability and pose a significant threat to a business's reputation. Although there are many industry-specific standards that apply to data security, we focus on one particular standard the violation of which has led to considerable media attention.

Payment Card Industry (PCI) Compliance

The five major credit card associations (American Express, Discover, JCB, MasterCard International, and Visa International), as members of the Payment Card Industry Security Standards Council, established a data security standard (PCI DSS) that merchants and acquirers, as members of each respective association, are required to satisfy for the security of data concerning prepaid, debit, and credit card transactions. Many of the standards are related to technological safeguards (e.g., firewall protection, encryption of data transmitted across public networks, and the assignment of a unique ID to every individual with access to cardholder data). Others, however, relate to physical security (e.g., restricting physical access to client data and implementing an information security policy).

PHYSICAL SECURITY

Technological advances and the ominous threat of a cyber attack have led to the creation of regulatory standards for the protection of information assets. It may appear to some that the regulators have overemphasized IT security at the expense of physical security. However, physical security is embedded in many of those regulatory standards. For example, physical security standards are set forth in GLBA and HIPAA security safeguard mandates. Physical security plays a prominent role in industry standards (e.g., PCI DSS compliance).

Additionally, most government agencies have issued physical security standards. For example, the Department of Defense has numerous physical security standards that apply to specific types of resources: DOD 5200.08-R for installations and resources; DOD 5210.41 for nuclear weapons; DOD 5210.65 for chemical agents; DOD 5210.63 for nuclear reactors; and

DOD 5100.76 for ammunition and explosives. The U.S. Central Intelligence Agency (and other federal agencies) has a physical security standard for sensitive compartmented information. The Department of Treasury has a standard (D.T. 72-56) for security related to international cargo. The Department of Housing and Urban Development (HUD) has a physical security handbook that sets forth several standards for various types of facilities within the jurisdiction of that agency.

The International Organization for Standardization (ISO), a network of national standards institutes in 159 countries, has established numerous standards relating to physical security. Though a nongovernmental organization, ISO is a widely respected authority on security standards, a respect grounded on its partnership between governmental standards bodies and professional organizations. Among the standards applicable to physical security are ISO 17799, which contains physical standards for information security; ISO 16936-3, which involves forced-entry security glazing requirements for glass in buildings; and ISO 19092, which involves security standards applicable to the use of biometrics in the financial industry.

Industry organizations within the United States also have developed specific standards for physical security. For example, a partnership led by the American Chemical Council has established site security standards for the chemical industry. The Institute of Electronics and Electrical Engineers (IEEE) has established a guideline or standard (IEEE 1402) for physical and electronic security of electric power substations.

Many of these standards do not include specific sanctions for a failure to comply with the applicable standard. However, the failure to comply can lead to civil liability and the imposition of regulatory sanctions.

WHY COMPLIANCE MATTERS

From an organizational perspective, there is every reason to have a robust compliance program. Indeed, in many respects it can be a matter of survival. A private-sector organization facing investigation and legal action is entitled to favorable consideration if it has an effective compliance and ethics program. Likewise, an organization convicted in a criminal case can receive a reduction in the sentence recommended by the Sentencing Guidelines if it has an effective compliance and ethics program. We consider each of these benefits separately.

Prosecutorial Discretion

The U.S. Department of Justice (2009) will consider the fact that an organization has an effective compliance program in determining whether or not to prosecute, whether to enter into a non-prosecution agreement (NPA) or deferred prosecution agreement (DPA), and whether to enter into a plea agreement. As stated in the U.S. Attorney's Manual (USAM § 9-28.300), prosecutors must consider nine factors:

1. nature and seriousness of the offense;
2. pervasiveness of wrongdoing within the organization;
3. history of prior similar conduct;
4. timely and voluntariness of disclosure of wrongdoing and willingness to cooperate in the investigation;
5. existence and adequacy of pre-existing compliance program;
6. the organization's remedial actions, including efforts to implement or improve an effective compliance program, replace responsible management, discipline wrongdoer employees and agents, pay restitution, and cooperate with government agencies;

7. collateral consequences, including disproportionate harm to shareholders, pensioners, or innocent employees;
8. the adequacy of prosecution of individuals responsible for the organization's wrongdoing; and
9. the adequacy of civil or regulatory enforcement actions.

The comment section of U.S. Attorney's Manual, § 9-28.800, also describes what prosecutors should consider in assessing the effectiveness of a compliance program:

> While the Department recognizes that no compliance program can ever prevent all criminal activity by a corporation's employees, the critical factors in evaluating any program are whether the program is adequately designed for maximum effectiveness in preventing and detecting wrongdoing by employees and whether corporate management is enforcing the program or is tacitly encouraging or pressuring employees to engage in misconduct to achieve business objectives. The Department has no formulaic requirements regarding corporate compliance programs. The fundamental questions any prosecutor should ask are: Is the corporation's compliance program well designed? Is the program being applied earnestly and in good faith? Does the corporation's compliance program work? In answering these questions, the prosecutor should consider the comprehensiveness of the compliance program; the extent and pervasiveness of the criminal misconduct; the number and level of the corporate employees involved; the seriousness, duration, and frequency of the misconduct; and any remedial actions taken by the corporation, including, for example, disciplinary action against past violators uncovered by the prior compliance program, and revisions to corporate compliance programs in light of lessons learned. Prosecutors should also consider the promptness of any disclosure of wrongdoing to the government. In evaluating compliance programs, prosecutors may consider whether the corporation has established corporate governance mechanisms that can effectively detect and prevent misconduct. For example, do the corporation's directors exercise independent review over proposed corporate actions rather than unquestioningly ratifying officers' recommendations; are internal audit functions conducted at a level sufficient to ensure their independence and accuracy; and have the directors established an information and reporting system in the organization reasonably designed to provide management and directors with timely and accurate information sufficient to allow them to reach an informed decision regarding the organization's compliance with the law.

In essence, the Department of Justice does not rely upon what is written on the paper. Compliance programs should be "designed, implemented, reviewed, and revised, as appropriate, in an effective manner" (USAM, § 9-28.800, Comment). Further, it should be emphasized that two of the nine factors considered by prosecutors involve the existence or improved effectiveness of a compliance program.

Sentencing Commission

The U.S. Sentencing Commission established Guidelines in 1991 for sentencing organizations in criminal cases. The Guidelines provide a methodology for the calculation of sentences based on such factors as the type of crime, criminal history of the perpetrator, and the extent of involvement of the defendant in the crime. With respect to the sentencing of organizations the

Guidelines provide for a significant reduction in the sentence that otherwise would be imposed if the organization has established and maintained an effective compliance and ethics program. The Guidelines, §8B2.1 (a), provides that, for a compliance program to be effective, the organization must:

1. exercise due diligence to prevent and detect criminal conduct; and
2. otherwise promote an organizational culture that encourages ethical conduct and a commitment to compliance with the law.

Section 8B2.1(b) of the Guidelines further provides that:

Due diligence and the promotion of an organizational culture that encourages ethical conduct and a commitment to compliance with the law within the meaning of subsection (a) minimally require the following:

1. The organization shall establish standards and procedures to prevent and detect criminal conduct.
2. **(A)** The organization's governing authority shall be knowledgeable about the content and operation of the compliance and ethics program and shall exercise reasonable oversight with respect to the implementation and effectiveness of the compliance and ethics program.

   (B) High-level personnel of the organization shall ensure that the organization has an effective compliance and ethics program, as described in this guideline. Specific individual(s) within high-level personnel shall be assigned overall responsibility for the compliance and ethics program.

   (C) Specific individual(s) within the organization shall be delegated day-to-day operational responsibility for the compliance and ethics program. Individual(s) with operational responsibility shall report periodically to high-level personnel and, as appropriate, to the governing authority, or an appropriate subgroup of the governing authority, on the effectiveness of the compliance and ethics program. To carry out such operational responsibility, such individual(s) shall be given adequate resources, appropriate authority, and direct access to the governing authority or an appropriate subgroup of the governing authority.

3. The organization shall use reasonable efforts not to include within the substantial authority personnel of the organization any individual whom the organization knew, or should have known through the exercise of due diligence, has engaged in illegal activities or other conduct inconsistent with an effective compliance and ethics program.

4. **(A)** The organization shall take reasonable steps to communicate periodically and in a practical manner its standards and procedures, and other aspects of the compliance and ethics program, to the individuals referred to in subdivision (B) by conducting effective training programs and otherwise disseminating information appropriate to such individuals' respective roles and responsibilities.

   (B) The individuals referred to in subdivision (A) are the members of the governing authority, high-level personnel, substantial authority personnel, the organization's employees, and, as appropriate, the organization's agents.

5. The organization shall take reasonable steps—
    (A) to ensure that the organization's compliance and ethics program is followed, including monitoring and auditing to detect criminal conduct;
    (B) to evaluate periodically the effectiveness of the organization's compliance and ethics program; and
    (C) to have and publicize a system, which may include mechanisms that allow for anonymity or confidentiality, whereby the organization's employees and agents may report or seek guidance regarding potential or actual criminal conduct without fear of retaliation.
6. The organization's compliance and ethics program shall be promoted and enforced consistently throughout the organization through (A) appropriate incentives to perform in accordance with the compliance and ethics program; and (B) appropriate disciplinary measures for engaging in criminal conduct and for failing to take reasonable steps to prevent or detect criminal conduct.
7. After criminal conduct has been detected, the organization shall take reasonable steps to respond appropriately to the criminal conduct and to prevent further similar criminal conduct, including making any necessary modifications to the organization's compliance and ethics program." (U.S. Sentencing Commission, 2009)

In sum, the development, implementation, and ongoing maintenance of an effective compliance program can make the difference between no prosecution and a full-blown criminal trial, and should an organization be convicted, the existence of an effective compliance program can significantly reduce the fine that otherwise would be imposed under the Sentencing Guidelines. States, likewise, consider compliance in exercising prosecutorial discretion and in sentencing.

Compliance is now a buzzword in corporate governance circles. Professional organizations have been formed, and certification programs have been developed for compliance officers and other organizational personnel engaged in compliance activities. Security personnel should investigate the benefits of such certification as well as training and awareness programs presented by those professional organizations.

Summary

Compliance is an essential function for public and private sector security services. Whether mandated by federal or state law or a voluntary standard established by a particular industry, security services should undertake the development and implementation of an effective compliance program.

Review Questions/Activities

1. How would you define compliance, and based on your definition, what role does security play in compliance? Provide some examples that illustrate how a failure of security amounts to noncompliance and, potentially, to civil or criminal liability.
2. What are the tangible benefits of an effective compliance program for an organization? For employees within the organization? For the government?
3. What is the relationship between the HIPAA security standards, compliance, and risk management? Is the same true for any organization?
4. Contact the person responsible for security operations in a local company or on a college campus. What are the compliance concerns of that individual and the individual's perspective of the importance of compliance held by top management of the company or college?

Web Searches

1. Conduct an Internet search for organizations which have compliance as their main purpose or focus. Develop a list of approximately five organizations, describe whether they are similar or have a distinct focus, and determine how long each organization has been in existence.
2. Conduct a Web search to ascertain whether there are professional certifications that exist for those who can demonstrate expertise in compliance. What are the areas of competence that are examined for each certification?
3. In the past decade numerous compliance failures have led to massive fines and/or civil penalties. Conduct a search for articles concerning a few such cases. After reviewing these cases, how many of them were compliance failures in security and what was the nature of the security failure?
4. Conduct a Web search for data breaches. What were the compliance failures in these breach instances and what role did security, or the lack of security, play in each breach?

References

Biegelman, Martin T. 2008. *Building a World-Class Compliance Program: Best Practices and Strategies for Success.* Hoboken, N.J.: John Wiley & Sons.

Bishop, Toby J. F., and Frank E. Hydoski. 2009. *Corporate Resiliency: Managing the Growing Risk of Fraud and Corruption.* Hoboken, N.J.: John Wiley & Sons.

Department of Homeland Security (2009). National Infrastructure Protection Plan. Available at www.dhs.gov/xlibrary/assets/NIPP_Plan.pdf (NIPP)

Federal Trade Commission (n.d.). "Fighting Fraud with the Red Flags Rule: A How-To Guide for Business." Washington, D.C.: Federal Trade Commission.

Tarantino, Anthony. 2007. *Governance, Risk, and Compliance Handbook.* Hoboken, N.J.: John Wiley & Sons.

United States Department of Justice. 2009. *United States Attorney's Manual.* Available at www.justice.gov/usao/eousa/foia_reading_room/usam/

United States Sentencing Commission. 2009. Federal Sentencing Guidelines Manual, vol.1. Eagan, MN: Thomson Reuters. West.

12

■ ■ ■

Training

KEY TERMS

basic, certified instructor, distance learning, diversity, executive development, field training, in-service, learning environment, occupational socialization, preservice, special topics, supervisory.

Training is important in any security service organization because it teaches personnel how to perform specific tasks and provides a sense of purpose for the mission of the organization. Training also presents the informal and formal rules of conduct and attitudes that are demanded by the organization and fellow employees. This training element is often referred to as *occupational socialization,* which is defined as the process by which an employee learns not only tasks, but also values and attitudes related to an occupation or profession. It is the process by which a nontrained person learns all the aspects of a job (McBride, 1986). Training is also important for morale. A person who has not been taught both the formal and informal norms and skills of the position has a blind spot with regard to dealing with clients and fellow workers. Failure to provide training is a significant cause of worker dissatisfaction and stress and can be linked to negative turnover and tort liability.

In today's litigious society, training has also become an important function for both the employee and the organization, depending on the facts or merits of a criminal or civil case. Lesson plans and training registration forms may be used as evidence to show what and how the employee was taught. In a disciplinary case, one of the authors had to testify as to the curriculum of a radio communicator's course and the rules of conduct for dispatchers in daily operations. In administrative hearings, criminal prosecutions, and civil lawsuits related to complaints about use of force and deadly force, lesson plans on the use of deadly weapons and impact devices become critical items.

In this chapter we present suggested curriculum requirements for security services training and the current issues regarding training topics. We also explore current and potential delivery systems, which range from the traditional classroom setting to online and virtual reality programs. While the topic of training often boils down to specific courses and curriculum, the authors see training as an ongoing process because employees in the field must constantly learn about new methods and technology related to security services.

GENERAL OVERVIEW OF SECURITY AND LAW ENFORCEMENT TRAINING

The broad expanse of training for security service personnel can be divided into five stages that reflect a person's career in the field: preservice/basic, supervisory, in-service, special topics, and executive. Please note that these programs and courses are "models" for the field insofar that many states do not require any training especially for unarmed security officers. For those states that have training requirements, the number of required training hours ranges from one hour in Texas to forty hours in California, Florida, and Oklahoma (Hall, 2003).

PreService/Basic

A handful of states, such as New York, have training requirements that require security service personnel to take training courses before they can obtain a license. These programs review fundamentals such as basic law, report writing, basic patrol techniques, and rules of conduct. Once this course has been completed, usually at the person's expense, he or she can apply to obtain a license. With this license, the person is then able to seek employment.

A trend has emerged to allow a candidate with police status, who has not been hired, to take a basic police training program and receive a certificate of completion. These preservice programs are offered at community and junior colleges and local police academies under state certification and oversight guidelines. The person is then able to seek employment with a basic school certificate. As will be discussed in the next section, this makes the person an attractive candidate because he has already completed somewhere between 500 to 1,000 hours of training. The hiring agency is then required to offer additional training in specific topics such as firearms, defensive tactics, counterterrorism, and department rules and procedures.

The length of a basic course often depends on whether the person is going to be granted law enforcement powers and permitted to carry a weapon. For public police personnel, a typical basic school in the United States encompasses approximately 600 hours of classroom training with an additional 417 hours in mandated field and agency training (Bureau of Justice Statistics, 2003: 6). Examinations are generally held at least once a week and include skills tests for firearms, emergency vehicle operations (EVO), arrest techniques, and physical agility. Most programs are offered on a full-time basis of forty or so hours per week, but there are those for smaller agencies that run part-time over the course of a six-month period. Regardless of whether the course is full- or part-time, recruits have classes on basic marching, personal appearance, deportment, and equipment care and review in addition to standard areas of curriculum.

Using this book's security service model, the following presents courses for Level I and Level IV agencies.

PRESERVICE/BASIC TRAINING—LEVEL I   As discussed in Chapter 3, agencies performing at this level provide basic watch and guard services but have no governmental powers. For these agencies, the following training topics are recommended:

Role of security services: Explains the various models of security that operate in the United States and the services that are provided.

Basic state law: Reviews state regulations related to security services, license requirements, rules related to the use of force and arrest, and definitions of major offenses.

Introduction to criminal justice: Explains the criminal justice system and the role of security services, courts, and court dispositions as well as common legal terms.

Basic first aid/CPR: Instructs in the use of Red Cross or state standard training modules including the use of defibulators.

Patrol and observation techniques: Teaches identification of suspicious persons and dangerous situations.

Emergency response: Instructs in responding to crimes in progress and emergency situations including fires and alarms, hazardous materials, and how to call for assistance.

Interviewing and communication techniques: Explains how to obtain information from a victim, witness, or client in need of services.

Report writing and procedures: Reviews typical incident reports and information needed for a complete report.

Officer safety: Reviews strategies to deal with difficult people and situations and when to call for assistance or retreat.

Field training: Introduces the officer to the operations of a particular agency or company. In addition to reviewing the geography and key personnel, the field trainer reviews the agency's mission, role of security to the mission, and response procedures for outside agencies. Field training presents specific, important topic areas, based on the client or agency, such as these:
  · Loss prevention techniques
  · Alarm system monitoring and response
  · Parking enforcement
  · Robbery prevention and defensive driving techniques for armored car and valuable asset couriers
  · Crowd control techniques, including personal searches at secure areas

During field training, each recruit is assigned to a senior field-training officer, who evaluates her on a daily and weekly basis. The purpose of field training is to measure how well the recruit reacts to situations and solves problems under direct supervision of a trained evaluator (Payne, 1999). The length of a field training period depends on the nature and complexities of the job. Security service personnel with police powers may spend anywhere from one to six months with experienced field trainers. In a highly organized program, the recruit receives daily evaluations followed by weekly summary evaluations.

BASIC TRAINING—LEVEL IV   The following is a general overview of the general topic areas that would be found in a police basic training program at this level. Again, the number of hours ranges from 500 to 1,000 hours according to agency mission and need.

Administration of justice—Topics include the history of law enforcement and security, the justice system with a focus on adjudication of cases, the main actors in criminal justice, and contemporary issues.

General law—Topics normally covered in this area are constitutional law, state penal law, criminal procedure and regulatory law, use of deadly and physical force, mental health regulations, and vehicle and traffic law. Courses under this topic should include an introduction to civil law and civil liability.

Patrol functions—This covers a wide range of topics such as the role of patrol, techniques, crimes in progress, and response to specific calls such as domestic violence, bombs and bomb threats, fires and hazardous materials, and crimes in progress.

Traffic enforcement—The main areas are traffic direction and control, accident investigation, impaired driving, racial profiling, and vehicle pullovers.

Security service procedures—Report writing, radio communications, fingerprinting and booking, and care of uniforms and equipment are covered.

Criminal investigative functions—Courses in this area include interview techniques, interrogation techniques, victim-witness rules and identification, case preparation and court demeanor, and the specific situations of robbery, injury and death, missing persons, auto theft, burglary, robbery, narcotics, sex crimes, arson, and computer and electronic communications.

Community policing—Topics include introduction to community policing programs and techniques, diversity, crime prevention, victim services, and holding meetings with constituent groups.

Firearms training—These areas include use of deadly physical force, nomenclature, range safety, firing positions, shoot/don't shoot scenarios, and qualification testing for the weapon that is issued to the officer. The focus of most programs is on .40 and .45 caliber semiautomatic pistols although some agencies still use .38 and .357 "wheel guns" such as Colt and Smith and Wesson. This training ranges from forty to eighty hours.

Defensive tactics and less-than-lethal weapons— These topics encompass weapons such as pepper spray, conducted energy devices, popularly known as Taser, and baton, and tactical techniques for subduing a person for an arrest. Courses of this nature range from forty to eighty hours, depending on the duties that the officer performs and the weapons that are issued. Arrest techniques introduce a wide range of tactics for students to obtain compliance from a suspect. Arrest techniques include voice commands, and the use of physical force such as takedowns and handcuffing.

Pepper spray is pressurized water/alcohol with concentrated pepper and is shot into a suspect's face resulting in incapacitation and compliance. Although very effective for most encounters, there are times when persons under drugs can withstand the effects of pepper spray. A Taser is a brand name of a conducted electric device that shoots two barbs into a suspect. These barbs contain 50,000 volts of electricity, which causes the person to be temporarily incapacitated. Some deaths of suspects under drugs or with cardiac medical histories have been attributed to the use of Tasers. However, there continues to be widespread adoption of this device by law enforcement and security services units authorized to carry less-than-lethal devices.

Emergency vehicle operations course (EVOC)—Topics related to this important area use every-day instruction on driving both under normal and emergency situations. Because most patrol is accomplished in vehicles, officers have to learn to drive, watch the area, and listen to the radio and take mental notes at the same time. The course often consists of classroom training followed by skills testing (e.g., backing and parking) and emergency driving and skidding.

Physical agility testing—Most Level IV agencies require some degree of physical agility. Many programs use the Cooper standard, discussed in Chapter 10, and require an improvement beyond entry level. For example, recruits who are hired at the 60th percentile for physical agility testing may be required to pass at the 70th percentile. The objectives of physical agility testing are to promote healthy lifestyles with officers and to ascertain that they are in physical shape for physical events that occur in defensive tactics.

Counterterrorism—These topics include responding to post-terrorist incidents and working with the community to develop information to prevent such attacks. The focus of this training is on those groups who commit offenses for a political or social cause, and ancillary training programs address organized crime organizations and youth gangs.

Supervisory Stage

Supervisory courses are for people who have been promoted from basic patrol or investigations to middle management. General topic areas include the role of supervisor, and leadership and supervision in tactical situations. Most programs devote a number of hours to constitutional law and civil liability as related to supervision. There has been much emphasis on supervisory training in issues related to emergency management.

SUPERVISORY TRAINING   Supervisors at whatever level must be given the knowledge and tools to provide leadership and supervise members in the unit. Thus, a working knowledge of agency rules and expectations is important as is having the ability to make critical decisions in emergency situations. Supervisors also must be trained on how to deal with their subordinates and provide positive coaching (Jordan, 2003). The following are general topic areas covered in supervisor training:

Role of security services supervisor—defines the roles of the supervisor in terms of leadership, assignments, counseling and discipline, reviewer of paperwork, and trainer.

Supervision in emergency situations—covers a number of actual situations such as fires, accidents, crimes against the person, and crimes against property. The role of the supervisor is explained to include providing first response and making appropriate notifications for assistance from the support resource network.

Administration areas—address a variety of agency-related issues such as scheduling, daily paperwork, operational planning, personnel rules, and agency notification protocols.

Regardless of the level of services, the supervisor plays a critical role in agency operations as he or she becomes the on-the-scene manager for emergency situations at all hours of the day and night.

For Level III and IV agencies, in addition to presenting topics just listed, training includes the following suggested topics:

Emergency response—It is anticipated that Level III and IV supervisors will provide assistance, expertise, and resources to other agencies. Thus, these personnel must be trained as on-the-scene managers of emergency situations that could include all levels of natural and human-caused disasters (see Chapter 9 for a full discussion of emergency management). Thus, supervisors must be thoroughly versed with first response, incident command system, weapons of mass destruction, counterterrorism, and major event planning. Such training programs often provide role-playing in specific scenarios and tabletop exercises.

Legal update—The emphasis here is changes in the law as well as an intensive review of administrative and liability cases related to the use of governmental powers in operations and with personnel. These topics include search and seizure and review of the use of force rules.

Human resource administration—The role of the supervisor often includes key human resource–related functions such as evaluations, hiring, field training, and employee disputes. Some attention also has to be paid to shift design and planning for adequate staffing for daily operations and special events. It is also important to have training in sexual harassment issues because the number of women continues to increase in the workplace.

Training management—How to plan for shift and department-wide training is emphasized, and training delivery models are updated. The presentation ranges from traditional classroom formats to long-distance and self-paced learning.

Special issues in security services—Depending on the mission of the agency, topics include domestic violence, workplace violence, stalking, people with mental illness, response to computer crime, and counterterrorism issues.

Ethical supervision—This addresses ethical awareness as it pertains to supervisors. It goes without saying that a supervisor has to be both a role model and trainer when it comes to ethical issues, especially if subordinates are to perform their duties in a just and ethical manner.

Executive Stage

Of all the training stages, executive-level training is especially lacking in many security service agencies. Agency heads often find themselves promoted to executive positions but can take few courses on how to be a successful executive or survive in this capacity. In recent years, many professional organizations have offered executive-level programs ranging from command to executive development. Typical course topics include management and leadership theory, budgeting, strategic planning, legal updates in constitutional law and administrative matters involving criminal investigations and personnel, employee motivation and client satisfaction, enterprise risk management, community relations, crime prevention, and security technology and planning. ASIS International provides a joint program with the Wharton School at the University of Pennsylvania entitled Making the Business Case for Security. The two-week certificate course program focuses on business applications for security operations (Wharton Executive Education, 2010).

Related Training

SPECIAL TOPICS   Courses on special topics can range from investigations programs to tactical situations to issues involving human relations. They are offered to impart a specific skill, review a new law or procedure, or address a problem being faced by the organization. These programs are offered by state training divisions or departments, professional associations, and colleges and universities. Of critical importance today are courses dealing with terrorism and weapons of mass destruction.

IN-SERVICE TRAINING   *In-service training* is a general term that denotes updated agency training on various topics previously offered in basic or supervisory courses. It is also used to denote requalification in proficiency areas such as firearms, nonlethal weapons, and emergency first aid. Generally, departments require their officers to recertify firearms skills at least twice a year. In-service training may also be associated with roll-call training, whereby an updated or new topic area is formally presented before a shift "turns out" to its assignments and posts.

WHAT TO TRAIN FOR   A group of trainers discussing training will inevitably bring mention of how much time should be spent in training, what should be taught, and who should do the teaching. Ultimately, the discussion will come down to what should be learned and how to test that the student knows the material. Security service training, as with other law enforcement–related training, deals with topics that apply to a job-related situation or show that the student can perform a task or skill. The basis of training is that its learning objectives should relate to the job or tasks that personnel are required to perform.

TRAINING FOR INVESTIGATIONS PERSONNEL

Many security service organizations have designated personnel who perform investigations related to serious crimes, internal reviews of fraud or potential criminal activity by employees, and reviews of complaints filed by customers of the agency or organization. If the organization does not have law enforcement powers, the investigator is also the main liaison with the external agency that may ultimately prosecute the case. The following are some courses that might be offered to these personnel:

Role of the investigator in the organization—This module explains the role that will be required and how they fit into agency operations.

Constitutional law—This course pays special attention to search and seizure situations.

Agency rules and regulations for investigations—Many organizations have specific rules based on state law or employee contracts that cover privacy, computer use, interrogation rules, and how and when investigations are conducted. The role of the ethnical investigator must be explored in terms of dealing with people and conducting investigations.

Crime scene analysis and investigative techniques—Many investigators are called to an area that may be a crime scene and must know the proper procedures required.

Reports and testimony—The course instructs in preparing the myriad of reports that must be filed in an investigation, presenting information, and testifying in a trial as well as various state and company administrative hearings.

Interview and interrogation skills—Because the chief role of an investigator is to gather information from various kinds of people including victims, witnesses, and suspects, this course teaches related techniques.

Laws of evidence—This course deals with the correct collection, preparation, and presentation of evidence including the standards of proof needed for prosecution.

Basic response to electronic crimes—This course presents basic do's and don't's of dealing with Internet and computer crimes. Personnel skilled in this area need further training in specialized courses related to detection and response techniques. A major topic is dealing with seized cell phones.

SPECIFIC PROGRAMS FOR ALL LEVELS AND POSITIONS

The following describes a few in-service courses that have been presented by security service organizations and professional associations in special seminars or in-service training programs.

Diversity

We continue to become a diverse and global society in terms of transportation, manufacturing, movement of people, and exchange of ideas. Demographic trends in the United States indicate that its retired population (fifty-five years of age and above) and peoples from various races and ethnic groups continue to increase. Because of peoples' differences in culture and experience with and reaction to authority, security service employees have to be trained to deal with people and to be aware of various cultural mores. Most diversity programs may provide a list of do's and don't's for various cultures such as distance positioning and whether to use hand gestures or certain phrases. In areas with a concentrated population of new immigrants, basic phrases may be taught. Many programs include how to deal with people with physical disabilities in such areas as evacuation, victim treatment, and referral assistance.

Quality diversity programs, however, go beyond "do's and don't's" and try to review major concepts in their application to the officer's or supervisor's daily work life.

Another area that is often presented in diversity training is investigating *hate crimes*. As defined by the Department of Justice, a *hate crime* is a criminal act committed against a person or institution on the basis of race, ethnicity, religion, sexual orientation, gender, or disability. The key to hate crime training is identifying its causes, recognizing incidents, and taking proactive steps in dealing with victims and the community. The most common hate crimes are related to race and sexual orientation.

Electronic Crimes Investigation

As violent and traditional crimes decline in number, electronic crimes increase. Technology changes rapidly, and it is critical that security service personnel be trained in technologies (hardware and software) that can be utilized to perform computer and network security services and to investigate cyber crime and forensic-related incidents.

Domestic Violence

Domestic violence incidents continue to require law enforcement response or workplace security investigation. The response to and investigation of those incidents require specialized training. *Domestic violence* has been expanded to include a wide range of living arrangements between married or nonmarried partners and same-sex relationships, both with or without children. Domestic violence is a leading cause of murder, assault, and violent workplace incidents. Through legislation and operational policy, many states and law enforcement agencies have proarrest policies if personnel are called to a scene where an assault, harassment, or disorderly conduct is occurring. Training courses also review agency and company policies and plans that alert security service units to the existence of an order of protection or the potential for violence against an employee by a current or former partner.

Sexual Harassment

As discussed in Chapter 10, the key element to deal with sexual harassment issues is with strong and clear workplace policies followed by training of line and supervisory personnel. Training programs of this nature go into the nature of harassment, examples of prohibitive behavior, and a candid discussion of gender issues in the immediate workplace.

Terrorism—Prevention and Response

Since 9/11 a number of courses have suddenly been offered by both state and private sector agencies that come under the headings of counterterrorism, emergency management, and homeland security. The level of training needed in this area depends on the person's rank and the assignment of duties. The following are topical courses for personnel based on rank:

Patrol and Supervisors—Terrorism, basic patrol issues, and responding to potential weapons of mass destruction are introduced.

Investigators/Specialists—Counterterrorism issues such as intelligence gathering, identity theft and forged documents, and VIP protection are presented.

Executives—Executives have to be aware of target assessment, equipment and response capability analysis, interagency intelligence gathering and sharing, and grant applications for equipment and training.

EXECUTIVE DEVELOPMENT

As previously stated, there has been a lack of executive development programs for all levels of security services personnel. While we realize that variables are unique in each agency, factors that must be considered include how to get along with the boss, how to sell security programs to policy makers, and how to get promoted to the next level in the organization. The unfortunate reality is that many policy makers often do not believe that security service is part of the core mission of the company or organization. Often it is viewed as an add-on responsibility because it does not sell products and often costs money. These same policy makers become concerned, however, when terrible things happen in the organization or to employees, and often there is a knee-jerk reaction to provide increased protection, hire more officers, and install technology.

The important thing to be learned from these courses is how to achieve a balance among addressing the need for security, providing access for customers and visitors, and satisfying the needs of general agency or company management. Specific topic areas for executives in this area include personnel administration, planning, risk and vulnerability assessment, research methods, planning (long-term and strategic), relations with outside agencies, fraud, trends in security technology, investigative resources, civil liability, and contractual responsibilities. Ideally, these programs should be offered in settings that induce interaction between instructors and attendees.

TRAINING FOR LEVEL II AND III AGENCIES

Having presented the overall general training programs for Levels I and IV organizations, one might wonder about the training for the other two models. The training is based on the agency's defined mission, the powers its employees have, the daily tasks personnel are required to perform, and the expectations for what security service responders are to do in critical situations. By *agency mission*, we are addressing the general goals of the security service organizations as they relate to the goals of the organization or agency. Generally, most goal statements have some concept of protecting the property and assets of the company or agency, employees, residents, and guests. The key is to realistically review all the duties and responsibilities that personnel have.

The real crux is presented in the main issues presented in our model in Chapter 3. What is the extent of governmental powers for the agency and what are the expectations for agency personnel to respond to "routine" and emergency incidents? Such emergency situations include responding to alarms when there may be potential for the use of force, traffic enforcement, and overall perimeter security. There also has to be a realistic assessment of the capabilities of the agency. Let's take one scenario of an emergency event that tests this capability.

At a major corporation, a disgruntled employee takes her boss hostage with a handgun and threatens to kill him and other co-workers. Security services personnel, who fit the Level II services model, immediately respond to the area and set up an inner and outer perimeter. The supervisor on duty, who has been trained in hostage negotiations, begins a dialog with the suspect. Other security personnel gather information related to what caused the suspect to do this. In the meantime, employees are evacuated from the area, and the local police department is summoned to provide additional assistance through a hostage negotiation team and an emergency services unit.

Both the local police and the corporate security force have done joint training and an event of this nature involving an active shooter had been role-played just one year before this incident. The corporate security service force has armed officers based on an assessment of risks that could occur in the company and the need for an emergency first response.

Company personnel and the local police set up a command center, and the highest ranking member of the security department and the captain of the emergency services team begin join incident command operations to address the situation. After three hours, the negotiations are successful, and the employee releases her captive and surrenders without further incident. The local police take the suspect into custody and file attempted assault and kidnapping charges against her.

If this were a Level I agency, the entire management of the event would have been handed to the police department with little assistance from security. In a Level III agency, the entire event could be handled by agency personnel with perhaps some technical assistance in hostage negotiation by a Level IV agency. A Level IV agency would have both the skills and resources to handle the entire situation from start to finish. The key factors here are the time for responders to appear and the level of training and equipment the organization is willing to make available to responders.

The question that arises is whether to review the expectations of the agency or the organization if such an event were to occur. There also must be a realistic assessment of agency staffing and capabilities. A local police department with two vehicles on patrol would not be able to deal with other calls if the same scenario occurred in their jurisdiction. Likewise, an agency or organization without armed officers will not be able to respond and must rely on outside assistance. These capability issues must be realistically addressed through risk assessment, and then follow recommendations by offering the proper level of training and adequately equipping security service personnel.

Often in reviewing the training for security service organizations, the authors find overtraining or undertraining based in relation to the organization's mission and purpose. In one situation, the organization spent inordinate amounts of time on law and criminal procedure even though its personnel had no law enforcement powers. The question of what is the right type of training often is asked with regard to the use of arms and nonlethal weapons. Using our model, it is apparent that all security services personnel with law enforcement powers must be armed and properly trained and supervised. A number of organizational entities, particularly in college and hospital settings, grant full police powers to their security service employees but do not wish to arm them. The reason for this is based on what is called the *Kent State syndrome,* referring to a 1970 incident at Kent State University when national guardsmen fired their rifles and killed four people while attempting to disperse a group protesting the U.S. incursion into Cambodia. This event, in concert with other anti–Vietnam War actions, resulted in many student takeovers of campus buildings and the virtual shutdown of campuses all over the country. The fear today is that a misguided officer will accidentally shoot a student resulting in a similar violent reaction. Situations of this vein cause much conflict between organizational management and security services staff with regard to responding to serious calls unarmed. It is our contention that organizations dealing with the Kent State syndrome should either arm their officers or change the security mission to that of a Level II or I.

HOW TO TRAIN

When we say *training,* we are referring to the process by which a person learns how to do a task for a job. There are a number of factors that go into training courses and programs.

Learning Objectives

The first step in training is the creation of learning objectives, which simply stated, determines what the trainer wants students to do or know at the end of the training. Security service administrators and managers also have to conduct a needs assessment to determine whether there is a need for training, particularly for in-service personnel. As outlined by Watson (2002), the training program should be the result of intensive analysis related to job descriptions, performance reports, and after-action situations review. Most programs use a learning-by-objectives model in which the student must either perform a task or apply a concept to a learning situation to successfully complete a training model. As cited by Mager (1984), learning objectives have to be carefully thought out and integrated into the presentation of the material to assess trainee performance under certain conditions. The training objectives for a course on constitutional law will be much different than those for one on the use of defensive tactics with an armed attacker. After the course of instruction there should be an assessment or test of whether the trainee has understood the course of instruction. For academic topics, a written test would be used. For courses as firearms, EVOC, and arrest techniques, the candidates should be required to demonstrate the training at a certain competence which is often reflected in a numerical score or pass/fail.

The Learning Environment

The learning environment includes the overall physical area where the training is taking place. Obviously, the classroom should be comfortable with the right room temperature for the season, good lighting, and room for students and instructors to move about. Breaks should be provided. The concept of the learning environment also deals with the interchange that occurs between instructors and students. Instructors have to know their materials and know their audience. In a popular article from the *FBI Law Enforcement Bulletin,* Kennedy (2003) addresses the overall concerns of adult learners. In all, because they have more life experiences and fear failure, adult learners enjoy active learning environments, especially in those topics that have immediate application to their lives.

Certified Instructors

The term *certified instructor* in a general sense indicates that the person knows the information and can present it to a class. In the academic sense, certified means that the instructor has been found to be qualified to teach a program of study because she has both work experience and formal education that has been reviewed by a state board or professional group. For security service training, certification means that the instructor has both work experience and training in the presentation of material and development of learning objectives. Additional certification is often required to master and teach the various techniques for firearms, nonlethal weapons, first aid, and drug recognition.

Active Learning

A current buzzword in higher education today is active learning in which the student works on a problem either alone or in a group setting while the instructor acts as both teacher and facilitator. Passive learning consists of instructions where the instructor lectures the class and students write the main points of the presentation. After the lecture, students are tested on their ability to recall the facts or main points. Consider the following examples of passive and active learning experiences. This is reported to be more effective than passive learning.

Passive vs. Active

The topic of the lecture is search and seizure. The learning objectives are for each person to list the main exceptions to the search warrant requirement as developed in Fourth Amendment jurisprudence. Such exemptions include administrative searches, emergency or exigent searches, open fields, search incident to arrest, and so on. The instructor lists each exemption and the student writes it down. The student is later given a written examination on this information at the end of the instruction.

In an active environment, the topic here is the same with the same set of learning objectives. The instructor requires each student to review a handout and a textbook, which discusses the various exemptions. At the beginning of the class, the instructor presents a scenario obtained from a learning site link or a video. The students see an officer ask to go into a laboratory area that is occupied by a researcher to check for a missing laptop computer stolen hours before. The researcher is quite hesitant to admit the officer, but the officer persists. The officer finds the missing laptop in a closet off the laboratory area, accuses the researcher of theft, and makes an arrest for larceny.

The instructor asks the class to discuss why the search is or is not legal. Each student must give a review based on the facts and her understanding of these exceptions. Often groups will be developed to discuss the issue.

Simulation

Technology today allows simulation training to be accomplished in a cost-effective manner at regional training sites. For years, airline pilots and driver education students were placed in cockpits and driving seats and presented with various situations to respond to on screen. Using a combination of video, audio, and computer technology, trainees can be assessed not only in driving skills but also emergency decision making in "shoot/don't shoot" situations. Based on situations presented on the screen, the student's ability to react to a person coming at him or her with a knife can be assessed. The students' ability to give audible commands, unholster the weapon, take a position stance, and fire at a target can be assessed by the instructor and scored by computer.

Distance Learning

This book may be used as an "e-pack" in a distance learning course in which student and instructor live thousands of miles apart. The general lectures are created on the computer of a faculty member and distributed by course management software or systems over the Internet to students located at any place where Internet access exists. The student's assignments are graded every week based on responses to questions and participation in a chat room or threaded discussion, and tests can be taken and graded electronically. An electronic version of the text may be available to students enrolled in the distance learning course.

There is debate concerning the effectiveness of the distance learning method of delivering education or training and the types of students who benefit most. Studies on these issues have produced conflicting results. The number of online courses nevertheless continues to increase significantly, and there are some estimates that by 2005, more than half of all college students will be enrolled in one or more courses offered by distance learning methodology. Today many students demand such courses (*Chronicle of Higher Education,* 2004).

Webinars are Internet-based courses whereby participants log into the course at a specific time and location and watch and interact with the instructors from home or office. Using cameras, the faces of the presenters, students, and PowerPoint aid can also be included in presentations. These are effective methods in dealing with students from national or international locations.

The use of this technology is ideal for the education and training of security personnel because they can schedule it around their shifts or rotations. For national and global companies and interaction agencies, training programs can be delivered simultaneously to all locations.

Smart Classrooms

More often than not, training is presented in a classical style in "traditional classrooms" with rows of desks and a chalkboard. Today's classrooms have been technologically updated with data projectors, Internet access, wireless computer networks, and video conferencing that enable instructors to utilize different instructional media without wasting time or effort. Seating is meeting/conference style in which attendees can confer with one another around a rectangular or circular table setup. This is ideal for student–instructor interaction and provides access "at one's fingertips" if an instructor wishes to present material from the Internet.

TACTICAL TRAINING

Tactical training involves security services personnel dealing with serious field problems such as an active shooter, barricaded or fleeing suspect, hostage situation, and other related situations. Participants are required to respond to the situations and instructors portray the suspects. For example, an abandoned or vacant school or residence hall would be ideal for active shooter training. Security services trainees would be required to seek out and intercept the suspect. In these training sessions, simulated ammunition or plastic bullets are used for realism. In some cases, volunteer actors are used to portray victims.

DRILL

In a drill situation, an emergency response plan would be tested and evaluated among various agencies to test equipment, tactics, and agency roles. For example, a hazardous materials drill would require a simulated chemical spill with actors portraying victims. This would be a joint exercise involving fire, police, emergency medical services, social services, and others. Drills of this nature require planning and expenses must cover the use of equipment, props, and disposal items such as bandages and other first aid equipment.

Summary

This chapter discussed the areas of training for security service agencies. It presented suggested course topics based on the security services organizational model as presented in Chapter 3. Training curricula for preservice/basic, supervisory, special topics, in-service, and executive are based on agency resources, powers, and responsibilities. Specific attention was paid to a wide range of topics for training of supervisors and managers. The chapter also discussed the current issues in delivering training programs both in traditional classrooms and by long distance learning.

Review Questions/Activities

1. Based on the general training requirements in your state, obtain a general description of the curricula for police, security officers, and supervisors. How do they compare with the courses presented in this chapter?
2. Under the supervision of your instructor, make a training course outline that would be appropriate for security services or student services personnel at your campus. Your instructor will show you how to develop instructional objectives and the general format for a training outline based on model programs that exist in your state. Before you begin the exercise, conduct a needs assessment through interactions with campus management personnel.

Web Searches

1. Review the types and topics for training courses offered by professional associations for their members. These organizations include ASIS International (www.asisonline.org), the International Association of Chiefs of Police (www.iacp.org), the International Association of School Resource Officers (www.nasro .org), and the International Association of Campus Law Enforcement Administrators (www.iaclea.org). What topics appear to be common to all security service organizations?
2. After reviewing the types of training programs offered by the associations in Question 1, analyze the details of one of the training programs. Describe its substantive content and objectives. Discuss whether in your view the content adequately meets the program objectives.

3. Using an Internet search engine, search for *information security training* and view the various professional associations and organizations that provide training in the area of information, computer, and network security. Prepare a list of certification programs in the area of information security offered for managers and describe the basic components, often referred to as *domains,* of those programs.
4. Consider the same certification programs located in Question 3. How many of those programs are offered through a distance learning or online format? Why is the availability of programs offered through this format important to security personnel?

References

Bureau of Justice Statistics. 2003. *Local Police Departments, 2000.* Washington, D.C.: U.S. Department of Justice, Bureau of Justice Statistics.

Chronicle of Higher Education. January 30, 2004. "Distance Education: Keeping Up with Explosive Demand." *The Chronicle Review: Information Technology.* (January 30): B8.

Hall, Mimi. 2003. "Private Security Guards Are Homeland's Weak Link." *USA Today.* Accessed January 23, 2004 at USA Today.com. 1/22/2003. Retrieved January 23, 2004.

Jordan, Johnson W. 2003. "Get the Most from Your Guard Force." *Security Management Online.* Accessed June 18, 2004 at www.securitymanagement.com/libay/001395. html.

Kennedy, Ralph C. 2003. "Applying Principles of Adult Learning: The Key to More Effective Training Programs." *FBI Law Enforcement Bulletin* (April): 1–5.

Mager, Robert K. 1984. *Preparing Instructional Objectives,* 2nd. ed. Belmont, Calif.: Lake Management and Training.

McBride, R. Bruce. 1986. "Perceptions of Discrimination within Occupational Socialization Processes As Held by Newly Appointed Police Officers in Selected New York State Police Departments." Dissertation, University of Albany.

Payne, Michael. 1999. *Field Training Program for Police.* Albany, New York: Office of Public Safety, Division of Criminal Justice Services.

Wharton Executive Education. 2010. Wharton/ASIS Program for Security Executives. Accessed on May 2, 2010, at http://executiveeducation.wharton .upenn.edu/industry-association-programs/Management/asis-security-executives-program.cfm

Watson, Scott. October 2002. "A Lesson in Training." *Security Management*: 75–81.

13

■ ■ ■

Global Security Issues

KEY TERMS

al-Qaeda, arms trading, cartel, Cold War, globalization, Group 4 Falck, Hamas, Hezbollah, Interpol, kidnapping and ransom, Mafia/La Cosa Nostra, narco terrorism, Xe.

This chapter discusses the current and future challenges and issues faced by security service organizations. We begin with a summary of recent global events and how they have affected security service operations. Transnational crime issues are then explored in terms of the challenges they present to international, national, state, and local law enforcement agencies. While various issues related to terrorism have been discussed throughout this text, the global issues presented by terrorism and counterterrorist measures are presented in terms of their impact on strategic and daily operations. We then offer a glimpse into the future with regard to national and international issues affecting security service agencies. These include the need for national standards for most private security officers and for greater cooperation between public law enforcement and security services.

GLOBAL OPERATIONS

In the mid-1990s the term *globalization* was used to describe the interaction of goods and services from one continent to another as well as the commercial and social interdependence between nations. The examples are numerous. The European Union has created a unified monetary system and is slowly breaking down border and tariff restrictions among member nations. Most clothing now sold in the United States is produced in China, Southeast Asia, and Latin America. Every major war or conflict in the Middle East impacts the petroleum trade of all nations. Commercial, social, and political interaction continues to increase with high-speed electronic communications and relatively cheap jet travel. The impact of globalization is significant for security service organizations, which face new challenges ranging from illegal transportation of goods and services to terrorism. As discussed in Chapter 1, many U.S. security service organizations with long historical traditions are today part of global conglomerates such as Securitas (Pinkerton, Wells Fargo, Burns) and Group 4 Falck (Wackenhut).

INTERNATIONAL RELATIONS

Growing up after World War II in the so-called Cold War period, the authors experienced a world divided into three camps: "the West" led by the United States, Canada, and their European allies, particularly Britain, Germany, and sometimes France; the Communist bloc countries led by the Union of the Soviet Socialist Republics (USSR), Red China, their eastern European allies, and occasional countries around the world such as North Korea and Cuba; and the so-called third world of underdeveloped nations in the Middle East, Africa, Latin America, and Southeast Asia, which were courted both by the West and the Communist bloc for commercial development, intelligence, and strategic military bases. Always in the background was the threat of the use of nuclear weapons by the superpowers.

Between 1970 and 1990, the scenario suddenly changed. The foundation of the Communist bloc, the USSR, crumbled because an inefficient military and overextended economic system could not keep pace with Western military developments and consumer goods production. The Communists also could not curtail the spread of Western culture and ideas, reflected in the sudden rise of democratic groups in Poland, Czechoslovakia, and elsewhere. The Berlin Wall, which exemplified the Iron Curtain between western and eastern Europe, was torn down as Russian army personnel left eastern Europe where new governments were formed. The USSR dissolved in 1991, resulting in the creation of the Russian Federation and new autonomous nations such as Azerbaijan, Kazakhstan, and Georgia. The People's Republic of China, long a strong bastion of Communist economic policy, has gradually allowed Western capital ventures and currently is becoming a manufacturing giant for the world. It is estimated that many manufacturing operations will continue to be transferred to China and other countries in South Asia. Another trend is the gradual transfer of financial service customer relations operations from the United States to India and other English-speaking countries with a well-educated workforce.

Despite the end of the Cold War, regional conflicts between rival political parties and ethnic groups continue, and terrorist incidents impact world public safety. For example, fighting between Serbs and Muslims in the former communist republic of Yugoslavia resulted in the wholesale slaughter and forced migration of Muslim populations. The conflict finally ended in 1999 after NATO aerial bombardments and intervention by the United Nations. In Africa, tribal and rebel fighting continues to result in politically related slaughter in many countries, such as Liberia, Sierra Leone, and the Congo. In the Middle East, although the Israeli government gave limited authority to Palestinians living in occupied territories in the early 1990s, fighting still continues between Israel and various Palestinian militant groups, such as Hamas, Islamic Jihad, Hezbollah, and others. These groups continue to use suicide bombings and sniper and rocket attacks. The Israelis in turn retaliate with bombings, occupation of Palestinian neighborhoods, and the construction of a security wall between Israeli territory and Palestinian settlements.

The United States has emerged as the "world police officer," supporting peacekeeping missions and aggressively waging a war on terrorism. Note that in the mid-1970s, the United States was reluctant to become embroiled in local conflicts and withdrew its military units from Vietnam and Cambodia after some twenty years of fighting with Communist regular army and guerrilla forces led by North Vietnamese armed forces. Since that time, there has been a slow and reluctant willingness in the United States to become involved in local and regional issues as exemplified by its leadership in ending the Iraqi occupation of Kuwait in Gulf War I in 1993. The al-Qaeda terrorist attacks of 9/11 resulted in U.S. military actions against nations that harbor terrorists, such as Afghanistan. In 2003, the U.S. military invaded Iraq allegedly because that nation harbored terrorists and was developing weapons of mass destruction. Although Iraqi forces were quickly defeated, the occupation of the country resulted in a number of civil wars between Sunni and Shiite religious groups and ethnic factions. In the meantime, the war in Afghanistan continues against the Taliban, the term used to denote a number of Islamic fundamentalist groups, and a military buildup has been ordered by President Obama to defeat Taliban forces that have reoccupied various strategic areas in that country.

INTERNATIONAL CRIME ISSUES

In addition to these historical events, a number of international crime trends have emerged, particularly in areas of political unrest. The most notable is the emergence of international organized crime groups involved in the trafficking of narcotics, weapons, counterfeit and stolen goods, and humans from one area to another for illegal immigration purposes, as well as the sale of human body parts for medical testing and surgical use. There is also the demand for prostitutes and children for adoption. In some cases, organized crime groups impose "economic slavery" whereby people are given jobs in factories and plantations in other countries and then forced to pay for their food, lodging, and transportation with interest; the payoff never takes place.

Some organized crime groups have a legendary history. Italian and Sicilian organized crime groups, commonly called the *Mafia* or *La Cosa Nostra*, have existed for centuries in Europe. The Italian-Sicilian crime groups expanded to North America during the latter part of the nineteenth century, as did other crime groups based on ethnic backgrounds and region of operation including those of Irish and German descent. The prominence and notoriety of those gangs became common knowledge during the Prohibition Era of the 1920s and early 1930s, motivated by the opportunity for lucrative profits from the manufacture, transportation, and sale of alcoholic beverages. Upon repeal of the Eighteenth Amendment in 1933, organized crime groups became more actively involved in gambling, prostitution, labor racketeering, cargo hijacking, loan sharking, and eventually narcotics trafficking. Organized crime groups infiltrated legitimate businesses such as casinos, labor unions, and waste cartage businesses and acquired various cash businesses such as laundromats, pizza parlors, and restaurants as conduits for laundering significant cash profits. Some organized crime groups, such as the Colombian drug cartels, control the political and socioeconomic climate of entire countries, often through intimidation or the use of actual violence.

The success of those criminal organizations has had two consequences. First, the media refer to other crime gangs throughout the world as Mafia: the Russian Mafiya, the Jewish mafia, the Bosnian mafia, or—in the case of organized crime groups focusing on drug trafficking—as cartels, such as the Colombian cartels named for their region of operation, the Cali cartel, and the Medellin cartel. The second consequence involves the enormous cash profits that have resulted in an exponential growth in international money laundering.

The Taliban in Afghanistan used the sale of opium grown in that region to purchase weapons for terrorist activities, which contributed to the term *narco terrorism*. Despite the initial defeat of the Taliban, Afghan gangs and warlords continue to deal in opium trafficking, which amounts to some $2.5 billion of export revenue (IMF, 2003). This will lead to further fighting and deaths to protect business turf. Civil war between the government and guerilla groups continue in Colombia and parts of Mexico because the guerillas are able to procure arms through narcotics production and kidnapping.

Arms trading is a leading cause of death and physical injury around the world. While legitimate manufacturers create arms and sell them to dealers in other countries, there is a subculture of arms trading that includes machine guns, pistols, small artillery, and rocket launchers. Most weapon sales begin with legitimate orders but then the shipment may be rerouted to another vendor. Some orders are stolen during shipment. Regardless of method, the weapons end up anywhere including in the possession of terrorists, drug lords, and rogue armies. While the United Nations has pledged to increase restrictions on small arms trading, nothing has been done (*New York Times,* 2003a). There is also great concern about the sale of shoulder-to-air rocket launchers as exemplified by an August 2003 arrest of a New Jersey arms dealer who sold rocket launchers to undercover operatives acting as al-Qaeda agents who wanted rocket launchers to bring down commercial jet liners in the United States.

Another burgeoning economic activity is kidnapping for ransom and the rise for executive protection. According to Schmidle (2009), the global economy has given rise to the kidnapping of politicians, wealthy individuals and their families, and employees of multinational firms working in remote areas plagued by crime in such countries as Nigeria, Somalia, Columbia, Mexico, and various areas in the Middle East. Tracking one incident, the author reports that workers of a construction company captured at gunpoint in Nigeria were held and negotiations progressed over the course of several days between the insurance company, which insured against kidnapping and ransoms, and a middleman for the captors. Eventually the workers were released for an undisclosed amount. In many cases, there is government collusion with the gangs which allows this activity to continue. Insurance policies against "K and R" are common among Fortune 500 companies, who pay premiums over $300 million. Kidnappings in these lawless areas are common, with Mexico reporting as many as 7,000 incidents. There will be a viable trade in those areas where the government either has not been able exercise law and order or enters into tacit agreements with "K and R" gangs.

TRANSNATIONAL CRIME ISSUES

There are few law enforcement resources to deal with transnational crime because there is a lack of legislative authority in the international community (Combs, 1999: 150). The United Nations, which is the world forum for debating national and regional differences and disputes, may act only on resolution by its Security Council for specific actions, including the use of military force. Individual countries must either deal with transnational crime on their own soil or barter agreements with other countries for joint investigations.

Contrary to popular belief, Interpol (the International Criminal Police Organization) is not an international police unit. It serves as an intelligence-gathering and collaborative research agency for law enforcement agencies in member countries throughout the world. Headquartered in Lyon, France, Interpol provides specific services such as the identification of operations involving counterfeit credit cards, computer crimes, money laundering, intellectual property crimes, and ethics and professional responsibility. On a smaller scale, the European Union has established its own criminal police organization, Europol, which is composed of law enforcement officials from member countries that basically share intelligence.

A promising transnational development is the Council of Europe's Convention on Cybercrime, which is an international agreement by members of the Council of Europe and non-member countries, including the United States, Canada, Japan, and South Africa. The convention (commonly known as a *treaty* in the United States) ratified on November 23, 2001, requires nations to enact criminal laws prohibiting nine specified crimes: child pornography, copyright infringement, fraud activity by computer, computer forgery, the misuse of computer devices by using items such as hacker software tools and passwords that would enable access to and penetration of a computer or computer system, interfering with the functioning of a computer system, the intentional destruction or damage to stored data, the intentional interception of nonpublic transmissions by computer, and unlawful access of a computer or computer system to cause damage or some other criminal act. The convention also contains provisions that member nations must adopt for the preservation of data and evidence and for the search and seizure of evidence of cyber crimes. Finally, the convention provides for mutual assistance between members in gathering evidence and extraditing accused persons.

The need for a worldwide security service and investigation organization remains apparent. A good example of this problem is the case of Victor Bout, who is an international arms trader residing in Moscow. Although Bout has "violated" numerous laws in trading millions of dollars worth of machine guns, pistols, and rocket grenade launchers in Africa and Asia, there are outstanding warrants for him only in Belgium for money transfer violations. To transport these shipments, Bout supervises an entire network of planes, shipping companies, and politicians who are on his payroll. Bout purchased arms in the Ukraine after the breakup of the Soviet Union in 1991. According to writer Peter Landesman, "the Ukrainian military was turned into a tool for revenue by a generation of politicians who took advantage of the factories and used them to manufacture and ship weapons for money to anyone who wanted them" (Landesman, 2003: 31). Before 2001, many of Bout's arms shipments were destined for Afghanistan, which was under the control of the Taliban. Even though the United States attempted to work with a number of foreign governments to arrest Bout, he is still free in Russia. Landesman concludes that the case of Bout reflects the problem encountered by investigations that have to go outside national boundaries.

INTERNATIONAL TERRORISM

Groups that operate without regard to national boundaries are termed *international terrorists*. Their goal is to attack targets anywhere in the world to create fear of and support for their cause. Terrorist groups are often supported or sponsored openly or covertly by various countries as exemplified by the most noted group, al-Qaeda.

Al-Qaeda

As discussed by Rashid (2001) and Bergen (2001), al-Qaeda was formed by Osama Bin Laden, the son of a wealthy Yemeni construction operator who had close personal and commercial ties to the Saudi royal family. Bin Laden fought with the mujahideen against the Russian army during its occupation of Afghanistan between 1985 and 1992. This call for a jihad against the Russians resulted in thousands of Muslims from many countries coming to the area to fight under the auspices of the World Muslim League. Weapons, including portable surface-to-air missiles, were financed and supplied by the United States and other Western allies.

Following the retreat of the Russian army, Bin Laden moved to the Sudan in 1992 and began focusing his attention on the United States and its Western and Middle Eastern allies for their role in the first Gulf War. Bin Laden and other Muslim fanatics believed that the presence of Western troops in the Holy Land defied religious tradition and political autonomy of Saudi Arabia and Islam. He condemned the current Saudi regime for allowing Western troops to remain there. Before September 11, al-Qaeda was responsible for attacks of the World Trade Center in 1995 and the bombings of U.S. embassies in Kenya and Tanzania in 1998. During this time, al-Qaeda also invested in a number of businesses in the Sudan and Middle East. Bin Laden and his followers migrated in 1996 to Afghanistan, which soon fell under control of the Taliban, a group of religious zealots, following a long series of civil wars between various factions. That same year Bin Laden was identified as a major terrorist, and his financial assets in the United States were frozen. He was also indicted by a grand jury for his involvement with the attack on the

World Trade Center in 1995. Efforts by the CIA to "snatch" or kill Bin Laden were unsuccessful. The refusal of Taliban rulers to turn him over to U.S. authorities after the attacks of September 11 resulted in a military attack on Afghanistan led by the United States. At the time of writing, he had not been captured or killed and was said to be in hiding somewhere in the remote areas of the Afghanistan–Pakistan border. Other groups that appear to have a working relationship with al-Qaeda include Hezbollah or the "Party of God," Islamic Jihad, and Hamas, which attack Israeli targets.

Other Groups

A number of terrorist groups operate all over the world. At this time, most limit themselves to a specific region or an area for their main activities but obtain financial and political support by various means including covert and overt state support, crime activities such as narcotics trafficking, and funds from expatriates and activities to support bogus refugee efforts. For many years, terrorist training camps were allowed to operate in Libya, Sudan, and Iran. It is well known that the Irish Republican Army obtained money from American Irish supporters in the northeastern part of the United States. There are a large number of groups that have been deemed terrorist organizations by the Department of State and their financial assets have been frozen in the United States. The reader will note that most have a basis from conflicts between the Israel and the Palestinian state, border disputes between India and Pakistan, and Islamic fundamentalism in South Asia. Based on an initial review by Sauter and Carafano (2005), what follows is a brief description of these major groups, their purpose, and their sources of economic and political support. Note that many of these groups have formal and informal interactions with each other. Combatants often have fought in many other conflicts such as the Soviet occupation of Afghanistan in the 1990s and the American occupation of Iraq. They also train and supply lone gunmen and bombers who have an affinity for their cause. For example, Faisal Shazad, who was arrested for attempting to set off a car bomb during the evening of May 1, 2010, far appears to have acted alone but may have received financing and training from an unknown terrorist group. What follows is just a small selection of groups that are currently active. For a current review of all groups, please see www.state.gov/s/ct/list/.

Ansar Al-Islam (Helpers of Islam)

> **Purpose:** Create an Islamic state in Iraq
>
> **Description:** Closely allied with al-Qaeda, this group is composed of Iraqi Kurds and Arabs who wish to create an Islamic state in Iraq
>
> **Base of Support:** Receives assistance from local supporters and from al-Qaeda

Abu Sayyaf Group

> **Purpose:** Promote an Islamic state in the southern Philippines
>
> **Description:** Operates in the south Asian area and responsible for a number of bombings, beheadings, and assassinations. This group has been responsible for kidnappings of U.S. citizens including an incident in Malaysia where 21 persons were kidnapped and held for ransom
>
> **Base of Support:** Allied with other Islamic groups and obtains funding from extortion

Hezbollah (Party of God)

Purpose: Liberate Jerusalem from Israeli occupation

Description: Founded in 1982 in response to the Israeli invasion of Lebanon, this group has been responsible for a number of attacks including the U.S. Marine barracks in Beirut in 1993 and the U.S. Embassy in 1994.

Base of support: Receives funding, weapons, training, and diplomatic assistance from Iran and Syria

Hamas (Islamic Resistance Movement)

Purpose: Create a Palestinian state and eliminate the state of Israel

Description: This political party of the Palestine State in Gaza has been classified as a terrorist organization by the U.S. Department of State. Created in 1987 during riots (Intifada) in opposition to Israeli occupation of the area since 1967, Hamas targets Israeli civilian and military targets with rocket attacks, ambushes, and suicide bombings. In June 2006, Hamas fighters attacked a border-crossing area and captured an Israeli soldier. The Israeli defense force, in turn, launched a series of air and land attacks and created a virtual blockade around the area demanding the return of the soldier. Hamas wants the release of prisoners held by the Israelis. The population of Gaza, which consists of about 25 square miles, continues to survive on humanitarian aid and a series of underground tunnels that bring consumer goods and military supplies (Wright, 2009).

Base of support: Worldwide donations come from expatriates and benefactors around the world

Jaish-e-Mohammed (Army of Mohammed)

Purpose: Liberate Kashmir from India and reunite the area with Pakistan

Description: Often aligned with the Harkat-ul-Mujahideen, the group has conducted a number of attacks in Kashmir and is responsible for the hijack of an Indian airliner. This group has close ties with the Taliban in Afghanistan.

Lashkar-e-Taiba/(LT) (Army of the Righteous)

Purpose: Liberate Kashmir from India and reunite the area with Pakistan

Description: Founded in 1989, this group has conducted numerous attacks on targets in India. The group was responsible for well-orchestrated attacks by ten or more gunmen in Mumbai, India, on hotels, tourist sites, and the main railway station. The attacks, which began on November 26, 2008, resulted in 173 persons killed over a two-day period.

Base of support: The Mumbai attacks showed that the group was trained and directed from sites in Pakistan.

COUNTERTERRORISM EFFORTS BY SECURITY SERVICES

The U.S. government has the responsibility to protect national borders and gather intelligence, identify terrorist groups, and, in some cases, attack these groups under the rules of war or through UN sanction and international diplomacy. As discussed in Chapter 2, the United States has a wide range of military and law enforcement assets that include the major branches of the armed forces, the FBI, and various law enforcement groups under the Department of Homeland Security. The post-9/11 rules of engagement include identifying and arresting individuals with terrorist affiliations and employing undercover activities against international and national terrorist groups. Additionally, the federal government has the power to seize financial assets of foreign groups in the United States. The federal government is also responsible for major recovery management—responding to disasters and directing recovery efforts—through FEMA if a major terrorist event were to occur.

State security service agencies, whether they be public or private, are charged with assisting in these federal efforts by gathering local intelligence, identifying possible suspects, and providing security at key infrastructure and symbolic sites. Local agencies are also empowered to address these same issues in their immediate areas. In order for this to occur under the program of homeland security, the federal government and various state and local entities participate in a number of activities. Perhaps the most crucial is data sharing among federal agencies and state and local police units. It is no secret that significant amounts of intelligence information have been gathered but there is still a need for improved analysis and sharing.

Another important activity involves identifying persons who enter the United States and who may have terrorist affiliations as well as tracking the whereabouts of foreign visitors. The al-Qaeda operatives who commandeered the four planes on September 11 had lived in the United States for almost a year, rented apartments, received traffic tickets, and had memberships in workout gyms. And as an initial step in the identification and tracking process, the United States began fingerprinting and photographing foreign travelers at entry points in January 2004 to identify who enters the country and how long they remain. The name, fingerprint, and photo are then matched to those on visas, terrorist watch lists, and criminal data banks. Initially, visitors from about twenty-seven countries were exempted from the identification and tracking process if they stayed for less than 90 days for tourist reasons (Goodnough and Lichtblau, 2004). There is also an important need for security services to concentrate on domestic groups. Timothy McVeigh and Terry Nichols demonstrated the need for this. They were not on any watch list, yet they conspired to "get back" at the federal government by bombing the Federal Building in Oklahoma City.

GLOBAL SECURITY SERVICE ISSUES

A company with holdings and assets in many parts of eastern Europe, Latin America, the Middle East, and Africa has to look at security from the perspective of survival in an unstable environment. In addition to providing normal perimeter and internal security to protect employees, offices, and production equipment, the company has to be attuned to the local political scene to review threats and perform risk management. Democratic processes and personal safety, as we know them in the United States and western Europe, are either very fragile in some regions or almost nonexistent in others. Military takeovers and civil war between rival political factions can erupt suddenly. Global companies are tempting targets for regional and international terrorists, as illustrated by bombings of hotels in Jakarta, Indonesia, and Mumbai.

Private corporations may face the threat of nationalization, which is a nice term for the government in power taking over foreign-owned production facilities and expelling the foreign owners and their employees. Often the national security service, aka the secret police, keeps surveillance on foreign nationals by bugging apartment buildings and telephone services.

In addition to obtaining intelligence on the local scene, security services have to be concerned with the following matters.

Travel Restrictions

The U.S. Department of State keeps an inventory of areas that pose a high threat to U.S. citizens because of ongoing warfare, violent political protests, or terrorist activity. The State Department issues travel restrictions on a weekly basis on their Web site at www.travel.state.gov. Based on these warnings, an organization may issue direct orders to employees not to travel to these areas.

Emergency Planning

Often there is a need to withdraw personnel immediately and suspend commerce or close factories or offices because of civil war or threats by terrorist groups. Factors to consider in planning include emergency transportation; removal, transportation, or destruction of important documents and equipment; and long-term caretaking of properties.

Background Checks on Workers

Often companies and government organizations hire primary staff and ancillary staff such as clerical personnel, drivers, translators, and housekeepers. Sometime foreign workers such as guards and escorts are hired to provide security. The greatest threat here is having information about the daily movement of workers and their families supplied to terrorists and criminals. Some companies take the stance that intelligence and company secrets have to be kept away from these workers to prevent being compromised. Security personnel frequently conduct background checks before prospective workers are hired.

Health and Disease Status

Companies operating in foreign countries must identify the types of vaccinations needed to protect personnel from prevailing health risks. Companies take this seriously as illustrated by the H1N1 flu outbreak, which resulted in cancellations of billions of dollars worth of travel and conference bookings. Although smallpox is under control, malaria, typhoid, yellow fever, and other diseases are still prevalent in many areas of the world.

Civil and Criminal Matters

As in the United States, employees in foreign countries can become involved in civil and criminal matters. People marry, have children, and die naturally or by accident. They also buy homes and cars and get into disagreements with purchasers and buyers. The security service organization provides these employees a unique service in a foreign country by having a thorough knowledge of local customs and legal procedures. For example, most U.S. high school and college students are surprised to learn that the Miranda rule and speedy trial do not exist in many countries of the world. Committing offenses considered minor in the United States can result in serious fines and jail time in other countries. Motor vehicle traffic laws and customs are also a real problem, as is corruption of traffic cops.

EXECUTIVE PROTECTION

An important aspect in both global and national security operations is executive protection. Simply defined, *executive protection* provides security to a person who has the high potential of being the target of assassination, kidnapping, or assault. There are also less serious concerns such as "get-in-your-face" confrontation and pie-throwing attacks at executives during public events. Executive protection encompasses three main models:

1. Twenty-four-hour-a-day, seven-day-a-week protection.
2. VIP coverage for major events such as corporate meetings, graduation speeches, and planned visits.
3. Specific threat to an executive or manager by a disgruntled employee or customer following from a plant shutdown, termination or layoff of employees, or personal action by the organization.

In certain countries, protection is needed for employees and their dependents against political assassination and kidnappings by criminal and terrorist groups. In high-risk areas, companies and government diplomatic missions have secured compounds and a force of armed security officers to protect employees and their families.

The U.S. Secret Service provides around-the-clock protection for the president and vice president of the United States and their families, former presidents, and certain political candidates. Agents are trained in all three types of protection models as well as event and threat assessment, defensive and escape tactics, communications, use of firearms in confined spaces, and protective movement plans in public and crowded areas. The number of agents assigned to the presidential detail is not public. However, when the president visits a city, the Secret Service is assisted by hundreds of state and local police for outer perimeter access control, traffic control, and emergency support as he travels from one site to another. Foreign dignitaries who travel to the United States often have their own protection details through diplomatic agreements. Governors and mayors of large cities have executive protection details, and sports and entertainment figures often employ bodyguards and/or drivers to protect them from stalkers and threats from deranged fans. Security service personnel assigned to these details immediately learn that their efforts to protect "the boss" and family involve diplomacy and achieving a balance between dealing with the family's personal needs and providing a safe environment.

USE OF PRIVATE SECTOR CONTRACTORS IN IRAQ AND AFGHANISTAN

Soon after the successful American attack on Iraq in 2002, the authors began to receive requests for employment to serve with private security contractors deployed to that country. The range of job duties based on our educational and training backgrounds included training, intelligence analysis, planning, guarding convoys, and protecting executives and government officials. Following the invasion and the fall of the Saddam Hussein regime, civil war broke out between ethnic and religious factions and against the newly installed government. Attacks involving shootings and bombings continue to be directed toward American and coalition troops and private security contractors. Private contractors often became the center of media attention both as victims and perpetrators. Many private security personnel have lost their lives in bombings by improved explosive devices, sniper fire, and mob violence. On the other hand, there have been charges of human rights violations against these contractors.

The use of armed and unarmed contractors continues today and has been expanded to Afghanistan, where a United States–led coalition is fighting the Taliban. As in Iraq, private contractors guard convoys and strategic locations and often get into firefights with the enemy. The use of private contractors in recent times is not new. Both the United States and the United Nations have used contractors in various conflicts such as the Bosnian civil war in 1995. As with private security officers, private contractors can be hired, trained, and placed into the field very quickly to augment the duties and responsibilities of military personnel. Hiring local personnel has the advantage of gaining intelligence of terrain, civilian customs, and the enemy. As with any contract, the employment ends when there is no longer a need for their services.

However, it is not clear how private contractors are held accountable for their actions other than the loss of an operating license by the employing government. Thus abuses toward civilians quickly erode confidence and support of population. An example of this occurred when members of a Blackwater International Security (now known as Xe) assigned to executive protection were charged with opening gunfire on a mob killing 17 civilians. Their license to operate in Iraq has since been suspended.

What is significant is the number of contractors in these two areas. Elsea, Schwartz, and Nakamure (2009) estimates that there are 50 or so companies employing some 30,000 armed employees from various countries. In Afghanistan, the number of contract security personnel is estimated at 70,000. These include former U.S. military and law enforcement personnel as well as third country nationals and local civilians. The exact number of contract security personnel is difficult to determine based on issues with inaccurate data, official definitions of a security contractor, and the actual number of personnel operating in the field at any given times.

Based on the Blackwater incident and other human rights abuse reports, Congress is reviewing the use of private contractors in armed conflict areas. The essential question is the use of contract personnel for essential military functions. In the future, contractors may be prohibited in operating in combat zones or limited to static positions for critical buildings, bases, and supply depots.

Summary

The world, particularly the "world" of the United States, has changed drastically since 9/11, and that change has impacted significantly on security service organizations and their personnel. Preparing for the threat of terrorism on a global scale and from new and innovative criminal tactics that can be initiated anywhere on the planet and enhanced and enabled by technologies that change every day presents a daunting assignment for security personnel. Continued employment prospects for security personnel will remain high and the educational and training requirements strenuous.

Review Question/Activities

1. Review current periodical literature for articles that discuss recent trends in international crime and prepare a brief description of one article on each of the following topics:
   a. The changing landscape of international criminal organizations or groups.
   b. The prevalence of international money laundering.
   c. The influence or involvement of international crime groups in money laundering.
   d. Current national efforts in the United States to combat international terrorism.
   e. Security companies that provide international services.

WebSearches

1. Visit the home page of the Council of Europe at www.coe.int. Review the resources available at the site, and search for the Council's Convention on Cybercrime. Describe the international crimes covered by this convention and the procedures available for international assistance in the investigation of attacks and the search for perpetrators.
2. At the same Web page, locate the Council's Convention on Mutual Legal Assistance in Criminal Matters. What procedures are available for

international assistance in the investigation of international crimes?

3. Access the Web site for the International Criminal Police Organization (Interpol) at www.interpol.int. Describe the types of assistance that Interpol can provide in the investigation of international or transnational crimes.

4. Through the media and with guidance from your instructor, review a recent terrorist attack. What was the group responsible for the event? What is their cause? What were the outcomes of the incident?

5. Visit www.travel.state.gov and select the travel warnings section. From that site, compare and contrast three areas where travel warnings exist.

References

Bergen, Peter. 2001. *Holy War Inc.* New York: Simon & Schuster.

Combs, Cindy. 1999. *Terrorism in the 21st Century.* Upper Saddle River, N.J.: Prentice Hall.

Elsea, Jennifer, Moshe Schwartz, and Kennon Nakamure. 2009. CRS Report for Congress: Private Sector Contractors in Iraq: Background, Legal Status, and Other Issues. Congressional Research Service. Web posted at //www.fas.org/sgp/crs/natsec/RL32419.pdf. Accessed November 22, 2009.

Goodnough, Abby, and Eric Lichtblau. 2004. "U.S. Institutes Fingerprinting at Entry Points." *The New York Times,* January 6: A1, A21.

International Monetary Fund (IMF). 2003. *Islamic State of Afghanistan: Rebuilding a Microeconomic Framework for Reconstruction and Growth.* Accessed at www.imf.org/external/pubs/ft/scr/2003/cr03299.pdf, on June 21, 2004.

Landesman, Peter. 2003. "Meeting Mr. Bout." *The New York Times Magazine,* August 17: 28–33.

National Advisory Committee on Criminal Justice Standards and Goals. 1976. *Private Security: Report of the Task Force on Private Security.* Washington, D.C.: U.S. Department of Justice, Law Enforcement Assistance Administration.

Rashid, Ahmed. 2001. *Taliban.* New Haven: Yale University Press.

Sauter, Mark A., and James J. Carafano. 2005. Homeland Security: *A Complete Guide to Understanding, Preventing, and Surviving Terrorism.* New York: McGraw Hill.

Schmidle, Nicholas. December 6, 2009. The Hostage Business: Kidnapping the Developing World Is a Crime by Product of Globalization, and a Strange and Shadowy Ransom Industry Has Grown to Protect and Retrieve the Victims. But Are All the Consultants and Insurers Really Just Part of the Problem? *New York Times Magazine,* pp. 45–48.

The New York Times. 2003a. "World's Deadliest Arms." August 11: A.14.

Wright, Lawrence. November 9, 2009. Letter from Gaza: Captives—a Report on the Israeli Attacks. *The New Yorker,* pp. 46–61.

14

■ ■ ■

Future Trends in Security Administration

KEY TERMS

computer forensic investigators, coyotes, crime rates, gaming industry, hate crimes, Madoff, posses, privatization.

Proactive security service planners must look at current and future trends to plan for financial and operational needs in their organizations. This chapter discusses the future of national and global security service trends from both an academic and operational standpoint. Our predictions are that demands for security services will continue to grow based on continued concerns for personal safety and homeland security. The main trends will be influenced by economic conditions, continued globalization, and new developments in security technology. Another factor that must be considered is the reduction of services normally provided by municipal, county, and state police organizations.

CURRENT ECONOMIC SITUATION

In 2008–2010 the United States suffered a catastrophic recession brought, in part, by national deregulation policies, poor investments by major financial institutions, and the issuance of mortgages and loans to customers with either poor credit ratings or the means to pay principal and interest. By summer 2009, a number of leading financial firms, such as Bear Sterns and Lehman Brothers, had "gone under" or were purchased by competitors. Other financial giants, such as AIG, managed to survive by U.S. government loans. Other industries also did not fare well. Bankruptcies or reorganizations with government loans were needed by General Motors, Chrysler, United Airlines, and others. Added to this economic misery were a number of major frauds such as the Ponzi scheme perpetuated by Bernard Madoff, who is currently serving a term of one hundred and fifty years in federal prison for a wide range of federal stock fraud charges. In brief, Madoff's finance company took in investment money from various clients and these early investors reaped super dividends. This opened the door for a wide range of investors, including charities, labor unions, and educational organizations, to also invest to seek similar dividends even though the high earnings and value of Madoff's company were fictitious. Despite warnings by certain analysts, the fraud was able to continue until 2008, when it was learned that there was not enough money to pay for redemptions. In all, investors lost about $50 billion.

The value of stocks and bonds in the U.S. markets tumbled by 25–30 percent and the number of mortgage foreclosures or payment delinquencies rose to 14 percent (Morgenson, 2009). The economic recession is by no means confined to the United States. Other countries have experienced similar trends based on the meltdown of the American market and their own economic problems. This has all affected the housing prices, consumer confidence, employment, and tax revenues. In January 2010, there was an approximate 10 percent national unemployment rate. Attempts to revive the economy have been made with stimulus funding under the auspices of the American Recovery Act, which earmarks funding for infrastructure and other improvements.

In the meantime, Americans continue to think and work globally. According to pollster John Zogby (2008: 91–119), Americans, particularly persons between the ages of eighteen and twenty-four, are exposed to more global ideas and trends through the Internet and travel. Based on a survey in 2007, 56 percent of respondents age eighteen to twenty-nine reported that they had friends or family who lived outside of the United States and, relatedly, one in three reported that they traveled abroad once or twice within five years (p. 94). Additionally, the number of passports issued to American citizens has grown over 400 percent. It comes at no surprise that more workers entering the workforce will be assigned to foreign posts, or work with overseas units as part of their assigned duties.

CURRENT CRIME TRENDS

For the time being, overall reported crime rates appear to be declining. *Crime rates* refer to national trends as reported in the Uniform Crime Reports (UCR) and the National Crime Victim Survey. While these sources have certain limitations in measuring and reporting procedures, they provide a barometer on violent and property crime offenses. Based on UCR data reported by participating police departments, the estimated number of violent and property crimes for 2008 declined for the sixth year. Violent crime including murder/negligent homicide, rape, aggravated assault, and robbery, and property crimes, such as burglary, larceny, and motor vehicle theft decreased 0.8 percent in 2008 when compared with 2007 crime reports. According to the FBI (2008), "The 2008 violent crime rate was 454.5 offenses per 100,000 inhabitants (a 2.7 percent decrease from the 2007 rate), and the property crime rate was 3,212.5 per 100,000 persons (a 1.6 percent decrease from 2007)."

The National Crime Victim Survey, which is based on a sample of reporting households in the United States, also showed long-term declines in violent and property related offenses. For a ten-year period, the violent crime rate declined by 41 percent and property crime rate fell by 32 percent. For violent crimes, such as murder and sexual assault, there was little change between 2007 and 2008 with victimization reports per 1000 of 19.3 and 20.7, respectively. Property crimes showed another decrease of victimizations of 135 for 2008 and 147 for 2007 (BJS, 2008).

Despite the overall decline in serious offenses, the security service industry will continue to show growth based on "regional pockets" of both population growth and increased crime activity in the West, Southwest, and South, and general need for specialized services in technology, fraud investigation, and computer related issues. Economic forecasters warn that the current recession will have an impact on job recovery which is expected to be slow. The high unemployment rate may result in increased property crimes. Because of the financial mishaps in these past two years, there will be more federal and state government regulation of the financial services industry based on the widespread mortgage related fraud and Ponzi-like schemes related to the Madoff case. It appears that there will be changes in medical insurance protection for all Americans especially those who do not have coverage. This will result in efforts to curtail medical fraud schemes. Medical programs such as Medicare and Medicaid already bring forth fraud as a major issue based on phony claims from doctors and patients.

Many communities are concerned about gang activity especially those gangs associated with Latin American immigrant groups such as MS-14 and Calle-13, or localized groups, who provide "protection" and transport and distribute illegal drugs and commit a host of crimes. Then there is the issue of terrorism. Although there has not been a major attack or incident in the United States, a number of plots have been uncovered. Observers point to a possible trend whereby terror groups thinking of attacking targets may switch to secondary targets as opposed to targets that have been hardened since September 11, 2001.

FUTURE JOB OUTLOOK

The most recent reports from the U.S. Department of Labor suggest that jobs in policing, security, and investigations will continue to increase by 17 percent between 2006 and 2016 (Bureau of Labor Statistics, 2009). Watch and guard services will remain the mainstay of the industry. As discussed by the Department of Labor, these positions are based on the need for increased security for private businesses, residential areas, and recreation facilities. It is noted that there is a high rate of turnover with unarmed security officers or what we term Level I positions. Recall that Level I positions generally do not require extensive training and part-time hours are available. Growth is also expected in the general area of "gaming surveillance" which includes security patrols and surveillance in the expanding casino industry. The report states that highly technically trained personnel will be needed to address casino fraud (Bureau of Labor Statistics, 2009).

Significant growth is expected for security services providing specialized, technical services in computer security, general and fraud investigations, and prosecution. Under the general topic area of "private detectives and investigators" job classification, the Bureau of Labor Statistics lists the following titles:

Private detectives—work for a specific client to obtain information on a target through computer searches, surveillance, and interviews with associates known to the target. Often thought of as mainly dealing with marital infidelity situations, private investigation companies conduct a wide range of investigations for clients such as personnel background checks, or technical expertise related to accident reconstruction, missing persons, and child custody.

Computer forensic investigators—recover, analyze, and present data from computers for use in evidence and deal with computer system intrusion and data recovery.

Legal investigators—assist in the preparation of civil and criminal cases through witness interviews, evidence review, and litigation preparation.

Corporate investigators—conduct investigations for private corporations related to personnel (e.g., frauds and background checks) and criminal matters affecting a business.

Financial investigators—develop and review information related to financial transactions by persons and corporations. These cases might include fraud and financial profiling.

Retail or loss prevention agents—control losses and protect assets in a retail establishment in public and stock areas.

The Bureau of Labor Statistics reports that these positions often require either college certification or a bachelor's degree. Positions in computer forensics and accounting require education in those requisite areas and additional training by the employer or specialized certification authorities. Computer forensics training must be ongoing due to changes in software and fraud intrusions into protected systems. Because of the various fraud cases that have emerged in recent years, such as the Madoff scandal, mortgage fraud, and the meltdown of various financial institutions, there will be the need for more personnel to be engaged in financial due diligence and compliance activities. In many states, licenses are required to perform this work. Employment in these areas is expected to grow because of the demand for specialized services and increased security concerns for property, business reputation, and the increase in computers and Internet for the transaction of business. Competition is slated to be keen as many persons entering the investigations field often have previous work experience and training in law enforcement and the military.

For policing titles of uniformed patrol officer and detective, which includes agencies providing security services at Levels III and IV, it is expected that job growth will increase 11 percent within the next ten years as current personnel retire and concern remains on personal safety. Job prospects are good for those who can meet physical agility and background check standards, which are a main stumbling block for many candidates. Jobs in federal and state law enforcement and security service agencies requiring high security clearances will remain competitive.

There will continue to be a need for security officers, managers, and technical personnel with managerial and planning/project skills. This will require education and training in budgeting, planning, human resource management, technology acquisition, and project development. At this time, many major positions are hired from former law enforcement personnel. While this fact of the security profession will continue, there will be a trend where people from security companies and the private sector will move into command and policy making positions rather than retirees from federal and state law enforcement.

PRIVATIZATION

Overall, the public sector cannot keep pace with the increased demand for specialized services because economic resources in the local tax base cannot fund needed law enforcement and other services such as medical and elderly care. Since the beginning of the economic recession of 2009, there have been layoffs and reduced hours given to public employees including police officers. For example, as reported by Copeland (2009: 1), state police forces in some states, such as Oregon and Michigan, have been reduced by 30 percent, thus reducing patrol coverage in suburban and rural areas despite population growth. Layoffs are also being seen in various municipal departments. Thus private companies may be called upon to fill the void for specialized services. Personnel who have been laid off will gravitate toward security services position until being recalled.

In the private sector there is increased demand for specialized services to protect company assets. Thus, there will be continued growth activity in security technology, particularly for bomb scanning equipment, antivirus software, identity authentication, and improved alarm systems. Support activities for governmental functions have risen since 9/11. For example, private companies have been conducting background investigations to deal with the sudden increase of federal employee candidates and current employees needing security clearances. In times of disaster, private security contract firms are often called upon to provide security in hardest hit zones.

However, there may been a greater transfer of more support services to private sector contractors. For example in 2009 G4S Wackenhut received a contract from ICE for prisoner transport busing of illegal aliens attempting to cross into Arizona from Mexico. In an ad in a well-read security newsletter, the same company advertises its personnel and services for courtroom services, juvenile detention facilities, inmate hospital security, and other services that can free up sworn officers (GSN, 2009: 18). All security service agencies must become adept at responding to computer crime and identity theft cases. Most law enforcement and prosecutorial agencies, such as the city, county, district, or state attorney, are ill-equipped to handle these cases because of the lack of training and forensic equipment. Most forensic analysts and managers report that they are backlogged with cases involving child pornography, theft of services, and violent and property felony crimes involving cell phones.

In the economic crime area, corporate and security fraud continue to make headlines. It is not uncommon to see headlines such as "Broker Charged in Fraud Case" or "Company Admits It Lied in Financial Reporting." This relates to inside and fraudulent trading practices and simple greed in some corporations and financial investment industries. Scandals involving such companies as WorldCom, Enron, Tyco, Adelphia, and Bank of America in 2002–2004, and Madoff in 2008 have had a profound impact on public confidence in investment in that the companies failed to disclose their true value to shareholders and the financial markets. In 2008, there was an implosion of the housing industry partially caused by mortgage fraud involving inflation over housing values by sellers, banks, adjusters, and loan officers. Thus there will be more efforts made in regulation and investigation of complaints by overseeing government entities.

Homeland Security

In many respects, the nature of security in the United States will depend on future terrorist attacks. Before 9/11 it was felt by some that there was too much complacency in addressing terrorism and natural and man-made disasters. Levin and Jensen (2006) and other futurists feel that a sudden rise of attacks could result in calls for more security including military intervention and greater surveillance of the general population. White and Collins (2008: 419) and others call for a degree of "normalcy" whereby security risks are continually evaluated, prioritized, and addressed. For example, in this past year, various terrorist plots have been uncovered through intelligence developed from informants, surveillance, tips, and suspicious overseas transactions. Target hardening, risk to CIKR industries, and greater security in transportation and air travel will continue to improve with new technologies. However, a sudden rise of attacks in this country could result in a "Fortress America" mentality, whereby greater security procedures would be employed that would have an impact on personal mobility and civil liberties.

While attention is focused toward terrorists groups from the Middle East, observers also caution that attention has to be paid to domestic groups and individuals who espouse hate for ethnic, racial, and religious reasons. Many point to the fact that Timothy McVeigh, who was executed for blowing up the federal office building in Oklahoma City in 1995, was an unknown suspect but part of a group that opposed the federal government. Citing a report from the Department of Homeland Security on domestic hate groups and terrorism, Chunovic (2009: 1, 16) reports that many groups are incensed that an African American president was elected in 2008. Current economic problems and the flow of illegal immigration into the country have created a number of vigilante or Minuteman groups along the Mexico–United States border. Thus far these "posses" report movement of migrants to the CBP but it may be a matter of time when these groups attempt to enforce the law and conflict with federal, state, and local law enforcement. The Southern Poverty Law Center publishes trends and names of groups that preach hate and the use of violence against Jews, Muslims, Catholics, and people who support abortion rights. This information can be found at www.splc.com.

ILLEGAL IMMIGRATION

Related to homeland security is the continued problem of illegal immigration. Citing the impact on health care, education, social services, and crime rates, many policy makers have called for very strict enforcement of immigration laws and greater security along the borders with Mexico and Canada, and increased sea patrols by the Coast Guard. In August 2009, the states of Arizona, New Mexico, Texas, and California were given $30 million for additional patrol officers, overtime, and related costs. Along the border in these states, greater technology is being deployed involving radar, video surveillance, thermal imaging and vibration sensing systems, and drone aircraft to stem the tide of migrants attempting to cross the border into the United States. Begun in 2005, the Southwest Secure Border Initiative consists of a high-tech virtual fence, which consists of sensors, cameras, and radar.

Despite these efforts, people from Mexico and other countries in Latin America using Mexican "jumping off" points, continue to try to enter the United States. Many of these migrants are preyed upon by Mexican gangs (coyotes) who offer their services to cross into the United States at exorbitant prices. Other gangs demand protection and rob migrants. The trafficking of illegal aliens often has deadly consequences, as illustrated by cases when migrants hidden in truck containers die because of the lack of proper ventilation and water. Others die because of exposure to the heat and sun in crossing the desert. From an economic standpoint, illegal migrants form the core labor force of many service industries such as landscaping, domestic service, food preparation, and agriculture. Their sudden absence would have serious negative economic effects. However, industries who fail to ascertain a person's identity and legal citizen status risk serious fines and possible imprisonment based on the enforcement of federal labor laws.

Assessing this problem from a homeland security policy aspect, former secretary Michael Chertoff (2009) writes that the federal government will have to adopt policies that allow illegal aliens to become citizens while at the same time increasing efforts to reduce illegal border crossings. Current secretary Janet Napolitano, the former governor of Arizona, echoed the same thoughts. Citing that illegal crossings have been reduced in the early part of 2009 because of the economic climate, Napolitano said that illegal activity will increase when the economy improves. Immigration reform efforts will include increased border protection programs while creating a program for illegal immigrants currently living in the United States to obtain citizenship (Trottman, 2009). In the meantime private vendors have entered into partnerships with property owners on the border by deploying their sophisticated detection equipment. The owners in turn will notify CPB of activity while the vendors have an opportunity to demonstrate their equipment (Goodwin, 2009: 1).

GREATER USE OF TECHNOLOGY

Given a review of equipment and technology presented at regional and national security conferences, there will continue to be increased development of new security technology. At this time, communications technology is readily available to the general populace due to improvements in cell phone technology and global communications. Conflicts and abuses by government officials are immediately photographed and sent to million via the Internet as illustrated by civilian protests over disputed election results in Iran in October 2009. Thus innovations are also translated to the security industry with wireless communications for alarms and CCTV systems. Patrol officers using wireless phone technology can now snap pictures of situations which can result in e-mail being sent to a command post. GPS tracking, which was one time reserved for government purposes, is now widely available for vehicles and individuals. What follows is a review of technology that will have increased application in the security industry.

CCTV

The use of CCTV shows no signs of abating as many organizations and municipalities increasingly continue to install CCTV systems to deter crime and catch criminals. Following a recent roundtrip by air to Washington, D.C., from Upstate New York, the authors estimated that they were photographed at least twenty times or more in air terminals, government buildings, hotels, and streets. This can result to what is called in Britain the "surveillance society with human activities being filmed and held in government computer banks" (Lyall, 2009). In England, it is legal for the government to secretly follow citizen targets for minor offenses such as dumping trash, barking dogs, using illegal fireworks, and so on. In a case involving some notoriety, a family was followed via CCTV in a community to ascertain if their daughter could legally enroll in a neighborhood school (pp. 1, 8).

According to a major vendor, digital wireless video systems will expand to include real time applications between communications or command centers and patrol vehicles, fixed and mobile posts, computers, and cell phones. Thus command personnel will be able to see an event as it unfolds from various locations. The use of CCTV for institutional purposes has resulted in some organizations to publish policies on the use of CCTV and the review of tapes for investigative purposes. At one college having some 250 cameras, faculty, students, and staff are advised that areas will be under video surveillance where the security of property and persons will be enhanced. Areas that are under general surveillance are public areas and restricted sites. Cameras are not to be installed in classrooms, bathrooms, locker rooms, and offices. The policy does give permission to install cameras in these areas "for exceptional circumstances" for criminal investigations through a review process with the campus president (Security Camera Policy, 2009). In the meantime facial image technology continues to be developed for CCTV applications. As outlined by Bryant (2007), face recognition software captures a face and then matches it to a data bank. This can be used to authenticate identity or match a person to a law enforcement data bank for warrants or "persons of interest." The applications for this are endless, such as searching for terrorists and criminals at border control crossings or high-security sites. An applied use of CCTV will be in the area of behavioral analytics, which is the study of human behavior by video surveillance. Advances will expand using artificial intelligence to analyze video images based on what the system has learned over a period of time and focus on suspicious or potentially violent behaviors. Thus the human element can be removed for video surveillance of a wide number of monitors over a period of time (Motorola, 2009). For example, St. Louis Metro reports that it is deploying this technology into railway tunnels to detect intruders (Resnick, 2009: 1).

Biometrics

Biometric security products, which have been developed to provide limited access to secure areas, have been greatly reduced in cost and thus offer a potential for a wide range of applications. Wagley (2009) reports that health clubs and retail stores are beginning to use hand and thumb biometric devices to authenticate those authorized to use facilities or make transactions. One major communications company has developed handheld units for field applications in determining identities of persons without official documents. For perimeter security, further developments are being made in thermal imaging, which allows security systems to see intrusions at night.

Robots

Related to the use of artificial intelligence for video surveillance is the use of robots for patrol. At this time, there are devices that can enter into barricaded or dangerous positions and relay images back to a secure position. Robots are also being developed to check pipelines for equipment fissures. According to Chunovic (2009), a robot snake is being developed that can move through tunnels or wriggle under fallen buildings to aid in search and rescue. Newer versions will be developed whereby robots can go on patrol and interact with humans. At this time, robots are being programmed to coach persons who have had strokes and need long-term therapy (Groopman, 2009). We may soon see the time as robots are available for patrol and to deter would-be intruders with incapacitating weapons.

Unmanned Surveillance Aircraft

Drones or unmanned surveillance aircraft are currently being used in Iraq and the Afghanistan war theaters. Programmed and "flown" from several locations in the United States, the drones can stay in the air for forty hours to survey and detect enemy movements. Drones can also be armed with air-to-ground missiles to strike at an enemy target. At this time, drones are being used by the CIA and the military to detect Taliban and al-Qaeda operatives in the remote border regions of Afghanistan and Pakistan. For domestic security, they can be used for the same purposes—albeit without weapons—to search for illegal immigrants crossing remote stretches of the New Mexico and Arizona border areas with Mexico, and along northern borders with Canada. As with any other device, the use of unmanned aircraft is dependent on human analysis and identification of a potential target. As reported by Mayer (2009), there have been errors with civilian casualties where Predator or Raptor drones have been used to kill enemy targets.

Explosives Detection

Another important technological development involves explosives detection, especially at airport sites. At this time explosives are traced by ion mobility spectrometry (IMS) and chemiluminescence. As outlined by Straw (2009), IMS test samples are heated to make them vaporize. IMS machines then pass the vapors through an electrical field and the unit identifies explosive substances based on the speed at which its ions travel. In chemiluminescence, machines expose a sample to its own luminescent chemicals that only bond with explosive molecules. Both methods are limited to certain explosive compounds. He reports that newer technologies involving spectroscopy, such as the XD 21–160, are being developed using Raman and Fourier spectroscopy to trace a wider range of newer explosive substances. These devices are now available in handheld devices that can be used in a variety of field situations.

SECURITY "OUTSIDE THE BOX"

In the preparation of this book, we began looking at security at places and locations that are often overlooked. One that came to the list was churches. Immediately after 9/11 several synagogues in our areas hired security services personnel to protect property and congregations from possible attacks during services. At the same time, mosques became targets for hate crimes. Over the past several years there have been killings committed during social activities and services at churches, synagogues, and mosques. As discussed by Stelter (2009: 11), a minister in Illinois was fatally shot during a church service. Houses of worship have also been targets for arson, burglary, and fraud. The reality is that they are virtually unprotected and large numbers of people congregate during specific periods of time. Thus church leaders and their advisory boards must review security practices such as perimeter security, fire safety, and threats posed from members of the congregation or immediate vicinity.

Another area that deserves attention is the care of the elderly. According to Alvarez (2009), the number of elderly is expected to grow to 72 million people. For certain areas in metropolitan New York, the number of persons over 65 is about 20 percent. This will require both the public and private sector to provide services to an aging population including security services in medical and retirement communities. Elderly persons are often viewed as easy targets for street criminals and fraudsters engaged in various scams such as identity theft. As shown by the experience of Hurricane Katrina, evacuation of the elderly posed many problems as many could not leave their homes because of medical conditions. For those that were eventually rescued, many needed immediate medical care and medications.

TERRORISM AND PRIVACY

Security planners remain concerned with further attacks on U.S. soil by al-Qaeda operatives, Muslim fundamentalists, and other anti-American sympathizers. Thus, training needs for local and state security service agencies addressing counterterrorism issues, fraudulent documents, emergency management, incident command, and weapons of mass destruction will remain high for many agencies.

The chief counterterrorism activity will continue to consist of obtaining and analyzing information by many federal, state, and local agencies that deal with terrorism and homeland security issues via fusion centers. The need to establish a master list of possible suspects including individuals living in and outside the United States continues. These data would be used for agencies in background checks, criminal investigations, and suspect analysis. There is also the need to conduct information reviews of potential terrorist activity that occurs overseas. One such program, the Terrorism Information Awareness program, is designed to analyze foreign intelligence and spread it to various governmental agencies in an effort to identify potential suspects.

The creation of these data banks will result in issues related to information security, privacy rights, and the right to amend or contest incorrect information. The issue of the extent to which federal and state governments will have access to and use of information on individuals is subject of continuing debate. In many communities there have been public discussions over the impact on personal privacy brought on by the PATRIOT Act and the actions of state and federal government agencies. At the initiation of the Act, librarians and others expressed great concern over the extent to which federal agents can review their clients' library use and the kinds of books people are reading.

NEED FOR NATIONAL STANDARDS

Against this background of growth in security services is the need for state and perhaps federal standards for individuals currently working in or supplying security services. Although it has improved, some states have requirements for employee background checks, licensing, and training, especially for Level I organizations. This lack makes both general security operations and homeland security vulnerable because anyone can become a security officer and gain access to all kinds of assets.

State regulatory agencies will have to use registration and licensing to create a database for tracking security service employees. Accordingly, there will be a need to hire and retain more qualified individuals, thus resulting in higher costs to provide employees a living wage and benefits package. The impetus for any significant change will have to come from the federal government because the "industry," especially those agencies in the private sector, obtains contracts based only on competitive bidding for hourly wages. What is necessary is the development of national standards for personnel providing basic security operations, investigations, alarm services, and security service with law enforcement powers. At a minimum, the following are required if the United States is to truly have "homeland security":

1. Sharing of state and FBI fingerprints records with the state criminal justice operations agency. These prints would be retained in both state and FBI fingerprint data banks. As previously discussed, *retained* means that the prints are kept on file and matched and reported to the licensing agency if an applicant is arrested or applies. Filing fees would have to be determined by each state. It is necessary, however, that these criminal history systems be kept up to date to be able to provide accurate and timely information to potential employers.
2. Completion of a basic security service training program that is administered by the state criminal justice training agency. The course would have a required number of hours and topics that include a mix of state and national topics.
3. Issuance of a license to security personnel by the state criminal justice services based on evidence of submission of fingerprints and completion of training program. A security service officer who moves to another state would have to apply for a license from that state and give evidence of training completion. He or she might have to take a course to learn about the criminal laws and security procedures of the new state.
4. A minimum of forty continuing education hours that must be taken every two years in courses on legal issues, dealing with the public, security techniques, and various homeland security issues. Completing these hours would be required for license renewal every three years.

COOPERATION BETWEEN LAW ENFORCEMENT AND SECURITY SERVICES

The tenuous relationship between public law enforcement and private security has been debated since the creation of different types of forces to provide protection and personal safety. The Task Force on Private Security summed up the debate in the 1970s in reporting that public law enforcement views security services as unprofessional and client driven. Security service personnel see public law enforcement as primarily concerned with making arrests, responding to emergency situations, and spending little time on crime prevention (Task Force on Private Security, 1976: 208). Many authors and observers have called for greater cooperation between the two in order to increase personal safety in a community. There are complementary roles between law enforcement and security organizations because both sectors provide personal safety for citizens (Fischer and Green, 2004). Can this really be achieved?

One must examine the professional roles of law enforcement and private security, which are at times the same but at others very different. For instance, on the executive level, police chiefs and superintendents and directors are professionally associated with state organizations that are affiliated with the International Association of Chiefs of Police (IACP). In addition to providing training and establishing standards, the IACP and its various organizational sections (e.g., state agencies, railroad, colleges and universities, and others) lobby for greater federal and state assistance from state legislatures and Congress. Security service executive professionals do the same thing under the auspices of ASIS. Seldom do the two groups meet. One of the authors is aware that both ASIS and the county chapter of the IACP meet at the same restaurant at different times.

If there is to be greater cooperation, security service and public law enforcement executives need to meet on a frequent basis. Some localities have law enforcement and security coalitions composed of agency heads that meet and discuss issues and share information on a weekly or monthly basis. As one member stated, the time to know your organizational partner is not during a major crisis. This by itself can be a major development because we know of many localities where public law enforcement has no idea what security service agencies might exist in its area, and security service supervisors do not personally know their public law enforcement counterparts.

Another stumbling block to greater cooperation deals with the sharing of criminal information. Public law enforcement agencies have monopolistic access to state and federal crime information as a result of historical practice and administrative rules. Data banks such as the National Crime Information Center, state databases, and the new fusion information network are open only to state-regulated police agencies. Thus, it is imperative that public law enforcement share data and information when possible. Even in the law enforcement community, the so-called silos between federal, state, and local agencies for information and operational cooperation still remain, although some breakdown has occurred since the events of 9/11. The FBI, the various Homeland Security agencies, and other federal agencies are sharing terrorist information and training with state and local agencies more frequently. In most states, there are federal regional counterterrorism areas, but there is little input from Levels I and II security service agencies.

Law enforcement remains suspicious and reluctant to share information and undertake joint investigations with security service agencies that have few or no standards or requirements for personnel selection and training. As one police chief said, "I am not going to share information with a security department that might hire felons or possible terrorists." On the other hand, some police departments are mismanaged and do not enjoy public support or cooperation. Police misconduct and a perceived lack of professionalism often deter cooperation even from other police departments! There is no broad answer to the state of affairs. This dilemma can be addressed only on a local agency-by-agency basis. Many security service directors want to know about crime trends and issues that affect their client area. They also want to know the status of investigations that are reported to law enforcement agencies by security service personnel. At times, the director or supervisor of a Level I or Level II agency has to be very proactive in obtaining information on crime trends and cases.

Another potential area of increased cooperation is training. Some area law enforcement coalitions have been able to offer joint training to all agency members on topics such as new laws, responding to serious incidents, and antiterrorism programs. Training cannot be seen as a one-sided undertaking because both instructors and students should be drawn from all sectors. Security service agencies, especially Levels II, III, and IV agencies in many areas, have much to offer in technical expertise and resources related to identity theft and computer crime. Multiagency training can be a great assistance in increasing cooperation.

SUMMARY

In this chapter we gave a summary review of international and national trends affecting security services into the next decade. There will be growth in the security industry based on concerns for crime, homeland security, and control of fraud in the financial industry. At this time, there is a trend for private companies to increasingly offer support services to public sector security and law enforcement agencies at less cost. Advances in technology will play an important role in this endeavor. While states have enacted various standards for security officer hiring and licensing, there is a need for national standards in this area. There is still a need for greater cooperative efforts between security and law enforcement agencies, especially to deal with natural and man-made emergencies and terrorist incidents.

Review Questions/Activities

1. Based on current crime data what is the crime rate for your community? How might this impact the delivery of security services?
2. How has globalization affected your community or campus?
3. What are the hiring and licensing standards for security service personnel in your state? To what extent do they vary between Level 1 and Level IV personnel?
4. Review one technological trend discussed in this chapter and discuss the advances and applications that have been made.

5. What areas of conflict exist between law enforcement and security services organizations? What can be done to resolve these issues?
6. To what extent has CCTV been used in your campus or community? Do you think it has an effect on crime?
7. Why are there concerns regarding privacy in this technological society?

WebSearches

1. Review the Web site for ASIS International and the Department of Homeland Security. What are the career openings in security? From your review of these Web sites, discuss three new technologies that are being developed.
2. Review the Web site for the Southern Poverty Law Center and determine to what extent hate groups

identified by the Center are found in your state or area.
3. With the guidance of your instructor, go to the agency Web site that regulates hiring standards for sworn and non-sworn security services personnel. What are the general hiring and training standards for these positions?

References

Alvarez, Lizette. December 6, 2009. Suburbs See A Challenge As Residents Grow Older. *New York Times*, pp. 1, 8.

Bryant, Lynn. January 2007. "The New Face of Surveillance–Incorporating Biometric Face Recognition into a Surveillance Video Camera System." Web posted at www.video-surveillance-guie.com/surveillance-video-camera-s. Accessed December 10, 2009.

Bureau of Labor Statistics, U.S. Department of Labor. 2008–2009. "Occupational Outlook Handbook, 2008–2009 Edition." Web posted at www.bls.gov/oco/ocos. Accessed October 31, 2009.

Bureau of Justice Statistics. 2008. Web posted at http://www.ojp.usdoj.gov/bjs/abstract/cv08.htm. Accessed on November 20, 2009.

Chertoff, Michael. 2009. *Homeland Security: Assessing the First Five Years*. Philadelphia: University of Pennsylvania Press.

Copeland, Larry. November 16, 2009. State Police Forces Shrink: Shortages Leaves Areas Unpatrolled. *USA Today*, p. 1.

Chunovic, Louis. October 2009. "Opinion / Get the 'Hate Out of the Debate'" *GNS: Government Security News*, Vol. 7, No. 10, pp. 1, 16.

Federal Bureau of Investigation. 2008. "Crime in the United States." Accessed November 20, 2009 at http://www.fbi.gov/ucr/cius2008/about/crime_summary.html.

Fischer, Robert J., and Gion, Green. 2004. *Introduction to Security*, 7th ed. New York: Elsevier-Butterworths.

GSN Case Studies. June 2009. Government Security News. Vol. 7, No. 6, p. 18.

Goodwin, Jacob. October, 2009. "Land Owners Use High-tech Gear to Spot Illegal Aliens." *GSN: Government Security News.* Vol 7, No. 10, pp. 1–13.

Groopman, Jerome. November 2, 2009. Medical Dispatch: Robots That Care: High-Tech Breakthroughs in Therapy. *The New Yorker,* pp. 66–77.

Levin, Bernard H., and Carl J. Jensen. 2006. "Homeland Security in 2015." In *Homeland Security, 2015: A series of working papers from the futures working group,* edited by Michael Buerger. Washington, DC: U.S. Department of Justice, Federal Bureau of Investigation.

Lyall, Sarah. October 24, 2009. Brtions Weary of Surveillance in Minor Cases. Accessed November 22, 2009 at http://www.nytimes.com/2009/10/25/world/europe/25surveillance.html.

Mayer, Jane. October 26,2009. The Predator War: The Risks of Covertly Targeting Terrorists. *The New Yorker,* pp. 36–45.

Motorola. 2009. "White Paper: Eyes on the Street: How Wireless Video Solutions Are Transforming Public Safety." Posted at GSN_Eyes on the Street_WiBB_120809. Accessed on December 9, 2009.

Morgenson, Gretchen. December 6, 2009. Why Treasury Needs a Plan B for Mortgages. *New York Times,* pp. 1, 8.

Resnick, Gary. June, 2009. "Detecting Intruders in Railway Tunnels." *GSN: Government Security News.* Vol. 7, No. 6, pp. 1,12.

Stelterok, Leischen. May 2009. "Watching over: Church Security a Balance of Hard and Soft Measures." *Security Director News.* Vol. 6, No. 5, pp. 11–12.

Straw, Joseph. August 2009. Assessing Explosive Detection. *Security Magazine,* pp. 46–53.

National Advisory Committee on Criminal Justice Standards and Goals. 1976. *Private Security: Report of the Task Force on Private Security.* Washington, D.C.: U.S. Department of Justice, Law Enforcement Assistance Administration.

Trottman, Melanie. November 14–15, 2009. Immigrant Bill is Back on Table. *The Wall Street Journal,* p. 5.

Wagley, John. November 2009. Hands-on Solutions. *Security Magazine,* pp. 59–64.

White, Richard and Kevin Collins,eds. 2006. *The United States Department of Homeland Security: An Overview.* Boston: Pearson Custom Publishing.

Zogby, John. 2008. *The Way We'll Be.* New York. Random House.

INDEX